| READING |

Basic   Intermediate   Advanced   Expert

| LISTENING |

 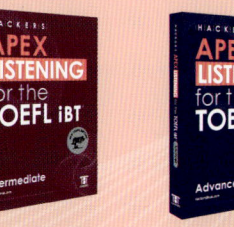  

Basic   Intermediate   Advanced   Expert

Informative passages

HACKERS APEX LISTENING includes informative and interesting listening passages on a variety of academic topics and everyday situations in a university setting.

Useful online study materials

HACKERS APEX LISTENING provides access to quality online study materials at HackersBook.com. These include streaming audio recordings of all passages accessible through QR codes in the book.

HACKERS
APEX LISTENING
for the TOEFL iBT®

Intermediate

Preface

Preface

Thank you for purchasing *HACKERS APEX LISTENING for the TOEFL iBT Intermediate*. The TOEFL iBT is a highly challenging exam, so it is important to select an effective study guide. All of us at Hackers Language Research Institute are confident that this publication will be an invaluable resource as you prepare for the TOEFL iBT.

HACKERS APEX LISTENING for the TOEFL iBT is a series of comprehensive study guides for students planning to take the TOEFL iBT or for those wanting to improve their general English listening skills. This series includes four books that progress in difficulty. Students can begin at the level that matches their current abilities and then move on to the higher ones. All of the books in this series provide step-by-step question-solving strategies for every TOEFL question type. These are based on thorough research and years of instructional experience. Each book also includes informative and interesting listening passages that enable students to improve their English listening skills and familiarize them with academic topics and spoken English used in everyday university settings. Furthermore, students will receive access to quality online study materials that are designed to help them get the most out of the books in this series. Key features of *HACKERS APEX LISTENING for the TOEFL iBT* books include:

- Detailed explanations and question-solving strategies for all TOEFL Listening question types
- A large number of high-quality TOEFL Listening passages and questions
- Two full-length TOEFL Listening tests
- Dictation exercises to enhance listening comprehension ability
- Vocabulary exercises to review essential vocabulary that appeared in the passages
- An answer book with complete scripts, Korean translations, and lists of key vocabulary
- Access to streaming audio recordings of all passages through QR codes
- Access to supplementary study materials online (www.HackersBook.com)

Thank you again for choosing *HACKERS APEX LISTENING for the TOEFL iBT Intermediate*, and we wish you all the best whether you are preparing to take the TOEFL iBT in the near future or simply hoping to develop your English listening skills overall.

Table of Contents

How to Use This Book — 6
About the TOEFL iBT — 8
NOTE-TAKING — 10

CHAPTER 01 — Main Purpose/Topic — 13
Example — 15
Listening Practice 1, 2, 3, 4 — 17
iBT Listening Test 1, 2 — 25
• Vocabulary Review — 32

CHAPTER 02 — Detail — 33
Example — 35
Listening Practice 1, 2, 3, 4 — 37
iBT Listening Test 1, 2 — 45
• Vocabulary Review — 52

CHAPTER 03 — Function — 53
Example — 55
Listening Practice 1, 2, 3, 4 — 57
iBT Listening Test 1, 2 — 65
• Vocabulary Review — 72

CHAPTER 04 — Attitude — 73
Example — 75
Listening Practice 1, 2, 3, 4 — 77
iBT Listening Test 1, 2 — 85
• Vocabulary Review — 92

CHAPTER 05	**Organization**	93
Example	95
Listening Practice 1, 2, 3, 4	97
iBT Listening Test 1, 2	105
• Vocabulary Review	112

CHAPTER 06	**Connecting Contents**	113
Example	115
Listening Practice 1, 2, 3, 4	117
iBT Listening Test 1, 2	125
• Vocabulary Review	132

CHAPTER 07	**Inference**	133
Example	135
Listening Practice 1, 2, 3, 4	137
iBT Listening Test 1, 2	145
• Vocabulary Review	152

- Actual Test 1   154
- Actual Test 2   164

How to Use This Book

1 Understand the Question Type

Each chapter includes an Overview page that provides essential information about the featured question type and key strategies for answering it. Make sure you fully understand the strategies before moving on to the Example section, where you can apply the key strategies to short conversation and lecture passages with one question each.

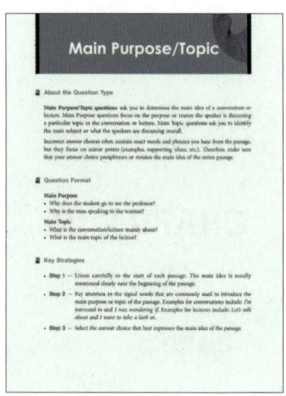

2 Improve Your Skills with Listening Practice Exercises

Each chapter includes four Listening Practice exercises, which consist of two conversation and two lecture passages. These will help you become more familiar with the featured question type, as well as other question types. Each exercise is accompanied by a dictation section so that you can enhance your listening comprehension ability.

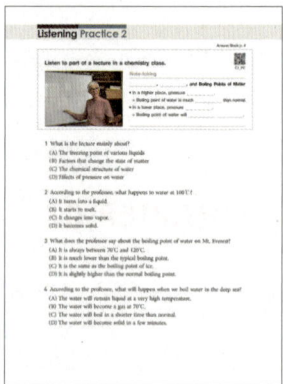

3 Take the iBT Listening Tests

Each chapter includes two iBT Listening Tests, which consist of longer conversation and lecture passages with 4 to 5 questions each that are similar to those that appear on the TOEFL iBT. Taking these tests will enable you to improve your listening comprehension skills and prepare for the TOEFL iBT.

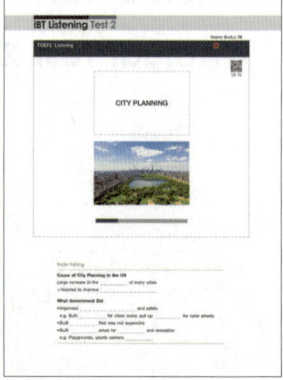

4 Review Essential Vocabulary

At the end of each chapter is a Vocabulary Review, which includes questions on essential vocabulary from the chapter. You will be able to easily memorize the vocabulary words through various types of questions.

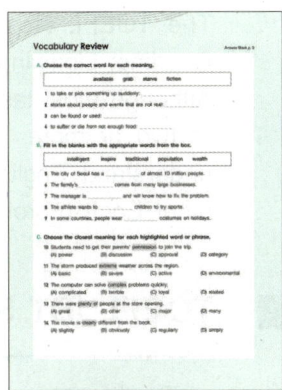

5 Evaluate Your Progress with Actual Tests

The book includes two Actual Tests, which are full-length listening tests that include passages and questions that closely match what appears on the TOEFL iBT. They provide an excellent opportunity to apply the skills you have learned and evaluate your progress.

6 Check the Answer Book

The Answer Book specifies the correct answer choice for all questions and provides complete scripts and Korean translations of all passages and questions. It also includes a list of key vocabulary words from each passage with definitions.

About the TOEFL iBT

What Is the TOEFL iBT?

The TOEFL (Test of English as a Foreign Language) iBT (Internet-Based test) includes Reading, Listening, Speaking, and Writing sections to comprehensively assess English ability. Although most tasks require the application of only one of these skills, some require the use of two or more. The TOEFL iBT is designed to measure a student's capacity to use and understand English at a university level and is, therefore, much more difficult than many other English proficiency tests.

TOEFL iBT Structure

Section	No. of passages and questions	Time (min.)	Score	Notable Features
Reading	• 2 Passages • 10 Questions/Passage	36	30	• Each passage is approximately 700 words long.
Listening	• 2 Conversations • 5 Questions/Conversation • 3 Lectures • 6 Questions/Lecture	41	30	• Speakers have various accents, including American, British, Australian, etc.
Speaking	• 1 Independent Task • 3 Integrated Tasks	17	30	• Independent Task asks you to state your opinion about a specific topic. • Integrated Tasks ask you to provide a response based on reading and listening content.
Writing	• 1 Integrated Task • 1 Academic Discussion Task	35	30	• Integrated Task asks you to provide a response based on reading and listening content. • Academic Discussion Task asks you to state your opinion about a specific topic in an online classroom.

Total Time: Approximately 2 hours / Total Score: 120

TOEFL iBT Listening Section

The TOEFL iBT Listening Section largely consists of conversations and lectures. Conversations mainly take place in university settings, and lectures discuss topics from different academic fields covered in university lectures. Note-taking is allowed while listening to conversations and lectures. Therefore, the ability to listen, understand, and organize information is more important than relying on memory. The test consists of 2 Parts with either 11 or 17 questions. Each Part has 1 conversation and 1 to 2 lectures.

TOEFL iBT Listening Question Types

Question Type	Description
Main Purpose/Topic	Choose the answer choice that best represents the main idea of the conversation or lecture.
Detail	Choose the answer choice that corresponds to specific information or important details introduced in the conversation or lecture.
Function	Choose the answer choice that best describes the underlying function or purpose of a speaker's specific statement.
Attitude	Choose the answer choice that best represents the speaker's attitude or opinion regarding a specific matter.
Organization	Choose the answer choice that best describes the overall organization of the passage or the relationship between ideas in the passage.
Connecting Contents	Choose the answer choices that correspond to related ideas clearly stated in the passage.
Inference	Choose the answer choice that can be inferred based on relevant information in the passage.

NOTE-TAKING

■ Strategies for Note-taking

1. **Write down the main idea using key words.**
   Listen carefully to the beginning of the conversation or lecture. Write down the main idea in a short sentence or phrase using key words.

2. **Organize information into subtopics and categories.**
   Identify the subtopics and organize the information into groups or categories. Listen for signal words (First of all, Secondly, Now, Later, Then, Another, etc.) used to introduce subtopics.

3. **Write down the supporting details.**
   Write down the supporting details for each subtopic or category. Especially for lectures, it is good to take notes according to how the lecturer gives supporting details. For example, the lecturer may give the definition of a term, compare two or more ideas, or give a list of important items.

4. **Do not try to write down everything.**
   Make your notes brief and do not try to write down every single word. Include only essential key words. It is also helpful to use symbols and abbreviations of your own.

Note-taking Example

Script

> P: Today we are going to continue our discussion on the differences between mammals and reptiles. One of the key traits that distinguish these two types of animals is the way that they control their body temperatures. I'm sure you have all heard the expressions "hot-blooded" and "cold-blooded," right? Well, it's actually a bit more complicated than that. Basically, mammals rely on their ability to burn fats and sugars to generate heat as required. In contrast, reptiles depend on external factors, such as the sun, to warm their bodies, or cold water to cool them. OK... Let's look at these functions in a bit more detail.

Note

diffs. bet. mammals & reptiles: way they ctrl. body temp.	— *Main Topic*
1. mammals: burn fat & sugar → heat	— *Type 1*
2. reptiles: ext. factors	— *Type 2*
e.g. sun → warm	
e.g. cold water → cool	*Examples of Type 2*

Common Symbols and Abbreviations

The key to note-taking is writing down only the essential information of the conversation or lecture. Using symbols and abbreviations will allow you to make your notes brief and accurate. With symbols and abbreviations, you can write down more information in a quick and efficient way. Below are some commonly used symbols and abbreviations.

1. Symbols
Symbols can save you time and increase the amount of information you write down about a passage.

=	equals; to be	K	1,000	X	not, no
+	and; plus	&	and	/	per, each
>	more than	∴	therefore/so	/day	per day
<	less than	←	from	/h	per hour
↑	increase	@	at	/w	per week
↓	decrease	#	number (of)	∵	because

2. Abbreviations
There are several methods to make abbreviations, but make sure to keep your method consistent. Here are some ways to make abbreviations.

- Omit latter part: European → Eu
- Omit vowels: movement → mvmt
- Omit middle letters: government → govt

e.g.	for example	usu.	usually	info.	information
prob.	problem	w/	with	sum.	summary
ppl	people	cf.	compare	psych.	psychology
rsn.	reason	c.	century	Qs	questions
etc.	and so on	max.	maximum	pics	pictures
i.e.	that is; in other words	min.	minimum	w/o	without
intro.	introduction	fr.	from	vs	versus
concl.	conclusion	tech	technology	ea.	each
b.f.	before	reg	regular	btw	by the way

www.HackersBook.com

HACKERS APEX LISTENING
for the TOEFL iBT
Intermediate

CHAPTER 01

Main Purpose/Topic

Main Purpose/Topic

About the Question Type

Main Purpose/Topic questions ask you to determine the main idea of a conversation or lecture. Main Purpose questions focus on the purpose or reason the speaker is discussing a particular topic in the conversation or lecture. Main Topic questions ask you to identify the main subject or what the speakers are discussing overall.

Incorrect answer choices often contain exact words and phrases you hear from the passage, but they focus on minor points (examples, supporting ideas, etc.). Therefore, make sure that your answer choice paraphrases or restates the main idea of the entire passage.

Question Format

Main Purpose
- Why does the student go to see the professor?
- Why is the man speaking to the woman?

Main Topic
- What is the conversation/lecture mainly about?
- What is the main topic of the lecture?

Key Strategies

- **Step 1** — Listen carefully to the start of each passage. The main idea is usually mentioned clearly near the beginning of the passage.

- **Step 2** — Pay attention to the signal words that are commonly used to introduce the main purpose or topic of the passage. Examples for conversations include: *I'm interested in* and *I was wondering if*. Examples for lectures include: *Let's talk about* and *I want to take a look at*.

- **Step 3** — Select the answer choice that best expresses the main idea of the passage.

Example

Answer Book p. 2

A. Listen to a conversation between a student and a librarian.

C1_ExA

Note-taking

Student's Problem
Can't find a book for my _____ class

Librarian's Solution
Copies were just _____ this morning.
→ Grab it from the _____

Why does the student go to the library?

(A) To get some book recommendations
(B) To determine which book to check out
(C) To ask about the location of a book
(D) To submit an order for a book

Answer Book p. 2

B. Listen to part of a lecture in a history class.

C1_ExB

Note-taking

The Czechs and Puppet Shows
The Czechs who performed _____ _____ continued to use Czech.
→ To preserve their _____ and culture
→ Helped them _____ their cultural identity

What is the lecture mainly about?

(A) Why the Habsburgs invaded the Czech Republic
(B) The importance of puppet shows to the Czechs
(C) The origin of the Czech language
(D) How a traditional puppet show was performed

Dictation

Answer Book p. 2

Listen again and fill in the blanks.

A.

W: Hi. I have a question... Um, I can't _____ _____ _____ that I need for my economics class. Could you tell me where to find it?

M: Have you checked our online system? It will show whether there are _____ _____ _____ or not. Other students may have checked out the book.

W: I have, and it showed that there are two copies right now. And they should be in the Economics and Business Section, but I couldn't find any of them...

M: OK. Let me have a look... Which book are you _____ _____?

W: Um, *Modern Economics and Business*, by Jack Harvey. I really need it today.

M: It looks like they were just returned this morning. They're probably not _____ _____ _____ _____ yet.

W: Oh, I see. Then when can I _____ _____ the book?

M: It's available now. You'll just need to grab it from the cart.

B.

P: From the 15th to 20th centuries, the Habsburg Empire ruled central Europe. The Czech lands were among the areas _____ _____ the Habsburgs. And interestingly, puppet shows _____ _____ _____ _____ here at that time. We'll talk about this today.

In the early 1600s, the Habsburg Empire _____ _____ _____ the Czech lands. The Habsburg rulers forced Czech people to use only German. So, the Czech people were _____ _____ German in official documents, laws, and even plays.

However, the laws did not apply to puppet shows. So, uh, people who performed puppet shows _____ _____ _____ Czech. And Czech people _____ _____ _____ in their native language through the puppets. Thus, puppet shows allowed the Czechs to _____ _____ _____ and culture. This led the Czechs to maintain their cultural identity even under Habsburg rule.

Listening Practice 1

Answer Book p. 3

Listen to a conversation between a student and a professor.

Note-taking

Student's Suggestion
Have a _____ session in class

Professor's Answer
- Take an _____ course
- Join a _____ _____ for the class

---

1 Why does the student go to see the professor?

(A) To complain about a change in class

(B) To ask about a paper assignment

(C) To discuss his class schedule

(D) To suggest an improvement to a class

2 What does the student say about the professor's class?

(A) Students have to memorize some information.

(B) There are too many reading materials.

(C) The group project is very difficult.

(D) Students need more explanations.

3 What does the student agree to do?

(A) Give a presentation in class

(B) Move to another professor's class

(C) Join a study group with classmates

(D) Choose an advanced topic for a paper

Dictation

Answer Book p. 3

Listen again and fill in the blanks.

S: Professor Sherman, do you have a few minutes? I'm Jacob Harrington, and I was, uh, hoping to _____ _____ _____ about our Introduction to Philosophy class.

P: Sure, of course. What can I do for you?

S: Um, I'd like to suggest _____ _____ _____ _____ in class. I think it would encourage a deeper understanding.

P: I see... Um, am I not _____ _____ _____?

S: No, no. Your explanations are great. Um, I just _____ _____ _____ what I've learned in the class with others.

P: Well, this is a beginner course. So, students will learn _____ _____ _____ in this class.

S: But it seems like we're just _____ _____ _____...

P: You see, memorization is important in learning because we cannot discuss anything _____ _____ _____.

S: Yeah. That makes sense.

P: If you want a discussion in class, I suggest you take _____ _____ _____. It will include a discussion and _____ _____ _____.

S: Oh, I didn't know that. I'll take one next semester.

P: Also, I recommend you _____ _____ _____ _____ for this class. That would provide you with, uh, a similar experience. You can _____ _____ _____ and _____ _____ on related topics with your classmates.

S: That sounds like a great option. Thank you, Professor!

Listening Practice 2

Answer Book p. 4

Listen to part of a lecture in a chemistry class.

Note-taking

_____, _____, and Boiling Points of Matter

- In a higher place, pressure _____.
  → Boiling point of water is much _____ than normal.
- In a lower place, pressure _____.
  → Boiling point of water will _____ _____.

1 What is the lecture mainly about?

(A) The freezing point of various liquids

(B) Factors that change the state of matter

(C) The chemical structure of water

(D) Effects of pressure on water

2 According to the professor, what happens to water at 100℃?

(A) It turns into a liquid.

(B) It starts to melt.

(C) It changes into vapor.

(D) It becomes solid.

3 What does the professor say about the boiling point of water on Mt. Everest?

(A) It is always between 70℃ and 120℃.

(B) It is much lower than the typical boiling point.

(C) It is the same as the boiling point of ice.

(D) It is slightly higher than the normal boiling point.

4 According to the professor, what will happen when we boil water in the deep sea?

(A) The water will remain liquid at a very high temperature.

(B) The water will become a gas at 70℃.

(C) The water will boil in a shorter time than normal.

(D) The water will become solid in a few minutes.

Dictation

Answer Book p. 4

Listen again and fill in the blanks.

P: We have already learned about the three _____ _____ _____: liquid, solid, and gas. For example, water can be a liquid, a solid as ice, or a gas as vapor. You see, what _____ _____ _____ in states are environmental factors... uh, like _____ _____ _____. Now, we're going to talk about them in more detail.

Temperature influences the freezing point, melting point, and boiling point of matter. Water's normal freezing point is 0°C, and water becomes ice at this point. Above 0°C, ice melts and becomes liquid. Um, its boiling point is 100°C, and water turns into _____ _____ at 100°C...

But, remember I mentioned temperature and pressure? Well, these conditions are true at normal pressure. What happens when the pressure is _____ _____ _____? The temperatures of the freezing, melting, and boiling points can change _____ _____ _____.

Before I explain this in more detail, there are some rules you need to remember. Pressure is _____ _____ _____.

When you are in a _____ place, pressure decreases. And when you are in a _____ place, pressure increases. Imagine that you are climbing a mountain. As you _____ _____ the mountain, you're in a higher place. So, uh, if you are on top of Mt. Everest, for instance, the pressure will be very low. At lower pressure, the boiling point of water is also _____ _____ _____ _____. On top of Mt. Everest, water will boil at around 70°C. Now, consider the opposite. As we _____ _____ to a lower place like the deep sea, the pressure increases. Then, the boiling point of water will _____ _____, too. There are places in the deep sea where water will not boil even at very high temperatures. In extreme cases, water can _____ _____ even at 400°C!

Listening Practice 3

Answer Book p. 5

Listen to a conversation between a student and a housing office employee.

C1_P3

Note-taking

Student's Problem
Wants to find a room in a dormitory because of a
_____ _____

Employee's Suggestion
- Find a _____ to share a house
- There is an _____ room in a dormitory.

1 What problem does the student have?

   (A) He has to find a roommate.
   (B) He has classes early in the morning.
   (C) He wants to find a room in a dormitory.
   (D) He needs to delay the deadline of his project.

2 Why does the student need to live closer to the campus?

   (A) To get a part-time job on campus
   (B) To live near his parents' house
   (C) To be able to walk to school
   (D) To work on a research project

3 What does the employee recommend that the student do?

   (A) Apply for a student ID
   (B) Rent an apartment
   (C) Share a house with a roommate
   (D) Place his name on a list

Dictation

Answer Book p. 5

Listen again and fill in the blanks.

M: Hi. I was hoping you could help me with something.

W: Sure. What do you need?

M: Uh, I want to _____ _____ _____ in a dormitory. I need to _____ _____ _____ because of a research project. I have to come to school _____ _____ _____ _____ to work on it.

W: Oh, but _____ _____ _____ _____ last week. The notice was on the board on campus and on the website.

M: I know it's a little late, but my parents' house is too far from here. It _____ _____ _____ _____ to get to school.

W: OK, but why don't you _____ _____ _____ to share a house near the campus?

M: Well, actually, I was going to live with my friend near the campus, but he _____ _____ _____ in a different state... All my other friends have already found roommates or _____ _____ _____ _____ .

W: I see... I'll have a look and see what I can find. If any student decided to leave a dormitory, then we can _____ _____ _____ for you.

M: I understand.

W: _____ _____ _____ ! It looks like there is _____ _____ _____ . Do you have your student ID with you?

M: Yes, here you are. Thank you so much.

Listening Practice 4

Answer Book p. 6

Listen to part of a lecture in a literature class.

Note-taking

Types of _____ in Literature
- Flat Characters: Shows only one part of their _____ that doesn't _____
  e.g. Dr. Watson in *Sherlock Holmes*
- Round Characters: More complex and more _____
  e.g. Jay Gatsby in *The Great Gatsby*

1 What is the purpose of the lecture?

   (A) To provide helpful tips for writing fiction
   (B) To explain the two main kinds of fictional characters
   (C) To give examples of famous characters in novels
   (D) To introduce the various categories of literature

2 What does the professor say about flat characters?

   (A) They have lively personalities.
   (B) They are usually main characters.
   (C) They show part of their personality.
   (D) They have positive characteristics.

3 What does the professor say about Dr. Watson?

   (A) He was originally created as a main character.
   (B) The character was based on a real person.
   (C) His personality does not change throughout the story.
   (D) The novel includes detailed information about his life.

Listen again to part of the lecture. Then answer the question.

4 What does the professor mean when he says this: 🎧

   (A) The characters in most novels are not complex.
   (B) The reason for their personalities is not a mystery.
   (C) The author uses real people's names for characters.
   (D) The readers expect characters to change in the end.

Dictation

Answer Book p. 6

Listen again and fill in the blanks.

P: I know that all of you have read fiction. But have you ever thought about the types of characters in novels? We're going to discuss two _____ _____ _____ _____ in literature.

First, there are flat characters. Flat characters are not complex. Imagine a photograph of a person. This can show _____ _____ _____ of his or her personality. If a person is smiling in a picture, then we might think that this person is nice. But we can't be sure about this because a person is _____ _____ _____ just a picture, right? Flat characters _____ _____ _____ what we see in a picture. We can only know one part of their personality, which doesn't change throughout the story. For instance, think about Dr. Watson in *Sherlock Holmes*. He is a good friend who helps Sherlock, the main character, solve crimes and mysteries. He is an _____ _____ _____ person, and this personality doesn't change. He keeps showing us this one side of his personality. We also don't know much about his life... The author doesn't tell us _____ _____ _____ _____ _____ in the novel.

Next, there are round characters. These are _____ _____ _____ flat characters, so they are more complex and, uh... more real. Since there is a lot of information about their lives, we can really know about their personalities. So, they seem more like _____ _____. Um, Jay Gatsby in *The Great Gatsby* is one example. The novel is about Jay Gatsby's effort to gain love and wealth. Gatsby had a poor childhood. So when he _____ _____ _____ _____ a girl from a wealthy family, he couldn't marry her. This made him have a strong desire to become rich. He even _____ _____ crimes. But we cannot say he is just a bad criminal because we know about his childhood and love story. We can easily understand him and his desire to become rich with this background.

iBT Listening Test 1

Answer Book p. 7

TOEFL Listening

Note-taking

Student's Request

Asks for _____ to change the topic of a paper

→ New topic: How _____ _____ will cause many _____ to die

Professor's Suggestion

- Will allow the change
- Talk about how _____ _____ can affect people
  → Add a few _____ at the end of a paper

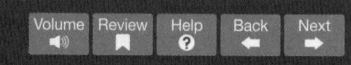

1 Why does the student go to see the professor?
   Ⓐ To give his thoughts about a lecture
   Ⓑ To request a different topic for a presentation
   Ⓒ To ask if he can write about a new topic
   Ⓓ To check facts about climate change

2 What caused the student to change his mind?
   Ⓐ A talk he attended
   Ⓑ A program he watched
   Ⓒ A website he visited
   Ⓓ An article he read

3 According to the professor, what could happen in the next 10 years?
   Ⓐ Scientists will develop solutions for climate change.
   Ⓑ Many sources of water will be unsafe to drink.
   Ⓒ Parts of the world will be too hot for animals to live in.
   Ⓓ Many people will not have enough fish to eat.

4 What does the professor ask the student to add to a paper?
   Ⓐ A possible result that is related to people
   Ⓑ Some ideas for fixing a serious problem
   Ⓒ A detailed explanation of climate change
   Ⓓ Some paragraphs about a documentary

Dictation

Answer Book p. 7

Listen again and fill in the blanks.

S: Excuse me, Professor Baker? I want to _____ _____ _____ _____ to change the topic of my paper. It's the one about natural disasters.

P: Sure, David. The paper is due in four weeks. You have _____ _____ _____ to write about a new topic... Um, what is your new topic?

S: I want to write about how climate change will cause many fish to die.

P: I'll allow it. Um, why did you _____ _____ _____?

S: Well, uh, I _____ _____ _____ a documentary that I saw on TV.

P: Tell me more.

S: Well, according to the program, many kinds of fish will die because of climate change. The, um, ocean will become _____ _____ _____ _____ to live. And, um, this could happen in the next 10 years.

P: That is terrible! And have you thought about what could happen if we lose a lot of fish _____ _____ _____ _____?

S: Um... No, I didn't think about it that much.

P: Well, _____ _____ _____ around the world eat fish regularly... So, if we lose a lot of fish, many people won't have _____ _____ _____.

S: Oh... That sounds like a big problem. Should I include that in my paper?

P: I think it will make your paper _____ _____ if you talk about how fish loss can affect people.

S: I see. Maybe more people will _____ _____ _____ _____ if it affects them, right?

P: Exactly. But, um, to be clear, don't write too much about it. Just _____ _____ _____ _____ at the end of your paper.

S: I understand, Professor Baker. Thank you!

iBT Listening Test 2

TOEFL Listening

ECOLOGY

Note-taking

_____ **Species**

- Predators

    e.g. _____ _____ maintain the _____ of sea turtles at a proper level.

- _____ _____

    e.g. Woodpeckers create _____ in trees, which other animals depend on.

- _____

    e.g. Flowers provide bees with _____, and the bees help flowers produce _____.

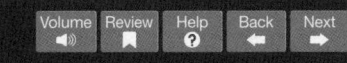

1. What is the main topic of the lecture?
   - Ⓐ The roles of sharks in an ecosystem
   - Ⓑ A few examples of endangered species
   - Ⓒ Several kinds of keystone species
   - Ⓓ The relationship between predators and prey

2. According to the professor, what happens if tiger sharks disappear?
   - Ⓐ The number of sea turtles will decreases.
   - Ⓑ Fish will start to lay eggs on seagrass.
   - Ⓒ Sea turtles will eat all of the seagrass.
   - Ⓓ Fish will not have any major predator.

3. What does the professor say about the woodpeckers' nesting holes?
   - Ⓐ They can harm the health of the tree.
   - Ⓑ Many other animals also use them.
   - Ⓒ Woodpeckers reuse them every year.
   - Ⓓ They attract a variety of insects.

4. What does the professor say about mutualists?
   - Ⓐ They have few natural predators.
   - Ⓑ They are most common in large forests.
   - Ⓒ They create a balance of predators and prey.
   - Ⓓ They are two organisms that benefit each other.

Listen again to part of the lecture. Then answer the question.

5. Why does the professor say this: 🎧
   - Ⓐ To make sure that everyone knows about beavers
   - Ⓑ To indicate that woodpeckers are more important than beavers
   - Ⓒ To highlight a particular type of ecosystem engineer
   - Ⓓ To explain the relationship between beavers and woodpeckers

Dictation

Answer Book p. 8

Listen again and fill in the blanks.

P: In every environment, there are keystone species. Keystone species are very important for ecosystems. If they are removed, many other species _____ _____ _____. Let's take a look at three types of keystone species.

First, there are predators. A good example is the tiger shark. The tiger shark is _____ _____ _____ of sea turtles. When there are enough tiger sharks, the population of sea turtles is maintained _____ _____ _____ _____. Uh, sea turtles eat seagrass... and, um, seagrass is important for many kinds of wildlife. For example, many fish _____ _____ _____ on seagrass, and, uh, young fish _____ _____ _____ _____ while they grow up. So, um, if tiger sharks disappear, the sea turtles have no major predator. If this happens, sea turtles will eat _____ _____ _____ _____, and the other organisms will have no place to _____ _____ _____.

Next, there are ecosystem engineers. Just like human engineers, these _____ _____ _____. An obvious example is the beaver. As you know, beavers build dams. Their dams _____ _____ _____, which, uh, other organisms depend on. But I really want to _____ _____ _____. Um, woodpeckers create holes in trees. They use their beaks to search for insects under the tree bark. And, um, they also _____ _____ _____. Then they _____ _____ _____ in these holes. Once they have raised their babies, woodpeckers do not use the nesting holes anymore. But _____ _____ _____ _____ other animals do. For instance, squirrels, owls, and snakes sometimes use woodpecker holes for shelter or to raise their babies.

Finally, we have mutualists. Mutualists are two types of animals that benefit each other. Thus, they have _____ _____ _____. Bees and flowers are examples of mutualists. Flowers _____ _____ _____ _____. And _____ _____, the bees help flowers produce seeds so that they can reproduce. So, uh, bees will _____ _____ _____. And the number of flowers will decrease without bees. But it also affects the entire ecosystem if _____ _____ _____ _____. For example, many birds _____ _____ flower seeds for food, and the number of these birds will be reduced. And other animals which eat these birds will decrease as well.

Vocabulary Review

Answer Book p. 9

A. Choose the correct word for each meaning.

available   grab   starve   fiction

1 to take or pick something up suddenly: _____

2 stories about people and events that are not real: _____

3 can be found or used: _____

4 to suffer or die from not enough food: _____

B. Fill in the blanks with the appropriate words from the box.

intelligent   inspire   traditional   population   wealth

5 The city of Seoul has a _____ of almost 10 million people.

6 The family's _____ comes from many large businesses.

7 The manager is _____ and will know how to fix the problem.

8 The athlete wants to _____ children to try sports.

9 In some countries, people wear _____ costumes on holidays.

C. Choose the closest meaning for each highlighted word or phrase.

10 Students need to get their parents' permission to join the trip.
  (A) power   (B) discussion   (C) approval   (D) category

11 The storm produced extreme weather across the region.
  (A) basic   (B) severe   (C) active   (D) environmental

12 The computer can solve complex problems quickly.
  (A) complicated (B) terrible   (C) loyal   (D) related

13 There were plenty of people at the store opening.
  (A) great   (B) other   (C) major   (D) many

14 The movie is clearly different from the book.
  (A) slightly   (B) obviously   (C) regularly   (D) simply

HACKERS APEX LISTENING
for the TOEFL iBT
Intermediate

CHAPTER 02

Detail

Detail

About the Question Type

Detail questions ask you to identify specific details or facts that are mentioned in a conversation or lecture.

Correct answers restate specific information explicitly mentioned in the passage. Incorrect answers contain new, contradictory, or irrelevant information. Some questions may require you to select more than one correct answer choice.

Question Format

- According to the conversation, what is ~?
- What does the professor say about ~?
- According to the professor, what are the reasons for ~? *Choose 2 answers.*
- What are the two examples the man gives of ~? *Choose 2 answers.*

Key Strategies

- **Step 1** — Identify the main topic and focus on important information supporting the main idea. For example, listen carefully for definitions, examples, reasons, results, and features.

- **Step 2** — Listen carefully for signal words that are commonly used to introduce supporting ideas. Some examples include: *For instance, To illustrate, That's because, As a result, Similarly,* and *On the other hand.*

- **Step 3** — Select the answer choice that best presents the information from the conversation or lecture. Remember, the correct answer often paraphrases information, or repeats it using different words.

Example

Answer Book p. 9

A. Listen to a conversation between a student and the director of campus activities.

Note-taking

Student's Problem

An _____ _____ is not on school website.

Director's Solution

Ask any professor for a _____

What was missing in the forms for the advertisement request?

(A) Costs for an advertisement
(B) A student ID number
(C) A signature from a professor
(D) Explanations about a lecture

Answer Book p. 9

B. Listen to part of a lecture in an astronomy class.

Note-taking

Jupiter's Great _____ _____

Why is it red?

→ The leading theory
: It comes from a combination of _____ in the clouds and _____ _____.

According to the professor, what are two factors that contribute to the color of the Great Red Spot? *Choose 2 answers.*

(A) Ammonia in the clouds
(B) Unique patterns on the surface
(C) Solar energy
(D) Red dust in the atmosphere

Dictation

Answer Book p. 9

Listen again and fill in the blanks.

A.

W: Hi. I'm looking for the director of campus activities.

M: That's me. What can I do for you?

W: I'm the head of the Literature Club. We applied to _____ _____ _____ _____ on our school website, but it's not there.

M: Um, did you _____ _____ _____ _____ _____?

W: I did. I _____ _____ _____. We really need an advertisement to _____ _____ _____ _____. A famous writer, Katherine Oliver, will be here to talk about her recent novel.

M: That sounds interesting. Let me take a look and find out what the problem is... Hmm... Did you _____ _____ _____ from a professor?

W: No, we don't _____ _____ _____ ... Is there anything I can do?

M: You can ask any professor for a signature. I'm sure that one of the literature professors would be happy to help you.

W: OK, I'll do that.

B.

P: If you look at the surface of Jupiter, you will see many unique patterns. Um, these patterns are _____ _____ _____. Jupiter is _____ _____ giant gas clouds that are _____ _____ _____ _____ the clouds on Earth. Among them, there is a giant red storm called the Great Red Spot. Why is it red, though?

No one knows exactly what creates this red color. But the leading theory suggests that the storm's color _____ _____ a combination of two factors: ammonia in the clouds and _____ _____. Um, ammonia forms the top layer of Jupiter's atmosphere, and it doesn't have any color. However, when it _____ _____ _____ from the Sun, a material is created that has a red color. Still, the theory has a weak point... So now, let's talk about what the weak point is.

Listening Practice 1

Answer Book p. 10

Listen to a conversation between a student and a professor.

Note-taking

Student's Problem
Cannot take the test because of a _____ _____

Professor's Suggestion
- Can double the student's _____ score
- Can give _____ _____ in class

1 Why does the student go to see the professor?
   (A) To ask for advice about missing a test
   (B) To invite him to an upcoming school event
   (C) To complain about the amount of schoolwork
   (D) To request help with preparing for a debate

2 Why does the professor congratulate the student?
   (A) She was accepted to study abroad.
   (B) She was asked to participate in a school activity.
   (C) She got the highest grade on a test.
   (D) She won a regional contest with her team.

3 According to the professor, how can the student earn extra points?
   (A) By writing a special report
   (B) By giving a class presentation
   (C) By joining class discussions
   (D) By taking a second exam

Dictation

Answer Book p. 10

Listen again and fill in the blanks.

S: Hi, Professor Anderson. I hope you aren't too busy. Do you have a moment to talk about next week's test? Uh, I don't think I can _____ _____ _____.

P: Oh? Is there a problem?

S: Um... I was chosen by the debate club to _____ _____ _____ _____ _____ next week. One of the other team members can't _____ _____.

P: I see. Well, it's important to participate in school activities, so _____ _____ _____. Um, is this a big contest?

S: It's a college championship. Our team will be _____ _____.

P: That's amazing! I hope you do well... But you'll need to _____ _____ _____ from the debate club to _____ _____ _____.

S: Yes, I have the letter right here, actually... But, um, what about the test? I could _____ _____ _____ on the topic instead.

P: Well, I can double your midterm score to _____ _____ _____ missing the final.

S: Um, I _____ _____ _____ _____ on my midterm. It may not be high enough... Is there any other way to _____ _____ _____?

P: Well, you can _____ _____ _____ in class, too. If you participate more in discussions, then I can give you extra points for that.

S: All right, Professor Anderson. That sounds fine.

Listening Practice 2

Answer Book p. 11

Listen to part of a lecture in a psychology class.

Note-taking

A _____ of a Black Swan

Conditions for a Black Swan
- Outside of our _____ _____
- Creates a _____ _____ on our society
  e.g. 'Earth is _____' → 'Earth is round',
       Paper and pens → _____

1. What is the main topic of the lecture?

   (A) A new species of bird
   (B) A theory about unexpected events
   (C) Views of reality in different cultures
   (D) New evidence about an old belief

2. What does the professor say about European explorers in the 17th century?

   (A) They had limited knowledge about geography.
   (B) They brought swans with them to Australia.
   (C) They had never seen a black swan before.
   (D) They were the first foreigners to arrive in Australia.

3. According to Taleb, what are two conditions of a Black Swan? *Choose 2 answers.*

   (A) It is outside regular knowledge.
   (B) It is imaginary rather than real.
   (C) It is not accepted by most people.
   (D) It has a big effect on society.

4. Why does the professor mention the Internet?

   (A) To highlight the importance of communication
   (B) To explain why people once refused new knowledge
   (C) To give an example of a dramatic change
   (D) To show how a new technology can create value quickly

Dictation

Answer Book p. 11

Listen again and fill in the blanks.

C2_P2_D

P: Who has heard of the Black Swan Theory? Well, as you might expect, it is related to a black swan. The Black Swan Theory is about a fact or event that _____ _____. But, the impossible becomes real with new information. And, uh, this changes people's psychology. In fact, it changes their _____ _____ _____ _____.

In the old days, Europeans thought that all swans were white. Imagine that you have seen thousands of swans, and all of them were white. You might think that all swans are white. Well, _____ _____ _____ for many years because there were no black swans in Europe. But, uh, when European explorers traveled to Australia in the 17th century, they saw black swans _____ _____ _____ _____. This changed their view about what a swan could be.

The theory was later _____ _____ Nassim Nicholas Taleb in 2001. In his book, he _____ _____ _____ for a Black Swan. At first, a Black Swan is _____ _____ our regular knowledge. We can never expect that it is real until we discover it. But once it is known, it _____ _____ _____ _____ _____ our society. Imagine that one day we find out something that turns our knowledge _____ _____. Everyone will be shocked and confused.

So, uh, here are some good examples. Once, people thought Earth was flat. But when they learned it was round, it changed their thinking completely. Similarly, most people could not imagine communication _____ _____ _____ _____. But the Internet changed all of that. It even changed the way we live. Um, think of how often you _____ _____ _____ every day. Before the Internet, no one knew how important it would become. It, uh, surprised everyone. A Black Swan will only have value after it is discovered, but its value will be very high.

Listening Practice 3

Answer Book p. 12

Listen to a conversation between a student and a food service manager.

Note-taking

Student's Problem
Won't be available to work at _____

Manager's Answer
_____ shift: Full
→ _____ shift: A position is available.

1 What is the main topic of the conversation?

(A) Looking for a new staff member
(B) Fixing a problem among the staff
(C) Changing some hours of work
(D) Adding items to a cafeteria menu

2 Why is the student unavailable at night?

(A) He is preparing for a music contest.
(B) He has to attend band practice.
(C) He usually studies late at night.
(D) He needs to take extra classes to graduate.

3 What was the student worried about?

(A) Missing a practice session
(B) Getting along with staff
(C) Working shorter hours
(D) Waking up early in the morning

Dictation

Answer Book p. 12

Listen again and fill in the blanks.

M: Hi, are you Ms. Stewart, the food service manager? I was told to come and speak to you about a question I had.

W: That's right. Uh, are you one of our _____ _____ _____? How can I help you?

M: Yes. My name is Ryan, and I work on _____ _____ _____ from 6 to 8 p.m. But I was wondering if I could _____ _____ _____ _____ of shift.

W: Are you _____ _____ _____ other staff members on the nighttime shift?

M: No... Um, you see, I won't be _____ _____ _____ at night. I _____ _____ _____ and, um, I need to practice in the evenings.

W: I see. So which shift are you interested in?

M: I want to _____ _____ _____ _____ _____ if it's possible.

W: Well, the lunchtime shift is full. It's _____ _____ _____ _____ among the student staff.

M: Well, what about the morning shift? I was _____ _____ _____ _____ so early, but if there's no other option...

W: One of the students on the morning shift just quit, so we _____ _____ _____.

M: I guess I'll have to take that one, then. Thank you for your help, Ms. Stewart.

Supplementary materials at HackersBook.com

Listening Practice 4

Listen to part of a lecture in a geology class.

Note-taking

Sediment
: Loose _____ and minerals that are _____ _____ over time

Sediment _____
- By wind e.g. Sand hills called _____
- By water e.g. At the bottom of a _____

1. What is the main topic of the lecture?
   (A) The places where sediment is found
   (B) What sediment is and how it moves
   (C) The importance of sediment for growing food
   (D) How sediment makes the environment healthy

2. What is a key feature of sediment?
   (A) It comes in many sizes.
   (B) It provides food for animals.
   (C) It is mostly made up of plants.
   (D) It is a collection of grains.

3. What happens when sediment is blown by the wind?
   (A) It pollutes the air.
   (B) It causes physical damage.
   (C) It breaks up into smaller pieces.
   (D) It forms into large rocks.

4. According to the professor, where can large amounts of sediment be found in water?
   (A) On the shore of a beach
   (B) Near the edge of a lake
   (C) Between rivers and the sea
   (D) At the top of a mountain

Dictation

Answer Book p. 13

Listen again and fill in the blanks.

P: People don't think about sediment, but it's very important. Sediment is rocky material that is _____ _____ one place to another. It can be found everywhere... in the mountains, the desert, and even the sea. It helps us grow food and _____ _____ a healthy environment... But, what exactly is sediment, and how does it move from one place to another?

So, first of all, sediment is made up of _____ _____ _____ _____ that are broken down over time. However, it also _____ _____ _____ of plants and animals that, uh, are _____ _____ after they die... Individual sediments come in many sizes, too. Sometimes, they are _____ _____ _____ a grain of sand. Other times, they can be as big as a large rock or stone.

Because sediment is made up of loose material, it is _____ _____ _____... The way that this happens, um, scientists call this process sediment transport... It occurs mainly through _____ _____ _____.

First, there is wind. Strong wind _____ _____ rocks and moves soil, sand, and dirt across long distances. As sediments are _____ the wind, they hit each other and break down into smaller pieces. Eventually, they collect into _____ _____ or are moved across a wide area. In fact, wind is the main cause of sediment transport in the desert. Wind mostly _____ _____ sand. This sometimes creates large sand hills called dunes.

Second, we have water. Heavy rains, ocean waves, and fast-moving rivers can cause rocks to become loose and _____ _____ _____... Um, you'll often find lots of sediment at the bottom of a waterfall. You know, the power of a waterfall is very strong, so it makes sediment _____ _____ _____ _____. But the largest amount of sediment is collected, um, where rivers _____ _____ _____.

iBT Listening Test 1

Answer Book p. 14

TOEFL Listening

Note-taking

Student's Question
Wants to study _____ as another major
→ Can you tell me how to apply?

Application Process
- Complete basic _____
- Meet with the head of each _____
- Write a _____ stating you will _____ your majors

1 What is the main topic of the conversation?
 Ⓐ Signing up late for a class
 Ⓑ Completing some courses
 Ⓒ Studying another field as a major
 Ⓓ Starting a small business

2 Why does the student want to study psychology?
 Ⓐ To complete requirements for graduation
 Ⓑ To improve her grades
 Ⓒ To prepare for a marketing assignment
 Ⓓ To become a better marketer

3 How does the professor help the student?
 Ⓐ By approving a request
 Ⓑ By providing detailed advice
 Ⓒ By writing a letter of recommendation
 Ⓓ By offering to teach the student

Listen again to part of the conversation. Then answer the question.

4 Why does the professor say this: 🎧
 Ⓐ He thinks a student can study two majors at the same time.
 Ⓑ He believes a double major will help the student's career.
 Ⓒ He is sure about how to apply for a double major.
 Ⓓ He knows that the student's request will be accepted.

Dictation

Answer Book p. 14

Listen again and fill in the blanks.

S: Hello, Professor Morris. Can I talk to you? I was in some of your classes before. My name is Alice.

P: Of course, Alice. I remember... You're _____ _____ business management, right?

S: Yes, that's right. I'm here to _____ _____ _____ _____... As I said, I took a few of your psychology classes before. Um, but now I want to study psychology _____ _____ _____.

P: Oh, is that so? I'm _____ _____ _____ that. But why do you want to study psychology _____ _____ _____ _____?

S: Well, I want to be a marketing professional after college. I, um, think _____ _____ _____ will help in that field. You know, marketers need to know how consumers think.

P: You're right, it will be helpful! In that case, majoring in both _____ _____ _____ _____ will be perfect for you. That way you can _____ _____ _____ in both areas.

S: Yes, but I'm worried too because it sounds difficult. Do you think I can do it?

P: I am sure of it. You're intelligent and you _____ _____. Um, how are your grades? Are they good?

S: Thank you, yes. I'm doing well in all of my classes. Um, can I ask one more thing? Can you tell me _____ _____ _____?

P: Well, first, you _____ _____ _____ all of the basic requirements for each major. Then, you should meet with the head of each department. Lastly, you should _____ _____ _____ stating that you promise to complete your double major.

S: Thank you for _____ _____ _____, Professor Morris. I'll give it a try.

iBT Listening Test 2

TOEFL Listening

ENVIRONMENTAL SCIENCE

Note-taking

_____ : Natural resources can be used today and in the future.

Natural Resources
- _____ Sources: Can easily _____ themselves
    e.g. Most plants and animals
- Non-renewable Sources: Cannot be created easily and take _____
    _____ years to form
    e.g. Gold, silver, _____, natural gas, and oil

1 What is the main topic of the lecture?
  Ⓐ The most valuable natural resources
  Ⓑ Threats to the world's forests
  Ⓒ The importance of sustainability
  Ⓓ Types of renewable energy resources

2 What does the professor say about most plants and animals?
  Ⓐ They are limited in number.
  Ⓑ They are renewable resources.
  Ⓒ They take many years to reproduce.
  Ⓓ They have various practical uses.

3 What does the professor say about cutting down trees?
  Ⓐ It is happening less quickly than before.
  Ⓑ It has become easier to do with machines.
  Ⓒ It requires people to plant more trees.
  Ⓓ It will make a renewable resource unsustainable.

4 What are two possible outcomes of forest misuse?
  Choose 2 answers.
  Ⓐ Species can be lost forever.
  Ⓑ Climate change will become more serious.
  Ⓒ Trees can suffer from diseases.
  Ⓓ Carbon dioxide will decrease oxygen.

Listen again to part of the lecture. Then answer the question.

5 Why does the professor say this:
  Ⓐ To emphasize the human causes of global warming
  Ⓑ To show that some forests have successfully recovered
  Ⓒ To highlight the importance of protecting forests
  Ⓓ To explain how people can protect forests

Dictation

Answer Book p. 15

Listen again and fill in the blanks.

P: Sustainability means that we can _____ _____ _____ or use something in the future. When we talk about natural resources, sustainability means we can use these resources today and in the future... possibly forever. But we must _____ _____ _____ of natural resources properly to keep them sustainable.

Generally, there are _____ _____ _____ _____ _____. The first is renewable, and the second is non-renewable. Renewable resources _____ _____ _____. For example, most plants and animals can reproduce, so they are _____ _____... This allows us to use them _____ _____. On the other hand, the amount of gold and silver on Earth is fixed. This means that these resources are not renewable. Once we use all of them, they _____ _____ _____ easily. Similarly, coal, natural gas, and oil take _____ _____ _____ to form. They may be produced someday, but not in one lifetime, so we can say that they are non-renewable.

So, uh, obviously we must _____ _____ _____ _____ non-renewable resources. But, um, we must also _____ _____ _____ how we use renewable ones. Renewable resources are only sustainable if we _____ _____ _____. Well, let's look at the example of forests. We know that trees naturally reproduce. But did you know that forests can disappear? Humans have always used wood for many things like paper and buildings. We also _____ _____ _____ for agriculture, which happens on a large scale. A recent study found that 18 million acres of forests are removed each year. If we _____ _____ this number of trees, forests will not be sustainable. For example, already 20 percent of the Amazon rainforest _____ _____ _____

_____.

So why is the sustainability of natural resources important? Well, let me continue explaining this with forests. They provide _____ _____ with a home. When we _____ _____ _____, many species can disappear forever as well. You know, living things _____ _____ _____ each other, so this will eventually affect us, too. Also, misuse can _____ _____ _____ _____. Trees _____ _____ carbon dioxide from the air and release oxygen, right? Global warming will _____ _____ _____ without enough trees. So, um, _____ _____ _____ is not just an option anymore... We cannot wait any longer.

Vocabulary Review

Answer Book p. 17

A. Choose the correct word for each meaning.

| promote | misuse | communication | prove |

1. to use something incorrectly or carelessly: _____
2. to encourage people to use or support something: _____
3. the act or process of giving or exchanging information: _____
4. to show that something is true or false: _____

B. Fill in the blanks with the appropriate words or phrases from the box.

| find out | renewable | belief | value | contribute to |

5. Passengers can go to a website to _____ the train schedule.
6. Many people had the _____ that there was life on Mars.
7. Information has a lot of _____ in today's economy.
8. The sun is a good source of _____ energy.
9. Scientists _____ the development of new medicines.

C. Choose the closest meaning for each highlighted word.

10. Cars are one of the leading causes of air pollution.
    (A) best (B) flat (C) loose (D) main

11. Amy went to library to collect information about the topic.
    (A) submit (B) release (C) gather (D) represent

12. Farming had a huge impact on the development of cities.
    (A) form (B) influence (C) shift (D) limitation

13. He eventually became a lawyer after studying for many years.
    (A) completely (B) finally (C) similarly (D) regularly

14. Einstein was a genius in the field of science.
    (A) area (B) atmosphere (C) position (D) requirement

HACKERS APEX LISTENING
for the TOEFL iBT
Intermediate

CHAPTER 03

Function

Function

■ **About the Question Type**

Function questions ask you to determine the true meaning or intention behind a speaker's statement. This is usually different from what the speaker states directly.

These questions require you to listen again to part of a conversation or lecture. Some examples of the possible functions of a statement include: to explain a concept, to give an opinion, and to make a comparison.

■ **Question Format**

Listen again to part of the lecture. Then answer the question.
P: **********************
Why does the professor say this: 🎧

■ **Key Strategies**

- **Step 1** — Listen carefully to the replay, and then identify the intention behind what the speaker has said within the context.

- **Step 2** — Focus on the words that the speaker emphasizes and the tone of voice that they use. They often indicate the true intention behind statements.

- **Step 3** — Select the answer choice that best represents the true meaning or intention of the speaker.

Example

Answer Book p. 17

A. Listen to a conversation between a student and a professor.

C3_ExA

Note-taking

Student's Question
Would like to ask for some _____ about my _____

Professor's Answer
A paragraph is not _____ _____ the topic.
→ Compare the _____ and the draft

Listen again to part of the conversation. Then answer the question.
Why does the professor say this: 🎧

(A) To recommend a different printer
(B) To confirm that a paper should be printed
(C) To say that she understands a situation
(D) To indicate that other students had the same problem

Answer Book p. 17

B. Listen to part of a lecture in a biology class.

C3_ExB

Note-taking

How Antelope Squirrels Control Their Body Temperature
_____ is not a good way to cool down.
→ Instead, they dig _____ _____ and go inside them.

Listen again to part of the lecture. Then answer the question.
What does the professor mean when she says this: 🎧

(A) The ability to control body temperature is important.
(B) The importance of moisture is obvious in dry places.
(C) The antelope squirrels can live without much moisture.
(D) The animals in dry places survive by sweating a lot.

Dictation

Answer Book p. 17

Listen again and fill in the blanks.

A.

S: Professor Ross, I'd like to ask for some advice about my paper. Here's my paper...

P: We _____ _____ _____ _____ 30 minutes ago... Why are you so late?

S: Uh, I had a problem with the printer. I _____ _____ the paper yesterday, but the library printer _____ _____ _____ this morning.

P: Oh, I know about that printer. I've had _____ _____ _____ myself... Well, it's fine. We can discuss your paper now.

S: Thank you for understanding.

P: Let's see... Overall, it seems fine, but the third paragraph is not exactly _____ _____ the topic.

S: Oh, I didn't realize that. I think I made the same mistakes in my last paper, too.

P: After writing a draft, you should _____ _____ _____ and the draft to make sure everything is related to the topic.

B.

P: Many animals can naturally _____ _____ _____ _____ through sweating. But not all animals have this ability. Instead, some animals depend on the environment around them. An example of this is antelope squirrels.

Antelope squirrels live in very hot, dry places like deserts. They _____ _____ _____ during the day under extreme heat, so their body temperature increases. But because of their small size, sweating is not a good way for them to _____ _____. If they sweat to reduce their body heat, they will lose _____ _____ _____. You know what happens when you lose moisture in dry places... It becomes _____ _____ _____. So, instead, these squirrels use the environment. They _____ _____ that are cool and dark inside. Once they go inside the holes, their body temperature _____ _____ _____.

Listening Practice 1

Answer Book p. 18

Listen to a conversation between a student and a registrar's office employee.

Note-taking

Student's Problem
_____ a class and received a _____ from the school

Employee's Suggestion
• Stay in a _____ on campus
• Take the class _____ next semester

1 What is the main topic of the conversation?

   (A) The wrong information on a letter
   (B) A school's system for testing students
   (C) The student's concerns about a class
   (D) A student's options for next semester

2 What does the employee suggest that the student do?

   (A) Take a different bus to the campus
   (B) Live in a school dormitory
   (C) Change his class schedule
   (D) Ask his professor for advice

Listen again to part of the conversation. Then answer the question.

3 Why does the employee say this:

   (A) To remind the student about an exam
   (B) To make sure the student's name is on a list
   (C) To tell the student he can take a class again
   (D) To confirm that the student can graduate

Dictation

Answer Book p. 18

Listen again and fill in the blanks.

M: Excuse me. I _____ _____ _____ from the school last week. It says that I, uh, failed one of my classes. Does the school usually send letters like this?

W: Yes, a letter is _____ _____ to students' homes when they fail a class.

M: Oh, I didn't know that… This is the first time that it has happened to me. Um, do you know why I _____ _____ _____? It wasn't explained in the letter.

W: You should ask your professor for details. But, the system shows that you were often _____ _____ _____ _____ and missed it several times.

M: That's true… I, uh, thought it would be _____ _____ _____ a 9 a.m. class. But, it was difficult to get to the campus _____ _____.

W: What seems to be the problem?

M: Um, I live more than an hour away from campus. So, I have to _____ _____ _____ _____ to get to school on time.

W: I see. Perhaps you could _____ _____ _____ _____ on campus. It would be much more convenient.

M: I will definitely consider that. But, what about the class? I need to _____ _____ in order to graduate.

W: Don't worry. There's always _____ _____. The class will _____ _____ _____ next semester.

M: All right. I'll _____ _____ _____ _____ then. Thanks!

Listening Practice 2

Answer Book p. 19

Listen to part of a lecture in an architecture class.

Note-taking

The _____ of Sagrada Familia

- Gothic style
- Art Nouveau: Lots of curved lines and _____
- Catalan Modernism: Shapes copied from _____
- Playful designs from Gaudi's own _____

1. What is the lecture mainly about?

   (A) The history of architecture in Spain
   (B) The career of a well-known architect
   (C) The biggest attractions of a city
   (D) The design of a famous church

2. According to the professor, what was unusual about Gaudi?

   (A) His use of sharp towers
   (B) His love of Gothic architecture
   (C) His age when he started a project
   (D) His disagreements with other architects

3. What does the professor mention as a feature of the Art Nouveau style?

   (A) Cross-shaped buildings
   (B) Pointed windows and towers
   (C) Playful and colorful designs
   (D) Curved lines and decorations

Listen again to part of the lecture. Then answer the question.

4. What does the professor mean when she says this:

   (A) The design of Sagrada Familia was difficult to build.
   (B) Gaudi's carefulness probably caused a long construction time.
   (C) The church builders asked Gaudi to make too many changes.
   (D) The final design of Sagrada Familia is unknown.

Dictation

Answer Book p. 19

Listen again and fill in the blanks.

P: Recently, we were discussing _____ _____ _____ _____ _____ around the world. One of the most famous churches is the one in Barcelona, Spain. It's called Sagrada Familia, and it attracts _____ _____ _____ a year. Let's talk about its design.

So, the construction of Sagrada Familia started in 1882. Its original architect was, uh, Francisco del Villar. He _____ _____ _____ in the Gothic style, which includes pointed windows and sharp towers. Unfortunately, del Villar _____ _____ _____ _____ the builders of the church. So, he was replaced by Antoni Gaudi in 1883. Gaudi was only 31 years old when he _____ _____ Sagrada Familia's construction, which was, uh, quite unusual. However, Gaudi was already known for his creative designs at this age. Gaudi _____ _____ _____ some of the original Gothic ideas, like, uh, the building plan in the shape of a cross. But Gaudi also changed many other features... He combined the Gothic style with Art Nouveau, which features lots of curved lines and _____ _____. So, um, you'll notice other characteristics of Art Nouveau throughout the building. There are lots of dramatic shapes and decorations... And, uh, he also included features of Catalan Modernism, such as shapes _____ _____ _____, as well as playful designs from his own imagination. Gaudi's idea was to have a church that was full of light and color. He was careful about every detail.

S: Um, is that why its construction was _____ _____?

P: Well, that's probably one reason. Gaudi worked on Sagrada Familia for over 40 years! What else can I say? _____ _____ _____ _____ of it was complete by the time he died in 1926. After his death, other architects were hired to _____ _____ _____ based on Gaudi's ideas.

Listening Practice 3

Answer Book p. 20

Listen to a conversation between a student and a registrar's office employee.

Note-taking

Student's Question
A class is _____. → What are my _____?

_____ of Online Courses
- Can save time on your _____
- Can _____ the course videos to review lessons

1 Why does the student go to the registrar's office?

   (A) To get information about a professor
   (B) To find out about moving to a new college
   (C) To change some registered information
   (D) To learn about options for taking a course

2 How does the employee help the student?

   (A) By providing the phone number of a professor
   (B) By checking for courses on a computer
   (C) By telling the student to go to an office
   (D) By writing down the student's information

Listen again to part of the conversation. Then answer the question.

3 What does the student mean when she says this: 🎧

   (A) She needs an explanation of some advantages.
   (B) She disagrees with the employee's idea.
   (C) She does not understand some course requirements.
   (D) She doesn't want to take an online course.

Dictation

Answer Book p. 20

Listen again and fill in the blanks.

W: Hello. My name is Victoria, and I have a question to ask you about a course.

M: Sure, Victoria. How can I help you?

W: Well, I wanted to _____ _____ _____ Professor Wilson's course on Russian history, but, um, I found out that the class is full. I'm wondering what _____ _____ _____.

M: Let me check on my computer to see if there are _____ _____ ... Hmm... That course is offered online. Does that _____ _____ ?

W: Um, I think that taking a course _____ _____ would be better... I can meet the professor and _____ _____ _____ _____.

M: I understand, but it is _____ _____ _____ about Russian history for this semester. Also, I _____ _____ _____ _____. You see, online courses _____ _____ _____.

W: What do you mean?

M: Well, you don't need to come to school, so you can _____ _____ on your commute... Um, you can even _____ _____ _____ _____ if you need to review class material.

W: I like that I can _____ _____ _____.

M: And even though it's online, all the lessons from the class will be the same. Your assignments will still _____ _____ _____ Professor Wilson, too.

W: That's true. I'll sign up for the online course, then.

Listening Practice 4

Answer Book p. 21

Listen to part of a lecture in an ecology class.

Note-taking

Wetlands
: Land areas that are _____ _____ water for a long time
- Types: _____ wetlands and _____ wetlands
- _____ for a variety of plants and animals

1 What is the lecture mainly about?
   (A) The different kinds of environments
   (B) The influence of water on wetlands
   (C) The characteristics of wetlands
   (D) The difference between wet and dry climates

2 According to the professor, when do tidal wetlands form?
   (A) When strong ocean waves hit parts of the coast
   (B) When rain falls in shallow areas
   (C) When fresh water mixes with salt in the ground
   (D) When water from the sea combines with fresh water

3 What does the professor say about Chesapeake Bay's oystercatchers?
   (A) They make nests in different areas every year.
   (B) They look for food on the beach.
   (C) They are decreasing at a rapid rate.
   (D) They prefer to live near fresh water.

Listen again to part of the lecture. Then answer the question.

4 Why does the professor say this:
   (A) To show the importance of an animal
   (B) To highlight the role of wetlands
   (C) To introduce more specific information
   (D) To bring up a separate point

Dictation

Answer Book p. 21

Listen again and fill in the blanks.

P: The natural world has many _____ _____ with, uh, different characteristics... For example, you have deserts that are very dry and hot, or uh, forests that are very green and cool... Well, today I'm going to focus on another environment called a wetland and talk about its features.

Wetlands are land areas that are _____ _____ _____ for a long time. They mainly form when water is _____ _____ _____ fast enough. So, a large amount of water collects in one area. In general, there are _____ _____ _____ _____. The first are freshwater wetlands. Fresh water is water that is _____ _____ _____, so you'll find freshwater wetlands near rivers, lakes, and other _____ _____ _____ _____. As you move near the coast, on the other hand, you'll find another kind called tidal wetlands. You know, tides are when ocean water _____ _____ _____. Every time this happens, some water from the ocean flows toward land and _____ _____ _____ _____, which creates tidal wetlands.

Now, wetlands are _____ _____ a wide variety of plants and animals, especially birds. Many birds spend their lives in wetlands because they find _____ _____ _____ there. Let me explain it in more detail. In the Chesapeake Bay, which is on the east coast of Maryland, you can find _____ _____ _____ _____. And more than 250 species of birds live there. Wood ducks are one of them. They're commonly found in freshwater wetlands near trees. They are the only ducks to _____ _____ in the holes of trees in this region. In the Chesapeake Bay's tidal wetlands, you will find American oystercatchers. The Chesapeake Bay produces about 14 million oysters every year along its muddy beaches. So, over 50 percent of the oystercatchers in Maryland come here to eat oysters.

iBT Listening Test 1

TOEFL Listening

Note-taking

Student's Question
Can I join the group for the _____ _____?
→ Any advice for _____ outside the classroom?

Professor's Suggestion
Talk to Professor Foster about his new _____ on artificial intelligence
→ _____ _____ him or come back tomorrow

1. What is the main topic of the conversation?
   - Ⓐ Submitting assignments on time
   - Ⓑ Asking advice for which class to take
   - Ⓒ Finding a school activity to join
   - Ⓓ Learning about new subjects

2. Why is the student surprised at the professor's suggestion?
   - Ⓐ He is excited about participating in a club.
   - Ⓑ He took a course about a project topic.
   - Ⓒ He did not expect any help with his request.
   - Ⓓ He does not feel confident he can perform a task.

3. What will the student probably do next?
   - Ⓐ Schedule an appointment for tomorrow
   - Ⓑ Check a notice posted on the wall
   - Ⓒ Come back after a class ends
   - Ⓓ Wait for a professor to return

Listen again to part of the conversation. Then answer the question.

4. Why does the professor say this: 🎧
   - Ⓐ To advise the student about choosing his career
   - Ⓑ To offer her assistance with a recent accident
   - Ⓒ To show that she understands the student's concern
   - Ⓓ To imply that the student needs to improve his grades

Dictation

Answer Book p. 22

Listen again and fill in the blanks.

S: Hi, Professor Greene. Here's my assignment. Um, I know it's late, but I _____ _____ _____ _____ yesterday.

P: I'm sorry to hear that, Ben, but I'll need an official document _____ _____.

S: OK, uh, I'll _____ _____ _____ _____ tomorrow... But anyway, um, I'm also wondering if I can _____ _____ _____ you've organized for the science fair.

P: Well, I'm afraid the group is already full... Many students wanted to join.

S: Oh, no... Um, I really need to do activities _____ _____ _____. I don't have much time left because it's _____ _____ _____ here at school. Um, do you have any advice?

P: Sure. Those activities will _____ _____ _____ _____ after graduation... Perhaps you could talk to Professor Foster. He is looking for students who can help him with his new experiment on artificial intelligence.

S: Oh, really? I took one of his classes about artificial intelligence last year, and I found it interesting. Do you know what kind of work I'll be doing?

P: You will probably _____ _____ and _____ _____ _____ of the experiment.

S: I think I can do that. I'll go to talk to Professor Foster right away.

P: I heard that he _____ _____ _____ this afternoon, so he will not be in his office right now. But he should be back soon. You can either _____ _____ _____ or _____ _____ tomorrow. I'll let him know that you stopped by.

S: Thanks, Professor Greene. I'll _____ _____ _____. I don't have any more classes today, anyway.

P: That's fine. Good luck!

iBT Listening Test 2

Answer Book p. 23

TOEFL Listening

HISTORY

Note-taking

In 1688

A _____ _____ king James II had a baby boy.
→ Some powerful Protestants formed a _____.
→ William and Mary agreed to _____ England.

In 1689

William and Mary made many important decisions:
- More _____ to the people in government
- The right to have free _____

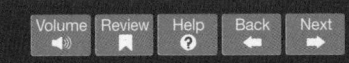

1. What is the lecture mainly about?
   Ⓐ The cause of a war between two different religions
   Ⓑ The rise and fall of the Roman Catholic Church
   Ⓒ A series of revolutions that happened in Europe
   Ⓓ A revolution in England that happened without a fight

2. According to the professor, why did Protestants become angry with James II?
   Ⓐ He tried to make himself more powerful.
   Ⓑ He banned Protestants from government.
   Ⓒ He sent his daughter away to a different country.
   Ⓓ He forced some people to become Catholics.

3. According to the professor, what caused England's powerful Protestants to form a plan?
   Ⓐ The death of James II
   Ⓑ The birth of James II's son
   Ⓒ The invasion of Netherlands
   Ⓓ The return of William and Mary

4. What is the professor's attitude toward William and Mary's decision?
   Ⓐ She thinks that it should have been made earlier.
   Ⓑ She is moved by their peaceful actions.
   Ⓒ She is impressed by its long-term effects.
   Ⓓ She believes that they were forced to make it.

Listen again to part of the lecture. Then answer the question.

5. Why does the professor say this:
   Ⓐ To show how hard it is to be the ruler of a country
   Ⓑ To explain why some politicians did not like William and Mary
   Ⓒ To emphasize the influence that William and Mary had
   Ⓓ To indicate that many people in England were still Catholic

Dictation

Answer Book p. 23

Listen again and fill in the blanks.

P: OK, where were we last time? Oh, we were talking about the late 17th century in England. Well, then, let's start with the Glorious Revolution. The Glorious Revolution happened from 1688 to 1689. At the time, England _____ _____ _____ a Roman Catholic king called James II, but England's people were mostly Protestant. Protestants are Christians who _____ _____ the Roman Catholic Church. The two groups, uh, _____ _____ some Christian beliefs and did not have a good relationship. James II made many Protestants angry by _____ _____ _____ _____ that benefited Catholics. He also wanted to change England's system of government to _____ _____ _____ _____ the king. _____ _____ _____, many Protestants thought they could wait until James II died. And, uh, after he died, his daughter Mary—who was Protestant—would _____ _____. Unfortunately, in 1688, James had a baby boy. This meant that the boy would _____ _____ _____ of England after James II died, not Mary. That is when some powerful Protestants _____ _____ _____. They did not want England to be ruled by another Catholic and asked Mary and her husband William, the ruler of the Netherlands, to _____ _____. William and Mary agreed. They, uh, _____ _____ from the Netherlands to England. James II _____ _____ _____ William and Mary, but he didn't _____ _____. So, he _____ _____ to France, where he eventually died. After James II ran away, William and Mary became the rulers of England without a war. Um, this is why it is called the Glorious Revolution. It happened _____ _____. Now, William and Mary _____ _____ _____ the country together, and they _____ _____ _____ _____ ... The biggest one was that William and Mary promised to _____ _____ _____ created by politicians. This decision gave less power to the king and queen and more power to the people in government. Isn't that incredible? This decision _____ _____ _____ _____. Because of the Glorious Revolution, England became a country ruled by politicians _____ _____ _____ ... And that's not all. William and Mary also gave people _____ _____ _____ _____ _____ _____. So, you can see that they had a big influence on England's way of life.

Vocabulary Review

Answer Book p. 24

A. Choose the correct word for each meaning.

playful   drain   architecture   experiment

1 the style or method of designing buildings: _____

2 lively, funny, and not serious: _____

3 a scientific test done in order to learn about something: _____

4 to remove the liquid from something gradually or completely: _____

B. Fill in the blanks with the appropriate words or phrases from the box.

recommend   supporter   automatically   moisture   take over

5 The cactus plant can survive with very little _____.

6 James is a big _____ of his city's basketball team.

7 Dentists _____ brushing your teeth three times a day.

8 Ms. Jefferson will _____ the project after Mr. Hart leaves.

9 The store's entrance doors open and close _____.

C. Choose the closest meaning for each highlighted word or phrase.

10 The hotel guests were able to get a taxi right away.
   (A) overall　　(B) naturally　　(C) immediately　　(D) unfortunately

11 The two friends had a disagreement and stopped talking to each other.
   (A) error　　(B) argument　　(C) report　　(D) grade

12 In the past, people hunted for animals with pointed sticks.
   (A) long　　(B) sharp　　(C) powerful　　(D) dramatic

13 The boy ran away from the dog that was chasing him.
   (A) escaped　　(B) flowed　　(C) organized　　(D) invaded

14 The education program will benefit students from difficult backgrounds.
   (A) extend　　(B) control　　(C) attend　　(D) assist

HACKERS APEX LISTENING
for the TOEFL iBT
Intermediate

CHAPTER 04

Attitude

Attitude

About the Question Type

Attitude questions ask you to identify the speaker's attitude or opinion regarding ideas mentioned in a conversation or lecture.

These questions require you to recognize the speaker's feelings, likes and dislikes, or reasons for particular feelings. These questions sometimes require you to listen again to part of the listening passage.

Question Format

- What does the man/woman mean/imply when he/she says this: 🎧
- What is the professor's attitude toward ~?
- What is the professor's opinion of ~?

Key Strategies

- **Step 1** — Pay close attention to parts of the talk where the speaker expresses personal opinions, suggestions, or feelings.
- **Step 2** — Listen to the speaker's tone of voice and way of talking. This can make it easier to identify the speaker's attitude towards a topic.
- **Step 3** — Select the answer choice that best illustrates the speaker's attitude or opinion.

Example

Answer Book p. 24

A. Listen to a conversation between a student and a professor.

Note-taking

Student's Problem
Doesn't know where to _____ with a project

Steps to Make an _____
1. _____ _____ everything to include
2. Find the _____ _____ to focus on

What is the professor's opinion of the Internet?

(A) It is often a waste of time.
(B) It has too much information.
(C) It is useful for making outlines.
(D) It should be a research topic.

Answer Book p. 24

B. Listen to part of a lecture in an oceanography class.

Note-taking

Causes of Waves
• Wind
  : Blows on the _____ of the ocean and _____ form
• Events like _____
  : Can create a large sea wave called a _____

Listen again to part of the lecture. Then answer the question.
What does the professor mean when she says this: 🎧

(A) She has talked about a topic in class before.
(B) She wants to remind students about a problem.
(C) She knows students may be confused.
(D) She asked students to read about a subject.

Dictation

Answer Book p. 25

Listen again and fill in the blanks.

A.

S: Hello, Professor Bailey. I need your advice on my research project.

P: Sure. What's the problem?

S: Uh, I _____ _____ _____ online about my topic, but there was too much of it. I don't know where to start... I feel like _____ _____.

P: I know the feeling. You always get more than what you ask for on the Internet, right? Well, how about making an outline first?

S: Um, how do I make an outline? Can you give me _____ _____?

P: Of course. First, _____ _____ everything you want to include in your project. And then find the main point that you want to focus on. Once you find it, you'll know what you need to support the _____ _____.

S: I can do that. It will _____ _____ _____ to search for information, too. Thank you for your help, Professor.

B.

P: So, let's talk about what causes waves... The most common cause is wind. When wind blows on the surface of the ocean, _____ _____. These are called wind-driven waves. They're also called surface waves because they only happen near _____ _____ _____ _____ _____.
These kinds of small waves usually aren't dangerous.
However, big waves are... Um, they start at sea and _____ _____ as they move toward land. Many times, they're caused by powerful storms. But they can also be caused by other events like earthquakes... Now, I know what you're thinking. Yes, these events don't happen _____ _____ _____, but they also happen underwater... Earthquakes underwater cause the ground to move. This movement makes _____ _____ _____ _____ move as well. The movement can be so strong that it creates a large sea wave called a tsunami.

Listening Practice 1

Answer Book p. 26

Listen to a conversation between a student and a professor.

Note-taking

Student's Problem
The group is not making good _____.

Professor's Solution
- Choose a leader who can make _____
- _____ for topics
- Give a _____ _____ to every member

1. What is the student's problem?
   (A) He did not submit an assignment on time.
   (B) He has a disagreement with team members.
   (C) He will have to miss some classes.
   (D) He is worried about a group's progress.

2. According to the professor, why should everyone brainstorm for topics?
   (A) To get a large number of ideas
   (B) To make sure there is agreement
   (C) To get a good grade
   (D) To make the research go faster

Listen again to part of the conversation. Then answer the question.

3. What does the professor mean when she says this: 🎧
   (A) She understands the reason for a problem.
   (B) She does not agree with a choice of leader.
   (C) She thinks her idea is better than the student's.
   (D) She is not sure why a leader left a group.

Dictation

Answer Book p. 26

Listen again and fill in the blanks.

S: Hello, Professor Stephens. Do you have time to see me now?

P: Hi, Oliver. Yes. How is your group assignment going?

S: That's what I want to talk about. Uh, our group is not _____ _____ _____. All the other groups have chosen topics and _____ _____ _____, but...

P: Are you _____ _____ _____?

S: Uh, we don't have one, actually.

P: Well, that makes sense... It's _____ _____ _____ _____ without a leader. You know, a leader can _____ _____ on things like, uh, what to do next.

S: I see. Uh, maybe I could _____ _____ _____.

P: I believe you'll _____ _____ _____ _____ _____. Um, also, I recommend that all of you _____ _____ _____. It's important that everyone is involved at this stage. That way, you can be sure that everyone _____ _____ the final topic.

S: That's true... Um, is there anything else we should do after _____ _____ _____?

P: Well, lastly, I would make sure every member is _____ _____ _____. They should know exactly what they _____ _____ _____.

S: You're right. I'll tell them what you've told me. I hope it _____ _____ _____.

P: It should... If you still have problems, let me know. I can speak to the group as a whole.

Listening Practice 2

Answer Book p. 27

Listen to part of a lecture in an ecology class.

Note-taking

Abiotic Factors
e.g. _____, light, water, and _____

Biotic Factors
- Producers: Change _____ factors into other things
- Consumers: Plant eaters, _____, or eat both
- _____ : Break down the materials

1 What is the main topic of the lecture?

   (A) Different types of living things
   (B) How certain organisms help each other
   (C) The two main factors in ecosystems
   (D) Why minerals are important in the environment

2 What does the professor say about abiotic factors of the ecosystem?

   (A) Healthy plants do not need them for growth.
   (B) Organisms depend on them for survival.
   (C) They are rare in most ecosystems.
   (D) They can be harmful to some living things.

3 According to the professor, what are two types of consumers? *Choose 2 answers.*

   (A) Predators that hunt prey
   (B) Animals that eat plants
   (C) Plants that create oxygen
   (D) Fungi that break down dead plants

Listen again to part of the lecture. Then answer the question.

4 What does the professor mean when she says this: 🎧

   (A) She thinks that she found the right information.
   (B) She forgot to mention an important point.
   (C) She expects the student to provide an explanation.
   (D) She is impressed by the student's answer.

Dictation

Answer Book p. 27

Listen again and fill in the blanks.

P: Now let's talk about ecosystems in more detail. I want you to understand the major factors in ecosystems. Uh, these are called abiotic and biotic factors. First, the word *abiotic* refers to _____ _____. So, uh, these factors include things like temperature, light, and water. Even though these are not alive, organisms depend on abiotic factors to survive, grow, and reproduce. Can anyone think about a specific example that illustrates this relationship?

S: Uh, how about soil and plants? If the soil does not have _____ _____ _____, then plants will not grow as well.

P: That's exactly what I was looking for… A good example is the minerals in the soil. Minerals are abiotic. They are _____ _____, but they are essential for healthy plants. Minerals help plants stay green so that they can create energy and grow.

Now, let's consider the biotic factors of ecosystems. These are the living things, such as plants, animals, and fungi. There are several types of _____ _____ in every ecosystem, and each of these has a unique and important role in the environment. Firstly, there are producers. They _____ _____ _____ _____ something else for organisms. For example, plants use abiotic factors like sunlight, water, and carbon dioxide to create oxygen, which is _____ _____ many organisms. Next, there are consumers, uh, like animals. Some consumers are plant eaters, while others are predators that get their nutrition only from hunting prey. And, some consumers eat both plants and animals. Finally, there are decomposers. Decomposers _____ _____ the materials created by producers and consumers. For instance, when a tree dies, it will _____ _____ _____. This is because decomposers, like mushrooms or earthworms, break down the dead tree into smaller pieces. Gradually, it will turn into dirt.

Listening Practice 3

Answer Book p. 28

Listen to a conversation between a student and a professor.

Note-taking

Student's Request
Needs advice about studying _____

Professor's Suggestion
Go somewhere that _____ you to learn new _____, like another _____

1. Why does the student go to see the professor?
   (A) To discuss a class project
   (B) To get help with a job application
   (C) To apply for a language program
   (D) To ask about studying overseas

2. According to the professor, what is an advantage of going to a new country?
   (A) Making new friends
   (B) Exploring different jobs
   (C) Learning new skills
   (D) Seeing various attractions

3. What is the student's opinion about going to Switzerland?
   (A) She is worried about the travel distance.
   (B) She still prefers to go to Scotland.
   (C) She believes that it will be helpful.
   (D) She thinks it is a boring place to visit.

Dictation

Answer Book p. 28

Listen again and fill in the blanks.

S: Good morning, Professor Parks. Are you busy? I want to _____ _____ _____ about something.

P: Sure, Riley. How can I help you?

S: Uh, you know that I'm _____ _____ _____ _____, right? Well, what do you think about studying in Scotland?

P: That's _____ _____ _____. Why there?

S: Um, I guess it would be _____ _____ _____ _____ _____, and they speak English too.

P: I see... I would _____ _____ _____ _____ there...

S: Oh? May I ask why? I thought Scotland would be an interesting place to visit.

P: That's true. But like you said, people there speak English like we do. It would be better to go somewhere that _____ _____ _____ _____ new skills, like another language. That's _____ _____ _____ _____ of going to a new country.

S: I don't know many languages. I mean, I learned some German and French in high school.

P: Then you should go to Switzerland. They speak _____ _____ _____ _____ over there.

S: Oh, I get it... I can _____ _____ _____ in Switzerland.

P: And, if you go there, you can still visit Scotland. It _____ _____ _____ _____ _____ by plane.

S: That's true! I think you've _____ _____ _____, Professor!

Listening Practice 4

Answer Book p. 29

Listen to part of a lecture in a history class.

Note-taking

1850 Fugitive Slave Act
: Required all _____ _____ to return to their owners even in free states

From 1850 to 1865, the _____ _____
: A _____ of people who offered food and _____ to slaves

1 What is the lecture mainly about?

(A) A difference between state laws
(B) A network of people that helped slaves escape
(C) The reasons people built a railroad
(D) The effort of the government to save slaves

2 According to the professor, what is true about the Fugitive Slave Act?

(A) It was required only in certain states.
(B) It offered slaves food and shelter.
(C) It applied even where slavery was illegal.
(D) It was ignored by railroad workers.

3 What is the professor's attitude toward the Underground Railroad?

(A) It had limited historical value.
(B) It needed to be improved.
(C) It was a meaningful effort.
(D) It should get more attention.

Listen again to part of the lecture. Then answer the question.

4 Why does the professor say this:

(A) To imply that a topic is hard to understand
(B) To suggest that the result of an action was unexpected
(C) To emphasize the difference between a name and the reality
(D) To explain the use of secret codes

Dictation

Answer Book p. 29

Listen again and fill in the blanks.

P: OK, so we previously discussed the 1850 Fugitive Slave Act in the US. Now, we are going to talk about the _____ _____ of this act. This is one of the most dramatic parts of American history: the Underground Railroad. But before we move on to today's topic, let me refresh your memories... So, there were about five million slaves in the US at that time, mostly in the South. The South _____ _____ _____ _____, especially cotton farms. However, about a thousand slaves _____ _____ _____ _____ every year. The Fugitive Slave Act required all escaped slaves to _____ _____ _____ _____ if they were caught. And it was required even in free states in the north. You know, slavery was _____ _____ _____ free states, so we can see _____ _____ _____ _____ _____. So, uh, this was a challenge for slaves who escaped to free states like Pennsylvania.

Now, uh, some people ignored the law. These people _____ _____ _____, so they developed the Underground Railroad. The Underground Railroad was a network that existed from 1850 to 1865.

When you hear the name, you might think that it was a railroad _____ _____. But that's not what it was. It was simply a group of people who _____ _____ _____ _____ to escaping slaves... um, along escape routes. Surprised, right? People _____ _____ _____ instead of writing things down. They also _____ _____ _____ to, uh, avoid slave catchers. About 100,000 people escaped this way. That may seem small compared to the millions of remaining slaves. However, the movement was still _____ _____ _____ by ordinary people who wanted justice.

iBT Listening Test 1

Answer Book p. 30

TOEFL Listening

Note-taking

Student's Problem

Wants to _____ a textbook to get money back
→ Won't have time to get the _____ today

Employee's Suggestion

Could _____ the return today
→ Bring the _____ tomorrow

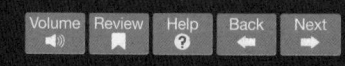

1. What is the conversation mainly about?
   - Ⓐ The problem with a credit card
   - Ⓑ The process for getting a refund
   - Ⓒ The cause of a product return
   - Ⓓ The policy for ordering a textbook

2. Why is the student unable to bring a receipt today?
   - Ⓐ Her credit card is missing.
   - Ⓑ She must attend a class now.
   - Ⓒ She is unable to access her room.
   - Ⓓ The bookstore will close soon.

3. What will the student probably do next?
   - Ⓐ Make an additional purchase
   - Ⓑ Provide an identification card
   - Ⓒ Fill out a student survey
   - Ⓓ Submit a written complaint

Listen again to part of the conversation. Then answer the question.

4. What does the employee imply when he says this:
   - Ⓐ A student doesn't have to follow a policy.
   - Ⓑ A manager will not be able to provide help.
   - Ⓒ A rule should apply to everyone equally.
   - Ⓓ A new policy is not really effective.

Dictation

Answer Book p. 30

Listen again and fill in the blanks.

W: Hi. I want to return this textbook. But, uh, I wonder if I will _____ _____ _____ _____ if I do.

M: Um, _____ _____. Could you show me your receipt?

W: Um, I _____ _____ _____ my room at the dormitory...

M: I need to know when you bought the book. You see, we only _____ _____ when it's _____ _____ _____. There should be a date on the receipt.

W: But I _____ _____ _____ _____ with a credit card. I think you have _____ _____ of the sale.

M: I will still _____ _____ _____, though. It's a store policy... And we're _____ _____ _____ _____.

W: Oh, no, I won't have time to go to my room and get the receipt today...

M: Is there a reason why you have to _____ _____ _____ today?

W: Uh, I bought the book two weeks ago. It will be _____ _____ _____ if I come back tomorrow...

M: Hmm... Well, this is a new policy, and the manager is _____ _____ _____ _____. But it doesn't _____ _____ in your case...

W: Is there anything you can do? I really need the money to _____ _____ _____ for another class. The class starts next Monday.

M: I guess I could _____ _____ _____ today. But you need to bring the receipt tomorrow morning. I could _____ _____ _____ if you don't... Um, actually, leave your student ID with me so that I know you're coming back.

W: Thanks so much! I can do that. Let me get it out of my purse for you.

iBT Listening Test 2

TOEFL Listening

SOCIOLOGY

Note-taking

Heinrich's Law

- First category: Accidents did not lead to an _____
- Second category: Accidents caused a _____ injury
- Third category: Accidents resulted in a _____ injury

e.g. A company with 330 accidents

: _____ were in the first category, _____ in the second, and _____ in the third.

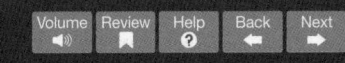

1. What is the main topic of the lecture?
    Ⓐ A way to improve workplace safety
    Ⓑ A study about workplace accidents
    Ⓒ The dangerous jobs in various industries
    Ⓓ The most common injuries in a workplace

2. What does the professor say about the second category?
    Ⓐ It is the most common category of accidents.
    Ⓑ It includes accidents that cause small injuries.
    Ⓒ It usually happens because of dangerous work environments.
    Ⓓ It results in the highest number of accidents.

3. According to the professor, how many serious injuries occur out of 330 accidents?
    Ⓐ One
    Ⓑ Twenty-nine
    Ⓒ Thirty
    Ⓓ Three hundred

4. What is the professor's attitude toward Heinrich's Law?
    Ⓐ She is impressed by the amount of research he did.
    Ⓑ She agrees that employees are the cause of accidents.
    Ⓒ She thinks that major injuries can be prevented.
    Ⓓ She feels that more companies should teach the law.

Listen again to part of the lecture. Then answer the question.

5. What does the professor mean when she says this:
    Ⓐ Accidents in the workplace are less common today.
    Ⓑ Employers often do not care about the safety of employees.
    Ⓒ Employees are not always to blame for accidents.
    Ⓓ A lot of companies have unsafe management practices.

Dictation

Answer Book p. 31

Listen again and fill in the blanks.

P: How many _____ _____ do you hear about on the news? Quite a few, right? It might sound like workplaces are dangerous. But, uh, it's important to _____ _____ _____. An industrial safety expert named Herbert Heinrich _____ _____ _____ accidents in the 1930s. He _____ _____ _____ different workplace accidents and discussed how they happen.

OK... So Heinrich first analyzed 75,000 workplace accidents. Then, he _____ _____ _____ three categories. The first category was any accidents that did not _____ _____ _____ _____. The second category was accidents that caused a minor injury, like hurting a finger. And can you guess the third category? It was accidents that _____ _____ _____ _____ _____, like breaking bones. This is Heinrich's Law, or Heinrich's Pyramid, and there are a couple of important points to remember about it.

Heinrich suggested that accidents _____ _____ _____ _____. Um, Heinrich used the example of a company with 330 accidents in total. According to him, 300 of those accidents were in the first category, 29 in the second, and 1 in the third. This means that _____ _____ _____ _____ did not cause any injury, but at least one of them was serious.

He also mentioned that each category of accidents is closely related... Uh, let's say that a painter _____ _____ _____ _____ because the ladder is broken. He is lucky and does not _____ _____ _____. So, his accident is in the first category. However, he does not _____ _____ _____ _____ and falls again. This time, he _____ _____ _____. Now he has an accident

in the second category. Still, he does not fix the ladder, so he falls again and
_____ _____ _____. He has a serious accident in the third
category. What does this tell us? Well, I think it means the worker could have
_____ _____ _____ _____ if he fixed the ladder.
Heinrich concluded that employees are usually _____ _____
_____ _____. He said that almost 90 percent of work accidents
happen because of employees' _____ _____. However, many
people do not accept this today. They think that Heinrich _____
_____ too much. They say that other factors like poor management
systems and _____ _____ _____ can also cause accidents...
not just employees' mistakes.

Vocabulary Review

Answer Book p. 32

A. Choose the correct word for each meaning.

brainstorm   blame   discourage   support

1. to help to show that a statement or a theory is true or correct: _____
2. to think of new ideas by having a discussion: _____
3. to make someone not want to do something: _____
4. to say that someone or something is responsible for a bad result: _____

B. Fill in the blanks with the appropriate words or phrases from the box.

gradually   nutrient   unexpected   fair   agree with

5. It was very _____ that it would rain today.
6. The planet _____ became warmer over millions of years.
7. It is not _____ to blame others for your mistakes.
8. I _____ the idea to have a party on Saturday.
9. Milk contains a _____ that is good for healthy bones.

C. Choose the closest meaning for each highlighted word.

10. The children's story illustrates the importance of being honest.
    (A) analyzes   (B) improves   (C) shows   (D) searches

11. Kyle was unhappy about the outcome of the game.
    (A) result   (B) act   (C) feeling   (D) route

12. Getting a high test score is essential to pass the course.
    (A) strict   (B) specific   (C) final   (D) necessary

13. Mr. Coleman is an expert in the use of computers.
    (A) advantage   (B) professional   (C) challenge   (D) producer

14. The river is very deep and is unsafe for swimming.
    (A) lost   (B) serious   (C) dangerous   (D) poor

HACKERS APEX LISTENING
for the TOEFL iBT
Intermediate

CHAPTER 05

Organization

Organization

About the Question Type

Organization questions ask you to identify how a speaker organizes a lecture or presents certain information. Alternatively, you may be asked the reason the speaker mentions a specific piece of information.

Sometimes, you may be asked to determine how specific information relates to the discussion as a whole. Common ways of organizing include: cause and effect, compare and contrast, and problem and solution.

Question Format

- How does the professor introduce/clarify/explain ~?
- How is the lecture organized?
- Why does the man/woman mention ~?
- Why does the man/woman talk about ~?

Key Strategies

- **Step 1** — While listening to the passage, identify the overall organization or structure of the discussion.

- **Step 2** — If the question asks about the organizational structure of the passage, identify how the main idea and its supporting details are organized. If the question asks about the reason why the speaker mentions a specific piece of information, identify how that information connects to the talk as a whole.

- **Step 3** — Select the answer choice that best describes the organizational structure of the passage or the purpose of a specific piece of information.

Example

Answer Book p. 32

A. Listen to a conversation between a student and an academic advisor.

Note-taking

Student's Problem
Tried to _____ _____ a class, but it was _____

Advisor's Suggestion
Add your name to the _____ _____

Why does the student mention Mr. Hanlon?

(A) To indicate which class she is interested in taking
(B) To explain how she heard about a waiting list
(C) To show that she did not get some information
(D) To prove that she put her name on a list

Answer Book p. 32

B. Listen to part of a lecture in a sociology class.

Note-taking

Ascribed Status
: Decided when you are _____
  e.g. A _____ has a high status.

_____ **Status**
: Based on your _____
  e.g. Oprah Winfrey has a high status.

How does the professor organize the lecture?

(A) By discussing how social status has changed over time
(B) By introducing concepts and then giving examples
(C) By describing the lives of world-famous people
(D) By emphasizing the importance of a particular concept

Dictation

Answer Book p. 32

Listen again and fill in the blanks.

A.

W: Hi, I was wondering if you could help me. You see, one of the classes I _____ _____ _____ _____ was full yesterday.

M: It was? What's your number _____ _____ _____ _____ ?

W: What? Oh, uh, I didn't know there was a waiting list...

M: Yes, when a class is full, students can put their names on a waiting list. That way, if someone _____ _____ _____, students on the waiting list can get in. It's an option you can select when you register online.

W: Oh, that must be the problem... I actually _____ _____ _____ at the registrar's office with, um, Mr. Hanlon, I believe?

M: Well, he should have let you know about that... Anyway, it's not too late. You can still _____ _____ _____ to the list.

W: OK, thanks. I'll do that right away.

B.

P: In sociology, there are _____ _____ _____ _____. There is ascribed status and achieved status.

First, there is ascribed status. This is decided when you are born. It includes being male or female, upper-class or lower-class, and so on. It is determined by factors like gender, race, and _____ _____. A prince, for instance, has a high ascribed status because he is born into a royal family. Second, let's consider achieved status. Achieved status is _____ _____ _____ _____. Oprah Winfrey is a good example. She was born a poor, black woman in the American South. But, she _____ _____ _____ _____ as a broadcaster. Eventually, she became a popular talk show host and producer. Her ascribed status was low, but she later had high _____ _____.

Listening Practice 1

Answer Book p. 33

Listen to a conversation between a student and a professor.

Note-taking

Student's Problem
Dr. Cooper can't give a _____ at the dinner party.
→ Needs to find a _____ _____

Professor's Solution
Professor Daniels will be able to do that.
→ Has been _____ for a long time

1 What problem does the student have?

  (A) She cannot meet a professor.
  (B) She has to miss an important dinner.
  (C) She needs to find a speaker.
  (D) She has no time to prepare a talk.

2 What is the professor's opinion of Professor Daniels?

  (A) He enjoys listening to her lectures.
  (B) He believes she will be too busy.
  (C) He is worried that she has little experience.
  (D) He thinks she can do a task well.

3 Why does the student mention a class from last semester?

  (A) To complain that a course was too difficult
  (B) To say that she knows how to find an office
  (C) To indicate that she is familiar with a topic
  (D) To explain her interest in hearing a talk

Dictation

Listen again and fill in the blanks.

S: Do you have a minute, Professor Taylor? I need your advice about _____ _____ _____ _____.

P: Sure, Ellen, what's the problem?

S: Well, Dr. Cooper _____ _____ _____ _____ a talk at the dinner, but now he can't come. He's, um, _____ _____ _____ that day.

P: I see. Have you found someone else yet?

S: No, and I only have three days left to find a new person.

P: Hmm... Have you considered _____ _____ _____ _____ at all? That might be _____ _____ _____.

S: Well, I thought of that, but I'm worried that the students will be disappointed. They're _____ _____ _____ a talk.

P: I understand. What about Professor Daniels? She _____ _____ _____.

S: Do you think she can prepare a talk in the next three days?

P: That depends... Um, what's the talk about, anyway?

S: Um, Dr. Cooper was going to talk about his _____ _____ _____ _____.

P: Professor Daniels will be able to do that, don't you think? She's been teaching for a long time... Would you like me to ask her for you?

S: Thank you, Professor. But, uh, maybe I should _____ _____ _____.

P: Very good. I believe she's in her office right now... Do you know where her office is?

S: Yes, uh, I actually _____ _____ _____ _____ _____ last semester. So, I know where it is. Thank you again, Professor.

Listening Practice 2

Answer Book p. 34

Listen to part of a lecture in a geology class.

Note-taking

Earth's Geological Structure
- _____ : Contains rocks and soil
- Mantle: Mostly _____ rock, but constantly _____
- _____ core: A liquid-like material
- Inner core: Heavy and _____

1 What is the main topic of the lecture?
   (A) Why Earth is made up of different layers
   (B) How Earth's surface makes life possible
   (C) The geological structure of Earth
   (D) The composition of Earth's surface

2 According to the lecture, what is true of the crust?
   (A) It is invisible to the human eye.
   (B) It is composed of solid rock.
   (C) It is a very small percentage of Earth.
   (D) It is thicker on land than in the sea.

3 Why does the professor mention oil and water?
   (A) To give the reason for differences in thickness
   (B) To explain the relationship of two layers
   (C) To show that the mantle is always moving
   (D) To highlight the high temperature of a layer

4 What is the professor's opinion of Earth's core?
   (A) The two parts are probably equal in size.
   (B) It contains more elements than scientists think.
   (C) The materials inside it are very valuable.
   (D) It will be impossible to study it directly.

Dictation

Listen again and fill in the blanks.

P: We live on Earth's surface, so we probably do not think about _____ _____ _____ very often. But, uh, Earth's structure is important because it makes life on Earth possible. So, let's learn about Earth's geological structure and its _____ _____ _____ ... the crust, the mantle, and the core.

Let's start from the outside. The outer layer of Earth is the crust. The crust is the layer that we can see. It contains rocks and soil, and this is where all of the plants grow. But surprisingly, it's actually quite small. Uh, it _____ _____ only around 1.4 percent of Earth.

Next is the mantle. The mantle is mostly solid rock. It is around 2,900 kilometers thick. The mantle is _____ _____ the crust. Thus, the crust _____ _____ _____ _____ like oil floats on water... uh, because oil is lighter than water. Um, even though the mantle is mostly solid, it is _____ _____ . Natural forces, such as gravity, cause the rock to move. Some sections of the rock go over or under the others. When they _____ _____, this creates heat. So it can be very hot, and the rock can _____ _____ _____ . When this happens, the hot liquid rock can move up to the surface... like in a volcanic eruption.

Lastly, there is the core. The core is _____ _____ _____ of Earth. The pressure in the core is very high. So, this makes the core extremely hot. Some parts of the core are _____ _____ _____ the Sun! The core can be _____ _____ _____ _____ ... the outer core and the inner core. The outer core consists of a liquid-like material. But, the inner core is heavy and solid. The inner core is _____ _____ _____ heavy metals, mainly iron. However, everything we know about the core has been _____ _____ . We cannot examine the core directly because it's _____ _____ _____ _____ . And to tell you the truth, I don't think we ever will...

Listening Practice 3

Answer Book p. 35

Listen to a conversation between a student and a professor.

Note-taking

Student's Problem
University _____ is different from high school.

Professor's Suggestion
- Decide on the main topic → Write an _____
- Make a clear _____
- Attend my _____ _____

1. What is the student's problem?

   (A) She needs help with writing a paper.
   (B) She wants to move to a different school.
   (C) She does not understand a class lesson.
   (D) She lost some files for her assignment.

2. How does the professor help the student?

   (A) By recommending topics to write about
   (B) By showing examples of other people's work
   (C) By giving detailed suggestions to follow
   (D) By discussing the experience of another student

3. What is the student's attitude toward attending the workshop?

   (A) She is not sure it will be helpful.
   (B) She is willing to participate in it.
   (C) She thinks it will take too much time.
   (D) She wants to tell others about it.

Dictation

Answer Book p. 35

Listen again and fill in the blanks.

S: Hi, Professor Brown. I have something I need to talk to you about.

P: No problem. My door is always open.

S: Thanks, Professor. Well, the problem is... I don't know how to start writing my paper. University writing is _____ _____ _____ writing in high school.

P: Yes, that's a common problem for first-year students. Um, let me _____ _____ _____ _____.

S: I'd really appreciate it, Professor.

P: Yes, so, the first thing is to decide on the main topic of your paper. Then, _____ _____ _____. That way, you can always _____ _____ _____.

S: That's interesting... Um, what else should I do?

P: OK, next, make sure that you _____ _____ _____ _____...

S: What do you mean by a clear plan?

P: Well, I'm saying that you should _____ _____ _____ _____. If you don't schedule time to work on your paper, you may not _____ _____ _____.

S: I see. OK...

P: And lastly, if you ever _____ _____ again, come see me right away or speak to the other students in class. I also suggest showing your first draft to a couple of other people. You can _____ _____ _____ _____. This can help you see things differently.

S: I like that, Professor. Thank you.

P: Why don't you _____ _____ _____ _____? I have plenty more advice. So, it could be very helpful.

S: Definitely. Can I _____ _____ right away?

Listening Practice 4

Answer Book p. 36

Listen to part of a lecture in a history class.

Note-taking

Different Western Calendars
- Roman calendar: Based on the _____ cycle
- _____ calendar: An extra day added to February every third year
- Gregorian calendar: An extra day once every _____ years

1. What is the main topic of the lecture?
   (A) The development of Western calendars
   (B) The advantages of the Julian calendar
   (C) The reasons a calendar was used for a long time
   (D) The difference between solar and lunar calendars

2. How does the professor introduce the Julian calendar?
   (A) By talking about the differences between seasons
   (B) By discussing an issue with a previous calendar
   (C) By explaining a process for counting days in a year
   (D) By describing the achievements of Julius Caesar

3. Why did Julius Caesar introduce a new calendar?
   (A) To gain more popularity among the Romans
   (B) To make the solar and calendar years match
   (C) To provide the Romans with longer holidays
   (D) To give farmers more time to grow food

4. What is the professor's opinion of Pope Gregory XIII?
   (A) He should not have changed a system.
   (B) He did not understand the Julian calendar.
   (C) He made an important improvement.
   (D) He should have gotten more respect.

Dictation

Answer Book p. 36

Listen again and fill in the blanks.

P: As you probably know, the Gregorian calendar is the most commonly used calendar today. Um, it was first introduced in 1582. But before this, the Western world _____ _____ _____ for more than 1,600 years. I want to take some time this morning to look at _____ _____ _____.

The first one was the Roman calendar. It had 355 days in a year. This was because it was based on the moon's cycle, which is how long it takes for the moon to _____ _____ _____. However, the calendar's length was shorter than a solar year... That's, uh, the period of time for Earth to _____ _____ _____ _____ around the Sun. This created problems because the calendar did not _____ _____ _____ of the year. People got very confused as a result. For instance, farmers sometimes celebrated harvest festivals in the middle of winter instead of in the fall.

So, in 46 BC, the Roman dictator Julius Caesar _____ _____ _____ known as the Julian calendar. The purpose of the Julian calendar was to make sure that the calendar year matched the solar year. So, he created a calendar with 365 days, uh, by _____ _____ _____ _____, February 29. This extra day was added to February every third year. Um, this was because the Romans believed that the solar year _____ _____ 365.25 days. Unfortunately, they _____ _____ _____ _____... It is actually 365.242 days. As a result, this calendar did not match the seasons, either.

This issue was finally _____ _____ the Gregorian calendar. It includes an extra day _____ _____ _____ _____ instead of every three years. This calendar was named for Pope Gregory XIII, who ordered a new calendar system in 1582. And it's a good thing he did... Otherwise, we'd probably still be using a less accurate calendar today.

iBT Listening Test 1

Answer Book p. 37

TOEFL Listening

C5_T1

Note-taking

Student's Question
Wants to know if I've met all of the _____ _____

Employee's Answer
You haven't completed a _____ _____ for your major.
→ Take the class this semester, and _____ _____ right away

1. Why does the student visit the registrar's office?
   - Ⓐ To ask about some requirements
   - Ⓑ To request a new student ID
   - Ⓒ To get directions to a department building
   - Ⓓ To make a payment for a class

2. How does the employee help the student?
   - Ⓐ By giving him a new ID card
   - Ⓑ By printing out some instructions
   - Ⓒ By searching for information
   - Ⓓ By helping him fill out a form

3. Why does the student mention the university's football team?
   - Ⓐ To suggest that he is good at sports
   - Ⓑ To explain why he could not take a class
   - Ⓒ To confirm that he would like to join an activity
   - Ⓓ To give the reason for missing a graduation

Listen again to part of the conversation. Then answer the question.

4. What does the student mean when he says this:
   - Ⓐ He thinks that a class should be required.
   - Ⓑ He remembered that he had finished a class.
   - Ⓒ He already knew he had missed a class.
   - Ⓓ He has heard the same information before.

Dictation

Answer Book p. 37

Listen again and fill in the blanks.

M: Excuse me, is this the registrar's office? I was hoping you could help me.

W: Yes, of course. What's your question?

M: It's about _____ _____ _____. Um, I'm not sure if I've _____ _____ _____. I want to be sure because this is supposed to be my last year here.

W: All right. If you give me your student ID, I can _____ _____ _____ _____.

M: Oh, I don't have my ID right now. It's back at my dorm room. But, um, I know my student ID number. It's, uh, 1860-4112.

W: That's fine. OK, so... I see here that you've _____ _____ _____ _____ _____. There's no problem there.

M: Yes, I made all the payments at the beginning of the semester.

W: That's good. Hmm... However, it seems you haven't _____ _____ _____ _____ for your major.

M: Oh, I thought so. I don't remember which class it is, though. Is it a history class?

W: Actually, it's _____ _____ _____ _____.

M: Oh, right. I think I _____ _____ _____ _____ _____ last year, but I was busy. I'm on the university's football team.

W: I understand. You must have been _____ _____ _____ and games... Anyway, you can still _____ _____ _____ this semester if you like. I guess it will be your last chance.

M: Right. I hope the class _____ _____ _____.

W: Let me see... Yes, there are a few spots left, but you should sign up right away. The class could _____ _____ _____ _____.

M: OK. I'll sign up right now, then.

iBT Listening Test 2

TOEFL Listening

CITY PLANNING

Note-taking

Cause of City Planning in the US

Large increase in the _____ of many cities

→ Needed to improve _____ _____

What Government Did

- Improved _____ _____ and safety

  e.g. Built _____ for clean water, put up _____ for safer streets

- Built _____ that was not expensive

- Built _____ areas for _____ and recreation

  e.g. Playgrounds, sports centers, _____

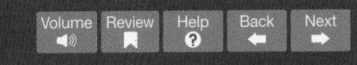

1. What is the lecture mainly about?
   - Ⓐ The advantages of living in a city
   - Ⓑ The construction of the American capital
   - Ⓒ The development of city planning in the US
   - Ⓓ The effects of the Industrial Revolution

2. According to the professor, why did the population of American cities increase?
   - Ⓐ Cities needed immigrants to build factories.
   - Ⓑ Houses were too expensive outside the cities.
   - Ⓒ Immigrants received money to buy homes.
   - Ⓓ Workers came from other areas to find jobs.

3. How is the lecture organized?
   - Ⓐ The professor asks questions and then answers them.
   - Ⓑ The professor talks about a personal experience that he had.
   - Ⓒ The professor describes the characteristics of an ideal city.
   - Ⓓ The professor compares and contrasts two different cities.

4. What does the professor imply about the government?
   - Ⓐ It did not allow many factories at first.
   - Ⓑ It controlled the number of people moving to cities.
   - Ⓒ It tried to provide more than just basic needs.
   - Ⓓ It built parks to attract more tourists.

5. What is the professor's opinion of Central Park?
   - Ⓐ It was difficult to build.
   - Ⓑ It was worth the high cost.
   - Ⓒ It needs some improvement.
   - Ⓓ It is good for the environment.

Dictation

Answer Book p. 38

Listen again and fill in the blanks.

P: OK... In the past, most cities in the United States were _____ _____ _____ settlers. This means that people built structures wherever it was convenient for them. As you can imagine, this was very _____ _____ _____. But in the 19th century, as the Industrial Revolution began, the US government _____ _____ _____. Let's look at how this happened.

Well, one of the key factors that led to this was the large increase in _____ _____ _____ _____ _____. This happened because millions of immigrants and people from the countryside _____ _____ _____. Uh, they wanted to live close to the factories that were looking for _____ _____ _____. However, there were _____ _____ _____ and facilities for all of the new people. Cities became dirty, crowded, and dangerous.

So, what did the government do to improve living conditions? Well, it first tried to _____ _____ _____ and safety. For instance, many people _____ _____ _____ _____ dirty water, so the government built pipes for clean water. Also, um, streets were _____ _____ _____ because it was dark. So, the government put up lights to make the streets safer... What else? Well, many of the people moving to the city were not rich. So the government _____ _____ _____ _____ that was not expensive. All of these things _____ _____. Government officials had to decide where to build everything in an organized way.

Now, was this all? No, the government also built outdoor areas for _____ _____ _____. People needed somewhere to enjoy breaks from work, to get together, and to exercise. So, the government used public

110 Supplementary materials at HackersBook.com

spending _____ _____ _____ _____ but also for leisure and recreation... Therefore, it built playgrounds for children and, uh, sports centers for adults. It also used a lot of land for parks. The most famous example of this is Central Park in New York City, which first opened in 1858. It cost millions of dollars _____ _____ _____ _____ _____. However, Central Park was _____ _____. It has become a place for people to escape the busy city environment. It's also now _____ _____ _____ _____.

Vocabulary Review

Answer Book p. 40

A. Choose the correct word for each meaning.

| float   status   leisure   crowded |

1. a position or rank, especially in a social group: _____
2. to stay on top of a liquid and not sink: _____
3. filled with people: _____
4. the time when you are not working and can relax: _____

B. Fill in the blanks with the appropriate words or phrases from the box.

| payment   celebrate   attraction   in time   successful |

5. The art museum is the city's most popular tourist _____.
6. Nora will _____ her birthday with a group of close friends.
7. People that work hard are usually more _____.
8. The product will be delivered after the customer has made a _____.
9. He got a low score on the assignment because he did not submit it _____.

C. Choose the closest meaning for each highlighted word.

10. Each group leader must select five members each from the class.
    (A) share   (B) choose   (C) practice   (D) remind

11. The planet Jupiter is mostly made up of gas.
    (A) loudly   (B) plenty   (C) mainly   (D) together

12. The ocean constantly produces waves.
    (A) quickly   (B) continually   (C) weakly   (D) indirectly

13. A few workers will examine the place of the accident to find out what caused it.
    (A) investigate   (B) introduce   (C) compare   (D) match

14. She decided to drop her language class because it was too difficult.
    (A) register   (B) make   (C) consider   (D) cancel

Supplementary materials at HackersBook.com

HACKERS APEX LISTENING
for the TOEFL iBT
Intermediate

CHAPTER 06

Connecting Contents

Connecting Contents

About the Question Type

Connecting Contents questions ask you to complete a table or chart that shows how the ideas directly mentioned in a conversation or lecture relate to one another.

List questions require you to identify whether the statements listed in a table are true or false. Matching questions ask you to classify the statements or identify which category they belong to, while Ordering questions require you to put the steps of a process or series of events in the correct order.

Question Format

List
- Indicate whether each of the following is mentioned/included/suggested/etc.
  Click in the correct box for each phrase.

	Yes/Included/Suggested	No/Not Included/Not Suggested
Statement A		
Statement B		
Statement C		

Matching
- Indicate for each example what type of ~.

Ordering
- The professor explains the steps ~. Put the steps listed below in the correct order.

Key Strategies

- **Step 1** — Pay attention to the important details and overall flow of the talk.
- **Step 2** — Identify the number of ideas being discussed, and predict which type of question will be asked. Types of questions include List, Matching, and Ordering.
- **Step 3** — Select the answer choices in the table or chart that best represent the information in the passage for each item.

Example

Answer Book p. 40

A. Listen to a conversation between a student and a professor.

C6_ExA

Note-taking

Student's Question
Finished my _____ → What's next?

Things to Discuss in Essay
- What the book can teach us in the _____ context
- How the book was _____

Indicate whether each of the following is mentioned as something the student should do when writing her essay. *Click in the correct box for each phrase.*

	Yes	No
(A) Include a summary of the book		
(B) Compare the book to other books		
(C) Research American history		
(D) Describe the life of the author		

Answer Book p. 40

B. Listen to part of a lecture in a sociology class.

C6_ExB

Note-taking

Effects of _____
- Positive: Can easily _____ anywhere, make products _____ and deliver them quickly
- Negative: Bad for the _____ and helps spread ideas like _____

In the lecture, the professor mentions some effects of globalization. Indicate whether each of the following is mentioned as an effect. *Click in the correct box for each phrase.*

	Yes	No
(A) It increases competition between countries.		
(B) It makes products faster to deliver.		
(C) It is good for the environment.		
(D) It allows bad ideas to spread.		

Dictation

Answer Book p. 40

Listen again and fill in the blanks.

A.

P: Hi, Beth. Did you have a question about writing your essay?

S: Well, Professor Adams, I finished my _____ _____ _____ _____, *The Blind City*. But, I'm not sure what to do next.

P: Yes, well... A summary is necessary, but the essay should also talk about what the book can teach us.

S: Um, like the book's _____ _____?

P: Yes, but also about _____ _____ _____. The book was written in 1929. So, what was happening _____ _____ _____ in America's history?

S: OK. I should _____ _____ _____ about that, then.

P: Exactly. Your essay should explain why the book was important for, uh, readers _____ _____...

S: All right... Is there anything else I should include?

P: You should also discuss how the book was written. Um, like what the writer did to _____ _____ _____ _____.

B.

P: Nowadays, people around the world are connected to each other in many ways... This happened because of a process _____ _____ _____.
There are both positive and negative effects of this. For instance, people can _____ _____ _____ in the world. Also, companies can make products cheaply and deliver them to customers more quickly than before. And _____ _____ help people communicate and enjoy culture... All of these, um, are positive. But, globalization can _____ _____ _____, too. Um, for example, many people travel on airplanes and companies move products on ships. This is bad for the environment because of pollution. And, um, globalization doesn't just help people _____ _____ _____. It helps them spread bad ones too, like terrorism.

Listening Practice 1

Answer Book p. 41

Listen to a conversation between a student and an employee in the university bookstore.

Note-taking

Student's Problem
Can't find a book for a _____ class

Employee's Answer
Sells books about _____, chemistry, and physics
→ Go to the _____ in the sociology department building

---

1 What is the conversation mainly about?

(A) Using a school computer
(B) Registering for a class
(C) Finding an item for a class
(D) Understanding school requirements

2 Why does the student mention a lesson plan?

(A) To talk about a school activity
(B) To confirm some information
(C) To make another request
(D) To explain a mistake

3 In the conversation, the student provides several pieces of information. Indicate whether each of the following is provided. *Click in the correct box for each phrase.*

	Yes	No
(A) The name of a class		
(B) The name of his professor		
(C) The day that a class starts		
(D) The major he is studying		

Dictation

Answer Book p. 41

Listen again and fill in the blanks.

M: Excuse me. I can't find a book I need for my class.

W: Oh, what's _____ _____ _____ _____ _____? I can look for it on my computer.

M: Um... It's called *Analysis of Structure*.

W: OK... Let me check... Hmm, that's strange. It seems we don't have the book. Um, to make sure, could you give me _____ _____ _____?

M: Um, yes... I believe it's, uh, Kay Fielding.

W: Are you sure about that name? I'm still not _____ _____ _____.

M: That's what it says on this lesson plan I got from class.

W: Oh, could I see that?

M: Of course... I really hope you can find the book. My class _____ _____ _____. But, I'm worried I won't be ready.

W: Aha! I see what the problem is. Is this for a sociology class?

M: Yes, that's right. I have to take a class in sociology, so I _____ _____ _____ Introduction to Sociology this semester.

W: Well, this bookstore only sells books about biology, chemistry, and physics. You _____ _____ _____ _____ the bookstore in the sociology department building.

M: Oh, I'm sorry. I didn't know that there were different bookstores... I'm _____ _____.

W: It's not a problem. Let me give you _____ _____ _____ _____ _____.

M: Thanks so much.

118 Supplementary materials at HackersBook.com

Listening Practice 2

Answer Book p. 42

Listen to part of a lecture in a biology class.

Note-taking

Four Stages of _____ Development

1. A mother fly lays up to 500 _____.
2. Develops into a _____, which is like a worm
3. Grows into a _____, covered in a hard outer skin
4. A fly breaks out of its _____.

1. What is the main topic of the lecture?
   (A) The lifecycle of a common insect
   (B) The eating habits of a housefly
   (C) Common habitats of houseflies
   (D) The effects of an insect on human life

2. Why does the professor mention a grain of rice?
   (A) To identify the food of young houseflies
   (B) To show why flies are difficult to see
   (C) To explain the appearance of a maggot
   (D) To show how flies can damage crops

3. According to the professor, what do the holes on maggots' bodies do?
   (A) They change the colors of the maggots.
   (B) They allow oxygen into the maggots' lungs.
   (C) They determine the maggots' body shape.
   (D) They help the maggots eat food.

4. In the lecture, the professor explains the stages of housefly development. Put the steps listed below in the correct order. *Drag each answer choice to the space where it belongs.*

Stage 1	
Stage 2	
Stage 3	
Stage 4	

   (A) The skin becomes darker.
   (B) A hard outer skin develops.
   (C) About 500 eggs are laid.
   (D) A shell is broken using the head.

Dictation

Answer Book p. 42

Listen again and fill in the blanks.

P: I'm guessing many of you have seen houseflies at least once before. About 90 percent of flies that fly around our houses are houseflies. Houseflies go through _____ _____ _____ of life.
The lifecycle begins with the egg. The mother _____ _____ _____ _____ _____, and this process takes three to four days to complete.
These eggs then _____ _____ the next stage... a maggot. Um, like a worm, a maggot has no legs. It looks like _____ _____ _____ _____. At first, the color of the maggots is white, but it changes into, um, a darker color _____ _____ _____. Here is a picture that shows this... Can you see _____ _____ _____ forming on its skin? Maggots have a number of tiny holes covering the body. These _____ _____ _____ that lead to the lungs and provide oxygen.
Now, let's move on to the third stage. Each maggot will eventually grow into a pupa. A pupa is similar to a maggot, but it is _____ _____ a hard outer skin. The color of the outer skin is slightly yellow at first, but it continues to _____ _____. And when the pupa is fully grown, it, uh, becomes a black color.
After this, the fly inside the shell will _____ _____ using part of its head. This shows that they've _____ _____ _____ and are adults. These flies are the fully grown version that we have all seen. You know, they have black skin and red eyes... And they have six legs and _____ _____ _____ _____. Their wings _____ _____ _____ _____ other insects... This is because most insects have two pairs of wings.
Anyway, this whole process takes about seven to ten days... And within 24 hours, adult flies _____ _____ _____ _____. Female flies will lay eggs after three days.

120 Supplementary materials at HackersBook.com

Listening Practice 3

Answer Book p. 43

Listen to a conversation between a student and a director of the student cafeteria.

Note-taking

Student's Request
Wants to join the _____ _____ festival

Instructions
1. Fill out a _____ form
2. Prepare _____ for the cafeteria staff to try
3. Give a list of the _____

1 What are the speakers mainly discussing?
   (A) How to use the school cafeteria
   (B) What kind of food is sold in a cafeteria
   (C) Benefits for an international student
   (D) How to participate in a food festival

2 Why does the man mention his mother?
   (A) To explain how he learned to make a dish
   (B) To show that he will need some help
   (C) To mention who will be attending an event
   (D) To indicate why he wants to join a festival

3 In the conversation, the woman gives the man instructions. Indicate whether each of the following is one of those instructions. *Click in the correct box for each phrase.*

	Yes	No
(A) Complete a sign-up form		
(B) Prepare samples of food		
(C) Get a parent's permission		
(D) Buy the ingredients for a dish		

Dictation

Answer Book p. 43

Listen again and fill in the blanks.

M: Excuse me. I heard there will be _____ _____ _____ _____ soon. Is that true?

W: Yes. It will happen here in the cafeteria. There will be booths serving traditional food from different countries. However, the event has been _____ _____ _____ _____.

M: Really? I thought the festival was this month!

W: Well, um, the students have _____ _____ _____ _____ to prepare. Are you _____ _____ _____?

M: Yes. I want to _____ _____ _____ from Brazil.

W: Wonderful. Here's _____ _____ _____ that you'll need to fill out... Um, what will you be making?

M: I want to make Brazilian-style cheese bread and chocolate balls.

W: Those sound delicious! Will you be _____ _____?

M: Yes. My mother taught me _____ _____ _____ them.

W: That's excellent. Um, you'll also have to _____ _____ for the cafeteria staff to try. Can you bring some on Friday?

M: Sure! How much should I make?

W: Um, five small samples of each dish will be fine. Of course, you'll have to _____ _____ _____ _____ for the food festival.

M: I understand.

W: I _____ _____ _____ _____ the samples... Oh, and one more thing. Please give us _____ _____ _____ _____ _____ as well. We're going to order what the participants need before the festival. That way, uh, students have one less thing to prepare.

M: I'll do that! Thanks!

Listening Practice 4

Answer Book p. 44

Listen to part of a lecture in an ecology class.

Note-taking

European Settlers' Activities and Effects in Australia
- Logging → _____ loss, soil loss, and _____ weather
- Mining → _____ of streams and rivers, and _____ chemicals
- Animals from _____ → Lowered _____

1. What is the main topic of the lecture?
   (A) The plant and animal diversity in Australia
   (B) The various types of Australian ecosystems
   (C) The impact of Europeans on Australia's environment
   (D) The history of European settlement in Australia

2. What does the professor say about most agricultural areas?
   (A) They originally had little soil.
   (B) They were close to the ocean.
   (C) They were far away from towns.
   (D) They eventually became deserts.

3. Why does the speaker mention rabbits and dogs?
   (A) To explain how these animals were harmed by Europeans
   (B) To give examples of foreign animals and their effects
   (C) To show that biodiversity increased after European settlement
   (D) To highlight that European settlers often had pet animals

4. The professor mentions several human activities and the outcome of each. Indicate the outcome of each activity. *Click in the correct box for each phrase.*

	Logging	Mining	Introducing animals
(A) Pollution of streams and rivers			
(B) Loss of animal habitats			
(C) Extinction of native species			
(D) Loss of soil			

Dictation

Answer Book p. 44

Listen again and fill in the blanks.

P: Europeans began to _____ _____ _____ in 1788. And, um, since that time, they have _____ _____ _____ in various ways. Uh, now let's talk about how their activities affected it.

Well... first, European settlers did a lot of logging, uh, which means that they _____ _____ large sections of forest. They did this for wood to build houses and towns. But they mainly did it to remove trees for agriculture. It was usually done in areas _____ _____ _____ because the soil there was good for farming. Cutting down forests, however, caused _____ _____, and forest animals had to move to new areas. Trees also protect soil. So, uh, removing the trees caused the soil _____ _____. Removing trees also caused long periods of dry weather, and the deserts in Australia got larger and larger...

Another major activity of the settlers was mining. Many miners moved to Australia to _____ _____ _____ because they believed they would become rich. But mining caused _____ _____ _____ _____ and rivers. This killed many fish. It also _____ _____ _____ into the soil, so plants could no longer grow.

Now, the outcome of this next part will surprise you. Settlers introduced animals, such as rabbits and dogs, from overseas. You might think that increasing the number of _____ _____ living in Australia would be good, right? For instance, um, if there are lots of different animals and plants, you have high biodiversity. But, actually, by introducing foreign animals, settlers _____ _____. Rabbits _____ _____ _____ and seeds, and dogs killed birds and destroyed their eggs. In the end, these animals _____ _____ _____ _____ of more than 100 native Australian species.

iBT Listening Test 1

TOEFL Listening

Note-taking

Student's Question
Wants to know about the role of _____ _____

What Volunteers Do
- Help with _____ like _____ _____ tables
- Check student IDs
- Help students use _____ _____

1 What are the speakers mainly discussing?
   - Ⓐ Problems with a registration process
   - Ⓑ What student volunteers will do
   - Ⓒ Results of a school election
   - Ⓓ How to join a school organization

2 According to the professor, what is the school planning to do?
   - Ⓐ Install more voting machines
   - Ⓑ Rent a large space outside school
   - Ⓒ Give some students an orientation
   - Ⓓ Move the deadline for an event

3 Why does the student mention a second form?
   - Ⓐ She made a mistake on the first one.
   - Ⓑ She needs to check some information.
   - Ⓒ She has a friend who wants to help out.
   - Ⓓ She wants to participate in two activities.

4 Indicate whether the statements below are mentioned as roles of election volunteers.
   Click in the correct box for each phrase.

	Yes	No
Ⓐ Giving forms to students		
Ⓑ Checking student IDs		
Ⓒ Counting the number of votes		
Ⓓ Helping students use machines		

Dictation

Answer Book p. 45

Listen again and fill in the blanks.

S: Hi, Professor Melrose! Could I talk to you about _____ _____ _____?

P: Sure, Olivia. What would you like to know?

S: Um, so, I know it's happening soon, but, uh, I'm interested in becoming a volunteer. Could you tell me about _____ _____ _____ _____ _____?

P: All right. I can explain it to you. It's really quite simple.

S: Do we have to _____ _____ _____ like, uh, setting up tables?

P: That's a part of it, yes. But, um, more importantly, you'll be _____ _____ _____. We have to be sure that everyone who participates is a student at this school.

S: That's because only students are _____ _____ _____, right?

P: Yes, exactly. Um, and next, well, have you ever _____ _____ _____ _____ before?

S: No, I haven't, but I think I can learn.

P: That's fine. The school is going to _____ _____ _____ for all the volunteers. Um, someone will _____ _____ _____ about the voting machines. That way, you can help students use them on election day.

S: Great! I think I can do all of that... Um, so how do I _____ _____?

P: I have a form right here. You can complete it _____ _____ _____. Just return it to me before the end of the week.

S: Thanks, Professor! Oh, could I get _____ _____ _____? My friend would also like to volunteer.

P: Certainly. We're still _____ _____ six to eight more volunteers.

S: Understood, Professor Melrose. I know some other students who might _____ _____. I'll tell them to sign up as well.

CHAPTER 06 | Connecting Contents 127

iBT Listening Test 2

TOEFL Listening

ART

Note-taking

Realism
- Represented the _____ world
- Focused on _____ subjects in the present time
e.g. Jean-Francois Millet

Impressionism
- Created a general _____ of what an artist saw
- Happy and pleasant _____
e.g. Claude Monet

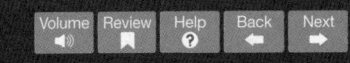

1. What is the main topic of the lecture?
   - Ⓐ The founder of Impressionism
   - Ⓑ The popularity of French Art
   - Ⓒ Two important art movements
   - Ⓓ The most famous French artists

2. How is the lecture organized?
   - Ⓐ By emphasizing the various goals of different artists
   - Ⓑ By discussing how one artist influenced the work of another
   - Ⓒ By explaining two art styles and then giving examples
   - Ⓓ By comparing the art styles in two different countries

3. What is an example of a subject of Jean-Francois Millet's artwork?
   - Ⓐ People at a social event
   - Ⓑ Farmers in fields
   - Ⓒ Colorful landscape scenes
   - Ⓓ Fields of flowers

4. Indicate whether each of the following describes Realism or Impressionism.
   Click in the correct box for each phrase.

	Realism	Impressionism
Ⓐ Did not capture all details		
Ⓑ Focused on subjects like common people		
Ⓒ Showed happy and pleasant scenes		
Ⓓ Tried to represent life truthfully		

5. What is the professor's opinion of Monet's *Impression, Sunrise*?
   - Ⓐ It has become more important over time.
   - Ⓑ It shows Monet's personality.
   - Ⓒ It did not take much time to complete.
   - Ⓓ It did not become famous during Monet's life.

Dictation

Answer Book p. 46

Listen again and fill in the blanks.

C6_T2_D

P: Today, we're going to talk about a couple of _____ _____ in art history. These are _____ _____ _____. And my examples will be from French art in particular.

As the name suggests, Realists tried to create art that _____ _____ _____ _____. What I mean is, um, how most people saw the world. Before, art focused only on the wealthy class or great events of the past. But, um, Realists _____ _____ _____ _____ in the present time. These included common people, like workers in a factory... The focus was on ordinary life, which the Realists tried to _____ _____ _____ _____. They were almost like photographers because of how they represented life...

In contrast, Impressionists created art based on, well, their impressions. Impressionists did not try to _____ _____ _____. Instead, the artists would _____ _____ _____ _____ of what they saw. Usually, the subjects were shown in happy and pleasant scenes like a picnic or a party... Either way, Impressionists wanted to give an impression of _____ _____ _____, like, um, the way sunlight looks in a field of flowers at sunset...

So, now for an example of each... Jean-Francois Millet was a Realist painter. His works mostly showed _____ _____ _____ _____. He had a clear intention to represent farmers at work realistically. The clothes, the fields, and even the sky looked real. It was as if you were _____ _____ _____ with the subjects when you looked at it... uh, like you were a part of the painting...

Now, I'm sure you are all familiar with the next one... Claude Monet. Monet is famous for his paintings of _____ _____ _____.

In fact, the Impressionist movement was _____ _____ one of his early paintings, uh, called *Impression, Sunrise*. This work shows a red sun far away and, uh, its reflection in the water. There are some boats in the picture, but there is _____ _____ _____. The lines are _____ _____ and the colors are not carefully _____ _____... The scene is mostly a gray fog. Overall, it seems as if the painting was done _____ _____ _____.

Vocabulary Review

Answer Book p. 47

A. Choose the correct word for each meaning.

summary   extinction   toxic   settle

1 a situation when an animal or plant no longer exists: _____

2 poisonous and harmful: _____

3 a short description that gives the main points or ideas about something: _____

4 to move to a place and live there, especially permanently: _____

B. Fill in the blanks with the appropriate words or phrases from the box.

preparation   participant   cheaply   lead to   spread

5 Jacob signed up to become a _____ in the contest.

6 In the 20th century, democracy _____ to many parts of the world.

7 Eating unhealthy food can _____ serious medical problems later in life.

8 The group studied all weekend in _____ for Monday's exam.

9 Houses that are built _____ do not last very long.

C. Choose the closest meaning for each highlighted word.

10 Everyone in the family had a pleasant day at the beach.
    (A) enjoyable   (B) effective   (C) wealthy   (D) general

11 David will take the role of team leader for the project.
    (A) subject   (B) purpose   (C) job   (D) major

12 The restaurant serves both Korean and Japanese food.
    (A) volunteers   (B) performs   (C) allows   (D) provides

13 Sharks take up to 15 years to develop into adults.
    (A) capture   (B) grow   (C) represent   (D) succeed

14 It was not my intention to hurt you.
    (A) scene   (B) election   (C) goal   (D) ingredient

HACKERS APEX LISTENING
for the TOEFL iBT
Intermediate

CHAPTER 07

Inference

Inference

About the Question Type

Inference questions ask you to infer the correct answer by using information that is implied, or not stated directly, in the conversation or lecture.

These questions require you to draw a conclusion based on a comprehensive understanding of the overall context and by connecting information mentioned in the conversation or lecture. Sometimes, questions may be about a speaker, an idea, or what a speaker will do next.

Question Format

- What can be inferred about ~?
- What does the professor imply about ~?
- What will the man/woman probably do next?

Key Strategies

- **Step 1** — Understand the overall context of the talk, and determine whether the question is about a speaker, an idea, or what a speaker will do next.

- **Step 2** — If the question is about a speaker or an idea, find information that is connected to the speaker or idea. If the question is about what a speaker will do next, listen to the statements that a speaker makes near the end of the conversation or lecture.

- **Step 3** — Select the answer choice that is best supported by information in the conversation or lecture.

Example

Answer Book p. 47

A. Listen to a conversation between a student and a university employee at the registrar's office.

Note-taking

Student's Situation
Applied for the _____ _____ _____

Missing _____
- Letter of recommendation from a professor
- One-page _____

What will the student probably do next?

(A) Revise an essay
(B) Make copies of a form
(C) Talk to a professor
(D) Take a language test

Answer Book p. 47

B. Listen to part of a lecture in an anthropology class.

Note-taking

Functions of _____
- For sleeping and _____ food
- Held large community _____
  e.g. Political _____, traditional _____

What does the professor imply about longhouses?

(A) They are no longer used today.
(B) They are also made with stone and clay.
(C) They were used to keep farm animals.
(D) They were the center of Iroquois life.

Dictation

Answer Book p. 47

Listen again and fill in the blanks.

A.

W: Hi, my name is Elizabeth Moore. I'm here about the student exchange program in Germany. I _____ _____ _____.

M: Ah, yes, Ms. Moore. We received your application form and your school transcript. However, you're _____ _____ _____ _____.

W: Oh, really? Could you tell me what they are?

M: Well, we need a _____ _____ _____ from a professor. It should include something about your _____ _____ _____.

W: OK. I thought Professor Muller _____ _____ _____ _____ that for me. I'll ask him about that right after I leave here.

M: And another thing is the one-page essay. Um, it should be about why you want to _____ _____ _____ _____ _____.

W: All right. I'll work on that later tonight.

B.

P: The longhouse was _____ _____, _____ built by the Iroquois people. The Iroquois people were a group of Native Americans. They became known as the People of the Longhouse because, well, they built many longhouses and lived in them.

Longhouses were _____ _____ _____. Some were even longer than a football field! Many families _____ _____ in one longhouse. Sometimes, there were 20 or more families in a single house. Longhouses were also _____ _____ _____ _____, like dried meat and corn. But, uh, they weren't just for sleeping and storing food. They had another _____ _____ ... Large like political meetings and traditional ceremonies were _____ _____ _____. Today, some Iroquois people still use longhouses for those reasons.

Listening Practice 1

Answer Book p. 48

Listen to a conversation between a student and a professor.

Note-taking

Professor's Suggestion
Submit your essay for the history department's
_____ _____
→ _____ the section on Turkey's modern history
→ Discuss Turkey's _____ history some more

1 What are the speakers mainly discussing?

(A) Helping a professor write an article
(B) Doing research for a class
(C) Preparing an essay for a publication
(D) Changing a presentation topic

2 In the conversation, the professor suggests some changes that the student should make. Indicate whether each of the following is a suggestion. *Click in the correct box for each phrase.*

	Suggested	Not Suggested
(A) Increase the length of an essay		
(B) Interview another student		
(C) Focus on a specific subject		
(D) Look for some books		

3 What will the student probably do next?

(A) Contact an expert
(B) Study for an exam
(C) Visit the library
(D) Check out a website

Dictation

Answer Book p. 49

Listen again and fill in the blanks.

P: Thank you for coming, Allan. I want to talk to you about your _____ _____ _____.

S: Sure, Professor Perlman. Uh, is there something wrong with it?

P: Actually, it's excellent. I think you should submit it for the history department's _____ _____.

S: Oh? Is it really that good?

P: Absolutely. It has some great points that were _____ _____ _____ _____ _____.

S: Thank you, Professor. Is there anything I should do before _____ _____ _____?

P: Well, the length is fine, but there is a part that needs to be changed.

S: OK. Which part?

P: Well, I'd like you to _____ _____ on its modern history... Another student will _____ _____ _____ about that.

S: All right. But, I'm worried that my essay might not have enough content then.

P: Yes, so you will need to discuss _____ _____ _____ some more.

S: Hmm... OK. What exactly should I write about?

P: I think you should focus on, uh, how Turkey's location affected its history. As you know, it's located _____ _____ _____ _____.

S: Thanks, Professor. I'll start _____ _____ _____ _____. I just need to return some books to the library first.

P: Good. While you're there, maybe you can _____ _____ _____ on Turkey's ancient history.

Listening Practice 2

Answer Book p. 49

Listen to part of a lecture in a biology class.

Note-taking

How Social Spiders Hunt

Hunt as a _____ and build two kinds of webs
- Main web: Spread out like a _____
- Another web: Acts as a _____
  → Can quickly find the _____ prey
  → Can kill _____ prey

1 What is the main topic of the lecture?

(A) How social spiders build their webs
(B) Different types of spiders in South America
(C) Special behaviors of a social spider
(D) The similarities between two spider species

2 According to the professor, what are two tasks done by the spiders? *Choose 2 answers.*

(A) Protect webs from other animals
(B) Build and repair webs
(C) Care for baby spiders
(D) Search for new homes

3 Why does the professor discuss a performance on a stage?

(A) To illustrate how social spiders catch their prey
(B) To demonstrate how spider webs are built
(C) To describe how quickly spiders move
(D) To explain why social spiders live in groups

4 What does the professor imply about the prey of the spiders?

(A) The spiders usually store it before eating it.
(B) The spiders sometimes fight one another for it.
(C) It often provides more food than the spiders need.
(D) It sometimes escapes from the spiders' trap.

Dictation

Answer Book p. 49

Listen again and fill in the blanks.

P: Next, I'm going to introduce you to some very interesting spiders. They are called *Anelosimus eximius*, a type of social spider. Most spiders like to stay alone, but these spiders _____ _____ _____ _____ in some rainforests of South America. Let's focus on some features of their _____ _____.

These spiders _____ _____ _____ in the rainforest. Thousands of spiders live together in these webs. They do various tasks, like, uh, make webs and _____ _____ _____ of the web. They also take care of baby spiders...

But the most interesting task that they do is hunt as a group. These spiders build _____ _____ _____ _____. Their main web is _____ _____ like a net. Below that there is another web, but this one is shaped like a bowl and _____ _____ _____ _____. This is brilliant because, uh, after insects _____ _____ in the main web, they fall into the trap. Once the prey is trapped, the spiders then do something amazing. They all _____ _____ _____ _____ together. First, they move a short distance, and then they stop... They do this repeatedly. The spiders _____ _____ _____ giving an organized performance on a stage...

With every motion, the spiders can _____ _____ _____ of the trapped prey. In this way, every spider knows where to find the trapped prey quickly. _____ _____ _____ _____ also helps them kill larger prey... Um, you see, social spiders are very small. That's why they usually attack their prey in large numbers. In some cases, they can catch prey that is _____ _____ _____ their own weight! So, there is usually _____ _____ _____ food for all of them...

Listening Practice 3

Answer Book p. 50

Listen to a conversation between a student and a librarian.

Note-taking

Student's Problem
Couldn't find a _____ collection for an English literature class

Librarian's Response
- Lost our only _____ of the book
- Try our _____ _____ system

1. Why does the student talk to the librarian?
   (A) To ask for help in finding a book
   (B) To find out how to use the library's website
   (C) To look for a missing item in the library
   (D) To return a book he borrowed

2. Why does the librarian mention the interlibrary loan system?
   (A) To complain about a program
   (B) To explain a recent mistake
   (C) To give the student an option
   (D) To show that the library is improving

3. What will the student probably do next?
   (A) Look for poems on the Internet
   (B) Visit a university bookstore
   (C) Go to speak with his professor
   (D) Make a request for a book

Dictation

Answer Book p. 50

Listen again and fill in the blanks.

C7_P3_D

M: Excuse me. I'm writing an essay for my _____ _____ _____. So, I need _____ _____ _____ called *The Tennis Court Oath*. It's by John Ashbury. Could you help me find it?

W: Umm... Did you check the library's website? You can _____ _____ _____ _____ _____ or author.

M: Actually, I already did. There is supposed to be one copy here. But I couldn't find it _____ _____ _____.

W: Just a moment... Ah, I see. It's _____ _____ _____.

M: What do you mean?

W: Uh, it means we've _____ _____ _____ of the book. But the library has _____ _____ _____ _____.

M: OK. When do you think it will arrive? My paper is _____ _____ _____, so I really need the book.

W: Uh, I'm sorry, but it will take _____ _____ _____ to get here.

M: Oh, no. Is there nothing I can do? It's _____ _____ _____ _____ the topic of my essay.

W: Why don't you try our interlibrary _____ _____ ? Our library is part of an interlibrary program. If you _____ _____ _____ for a book, a partner library will send it to us. Uh, if it's not _____ _____. I'm sure one of the other libraries will have it.

M: Thank you so much for your help! I'll do that now.

Listening Practice 4

Answer Book p. 51

Listen to part of a lecture in a photography class.

Note-taking

Innovations by Jacques Cousteau
- Aqua-Lung: A _____ device that allowed divers to move _____ and take better _____
- A new _____ camera: Light, easy to _____, with a _____ case

1. What is the lecture mainly about?

   (A) Scientific discoveries that changed the world
   (B) The methods used to take pictures in the water
   (C) The impact a person had on underwater photography
   (D) The role of photography in nature documentaries

2. According to the professor, what was one benefit of the Aqua-Lung?

   (A) It was easy for anyone to repair.
   (B) It gave photographers a clearer view.
   (C) It inspired some new inventions.
   (D) It was also useful outside the water.

3. How does the professor organize the lecture?

   (A) By comparing two different explorations
   (B) By showing the development of photography
   (C) By mentioning the names of famous photographers
   (D) By discussing the effects of some innovations

4. What does the professor imply about Cousteau's camera?

   (A) It was larger than earlier cameras.
   (B) It produced high-quality images.
   (C) It was made entirely of metal.
   (D) It could be attached to the Aqua-Lung.

Dictation

Answer Book p. 51

Listen again and fill in the blanks.

P: Since the 19th century, _____ _____ has been an important art form and a scientific tool. At first, it had many problems. The equipment was limited and color was _____ _____ _____ underwater. Then a French photographer named Jacques Cousteau _____ _____ that influenced and improved underwater photography. Let's discuss those today.
The first innovation was the Aqua-Lung. It was _____ _____ _____ that Cousteau developed in 1946 with Emile Gagnan, a French engineer. The Aqua-Lung allowed divers to _____ _____ _____ because they did not have to use difficult and heavy equipment. It also helped them _____ _____ _____. When they _____ _____ _____, the, uh, air bubbles went behind their head. The bubbles didn't _____ _____ _____, which allowed them to take clearer pictures.
Another innovation was in cameras. Before, most cameras didn't work very well underwater. They were, uh, slow and _____ _____ _____ _____. They also produced low-quality images. Well, in 1957, Cousteau and a Belgian inventor named Jean de Wouters developed a new kind of underwater camera. It was better in every way. It was light and _____ _____ _____... But what made this camera so special was its waterproof case. It made the camera _____ _____, which helped underwater photography significantly!
With these innovations, Cousteau _____ _____ _____ _____ and shared what he saw with viewers. This helped people have a better understanding of the underwater world.

iBT Listening Test 1

TOEFL Listening

Note-taking

Student's Problem

Missed the midterm exam because of an _____
→ Wants to take a _____ test

Professor's Answer

Tests can be missed for students' own _____ reasons.
→ Will review your _____ scores

1 What problem does the student have?

   Ⓐ She has to go to the hospital.
   Ⓑ She lost her notes for an assignment.
   Ⓒ She received a low score in a class.
   Ⓓ She did not take an important test.

2 What does the professor say about a university policy?

   Ⓐ It has recently been changed.
   Ⓑ Some students have complained about it.
   Ⓒ It allows exceptions for some situations.
   Ⓓ Some professors disagree with it.

3 What options might help the student's case? Indicate whether each of the following is an option or not.

   Click in the correct box for each phrase.

	Yes	No
Ⓐ Showing a note from a doctor		
Ⓑ Submitting an extra assignment		
Ⓒ Participating in more class discussions		
Ⓓ Having a good overall score		

4 What will the student probably do next?

   Ⓐ Call a doctor
   Ⓑ Fill out some forms
   Ⓒ Visit her grandmother
   Ⓓ Prepare for a test

Dictation

Answer Book p. 52

Listen again and fill in the blanks.

S: Hi, Professor Brown. I'm sorry about missing yesterday's midterm exam. Um, do you think I could _____ _____ _____ _____?

P: Hello, Carol. We can talk about that. But why couldn't you take it yesterday?

S: There was an accident. My grandmother _____ _____ _____ _____, and, uh, I had to take her to the hospital.

P: Oh, I'm sorry to hear that. I hope it's _____ _____.

S: Well, she _____ _____ _____, but she's doing fine. The doctors fixed her up, and she returned home today.

P: OK, good... Now, about the test...

S: Yes, I was wondering if you would let me take a makeup test. I'm prepared to take it _____ _____ _____.

P: Well, students can usually only miss tests for their own _____ _____. That's the university's policy. Um, makeup tests for other reasons are sometimes allowed, but _____ _____ _____ _____.

S: I understand, Professor. Um, what if I called my grandmother's doctor and _____ _____ _____ _____ _____? It will show that I was at the hospital yesterday.

P: That could help, but I don't think it will be enough.

S: But if you _____ _____ _____ _____, it's quite good... And I've never missed a test or assignment before.

P: Yes, that might help. I'll have to _____ _____ _____ _____ again, though. Um, if your scores are good and you've _____ _____ in class, I may allow you to take a makeup test.

S: Thank you, Professor. I'll let you know about the doctor's note in a few minutes.

iBT Listening Test 2

Answer Book p. 53

TOEFL Listening

HISTORY

Note-taking

1939 ~ 1940

Nazi-Soviet Pact: A secret _____ for control of Eastern Europe countries
→ Soviet Union _____ _____ of the Baltic countries.

1986

People _____ from the Baltic countries to the West.
→ Held _____ every year on August 23

1989

Baltic Chain: The Baltic people formed a _____ _____.
→ The Baltic countries declared _____.

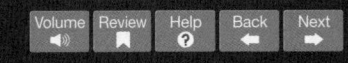

1 What is the lecture mainly about?
- Ⓐ The reasons for the Cold War
- Ⓑ The politicians in Baltic countries
- Ⓒ The role of Europe during the Cold War
- Ⓓ The story behind a large protest

2 How does the professor introduce the Baltic Chain?
- Ⓐ By explaining its importance to politicians
- Ⓑ By describing the events that led to it
- Ⓒ By comparing it to events in other countries
- Ⓓ By talking about the leaders who started it

3 What was the significance of the Nazi-Soviet Pact?
- Ⓐ It helped protect the Baltic countries from the Nazis.
- Ⓑ It gave some German lands to the Soviet Union.
- Ⓒ It let the Soviet Union take control of the Baltic countries.
- Ⓓ It eventually led to the end of World War II.

4 What does the professor imply about the Baltic Chain?
- Ⓐ It was organized by people in the West.
- Ⓑ It caused the Soviet Union to be violent.
- Ⓒ It made many people leave the Baltic countries.
- Ⓓ It was a peaceful form of protest.

Listen again to part of the lecture. Then answer the question.

5 Why does the professor say this:
- Ⓐ To suggest that he saw a protest in person
- Ⓑ To say that a protest was not shown on television
- Ⓒ To make a point about the size of a protest
- Ⓓ To explain that reports about a protest were wrong

Dictation

Listen again and fill in the blanks.

P: What happened in Eastern Europe during the Cold War? Um, in 1989, two years before the Cold War ended, three countries _____ _____ _____ the Soviet Union. These were Estonia, Latvia, and Lithuania. Now, these countries are called the Baltic countries because they are _____ _____ _____ of the Baltic Sea. The Baltic countries _____ _____ _____ that became known as the Baltic Chain.

Before we talk about this in detail, let's review some key events that _____ _____ _____ _____... The first one happened on August 23, 1939. This was when Nazi Germany and the Soviet Union _____ _____ _____ called the Nazi-Soviet Pact. This agreement promised that they would not _____ _____ _____. It also included a secret agreement for control of countries in Eastern Europe. So, in 1940, the Soviet Union _____ _____ the Baltic countries.

By 1986, many people who were unhappy with the situation _____ _____ the Baltic countries to the West. There, they held protests every year on August 23, which was the same day that the Nazi-Soviet Pact was signed. They wanted to tell the world about _____ _____ _____ the Soviet Union... Meanwhile, people who remained in the Baltic countries learned about these protests in the West and decided to _____ _____ _____. They _____ _____ for August 23, 1989. This was _____ _____ _____ of the Nazi-Soviet Pact. This protest became the Baltic Chain.

The Baltic Chain was actually _____ _____ _____. Many people formed a long line while holding _____ _____ _____... And there was a reason why the protest was done in this way. The Baltic people believed that a violent protest would _____ _____ _____ from the Soviet Union. So, instead of choosing violence, two million people held hands _____ _____ _____ _____. This line _____ _____ all three Baltic countries and was over 675 kilometers long. Now, imagine a human chain that long... It must have been _____ _____ _____! Well, various news media reported on the event and helped _____ _____ _____. This message was that the people of the Baltic countries wanted independence... Only seven months after the Baltic Chain, Lithuania became the first of these countries to _____ _____. It was followed by Estonia and Latvia.

Vocabulary Review

Answer Book p. 55

A. Choose the correct word for each meaning.

innovation   ancient   ceremony   waterproof

1 a formal event that is part of a religious or public occasion: _____

2 very old and having existed for a long time: _____

3 a new idea, method, or device: _____

4 not letting water enter or pass through: _____

B. Fill in the blanks with the appropriate words from the box.

violent   store   medical   protest   publication

5 George wrote an article for the school _____.

6 People _____ food in refrigerators to make it last longer.

7 The hospital needs to buy new _____ equipment.

8 _____ behavior is not allowed in school.

9 The group held a _____ about climate change.

C. Choose the closest meaning for each highlighted word.

10 Jamaica declared its independence from the United Kingdom in 1962.
 (A) searched (B) ignored (C) announced (D) followed

11 An employee helped the passenger find her missing bag on the train.
 (A) lost (B) social (C) overall (D) brilliant

12 The store sometimes replaces damaged items for free.
 (A) stopped (B) broken (C) prepared (D) careless

13 The old structure is mostly made of stone.
 (A) building (B) function (C) community (D) request

14 It is the school's policy that students wear uniforms.
 (A) theory (B) movement (C) media (D) rule

HACKERS APEX LISTENING
for the TOEFL iBT
Intermediate

Actual Test

Actual Test 1
Actual Test 2

Actual Test 1

Answer Book p. 55

TOEFL Listening

PART 1. Passage 1

Note-taking

Student's Request

Wants to find a _____ job related to _____ major
→ Will help future _____

Professor's Suggestion

- Apply for an _____
- Get a job with *Reflections* magazine
  → Looking for a _____ _____

Questions 1-5 of 11

1. Why does the student go to see the professor?
   - (A) She needs more time to decide on her career.
   - (B) She is thinking about working on campus.
   - (C) She wants work that is related to her major.
   - (D) She does not know what to do after graduation.

2. Why can't the student do an internship during the summer?
   - (A) She is taking a trip with family.
   - (B) She will be working on a project.
   - (C) She has to take some classes.
   - (D) She does not meet some requirements.

3. How does the professor make his point about a student assistant job?
   - (A) By explaining how it can affect a later career
   - (B) By describing the experience of another student
   - (C) By showing how it can improve a student's grades
   - (D) By warning that it involves a lot of hard work

4. The professor gives several suggestions to help the student. Indicate whether each of the following is a suggestion that the professor mentioned.

   Click in the correct box for each phrase.

	Yes	No
(A) Apply as an intern reporter		
(B) Find a full-time job during a break		
(C) Help the professor with a research project		
(D) Work for a magazine related to the school		

   Listen again to part of the conversation. Then answer the question.

5. Why does the professor say this:
   - (A) He wants to ask other professors' opinions about a job.
   - (B) He thinks an editor does not have enough experience.
   - (C) He wants to increase the student's chances of getting a job.
   - (D) He believes that the editor may not be in the office.

TOEFL Listening
PART 1. Passage 2

BIOLOGY

Note-taking

Photosynthesis

: A _____ that plants use to make their own _____
→ Needs four things: Chlorophyll, _____, _____, and carbon dioxide

How Plants Do Photosynthesis

1. Plants _____ water from the soil.
2. Leaves _____ carbon dioxide from the air.
3. Chlorophyll uses _____ to produce _____.
4. Plants _____ oxygen from their leaves.

Questions 6-11 of 11

6 What is the main topic of the lecture?
- Ⓐ Why plants make their own food
- Ⓑ The way plants create energy
- Ⓒ How plants help the environment
- Ⓓ The importance of plants to humans

7 What does the professor say about chlorophyll?
- Ⓐ It is the main nutrition for plants.
- Ⓑ It is absent in some plants.
- Ⓒ It makes plants green.
- Ⓓ It is produced in the plants' roots.

8 How does the professor organize the lecture?
- Ⓐ By emphasizing the stages of the growth of plants
- Ⓑ By explaining a process and describing its importance
- Ⓒ By mentioning a problem and giving possible solutions
- Ⓓ By comparing two roles of plants in the ecosystem

Listen again to part of the lecture. Then answer the question.

9 What does the professor mean when she says this:
- Ⓐ She believes the student's answer is creative.
- Ⓑ She wants the students to think of other examples.
- Ⓒ She thinks the student's opinion is not totally correct.
- Ⓓ She is not sure that the question is directly related to the topic.

10 In the lecture, the professor describes the stages of photosynthesis. Put the steps listed below in the correct order.

Drag each answer choice to the space where it belongs.

Step 1	
Step 2	
Step 3	
Step 4	

- Ⓐ Sugars are produced by using sunlight.
- Ⓑ Carbon dioxide is absorbed from the air.
- Ⓒ Oxygen is released from the leaves.
- Ⓓ Water is consumed through the roots.

11 What does the professor imply about a plant's ability to perform photosynthesis?
- Ⓐ It is limited if there is too much carbon dioxide.
- Ⓑ It is reduced in very hot and cold environments.
- Ⓒ It is usually about the same in all seasons.
- Ⓓ It is improved in cloudy or rainy weather.

TOEFL Listening
PART 2. Passage 1

Note-taking

Student's Request

Wants to change my _____; economics
→ Has to be something _____ _____ business

Advisor's Suggestion

Consider choosing _____ as a major
- Fill out some _____
- Read a _____ to learn more about the classes

Questions 1-5 of 17

1. Why does the man talk to the woman?
   - Ⓐ To get advice about leaving school
   - Ⓑ To find out about doing a double major
   - Ⓒ To ask about changing a major
   - Ⓓ To complain about some courses he took

2. What does the man plan to do after college?
   - Ⓐ Teach a business course
   - Ⓑ Go to graduate school
   - Ⓒ Work for a large company
   - Ⓓ Open a business

3. Why does the woman ask the man about his past classes?
   - Ⓐ To evaluate his performance
   - Ⓑ To determine his interests
   - Ⓒ To remind him of some requirements
   - Ⓓ To see if he qualifies for a program

4. What is the woman's attitude toward the man's decision?
   - Ⓐ She thinks the man should take more economics classes.
   - Ⓑ She worries that the man is not ready for a change.
   - Ⓒ She agrees that the man's friend gave good advice.
   - Ⓓ She thinks the man will be pleased with his choice.

5. What will the man most likely do next?
   - Ⓐ Suggest some ideas
   - Ⓑ Visit a professor's office
   - Ⓒ Read a document
   - Ⓓ Talk to his friends

Note-taking

The Law of Supply and Demand
- Price goes up.
    → Demand: Consumers buy a product _____.
    → Supply: Sellers make _____ products to sell.
- Factors that affect supply and demand
    → Demand: _____ of consumers and how much _____ they have
    → Supply: Cost of _____ and paying _____

6. What is the main topic of the lecture?
   - Ⓐ The ideal price for both companies and consumers
   - Ⓑ Why customers prefer certain products
   - Ⓒ An economic theory about buyers and sellers
   - Ⓓ How producers determine prices

7. According to the professor, what happens when the prices of goods increases?
   - Ⓐ The demand goes up.
   - Ⓑ People buy them less.
   - Ⓒ Sellers supply them less.
   - Ⓓ Their quality improves.

Listen again to part of the lecture. Then answer the question.

8. Why does the professor say this:
   - Ⓐ To criticize weak points of a theory
   - Ⓑ To point out a common problem
   - Ⓒ To introduce an opposite idea
   - Ⓓ To provide a clearer example

9. The professor explains the factors that affect supply and demand. Indicate whether each of the following is related to supply or demand.

   Click in the correct box for each phrase.

	Supply	Demand
Ⓐ Preferences of consumers		
Ⓑ Cost of materials		
Ⓒ Cost of paying workers		
Ⓓ Amount of money that people have		

10. According to the professor, what is the equilibrium price?
    - Ⓐ It is the price that most consumers prefer.
    - Ⓑ It is when sellers make less profits.
    - Ⓒ It is the lowest possible price.
    - Ⓓ It is when supply and demand are the same.

11. What will the professor most likely do next?
    - Ⓐ Introduce another economic theory
    - Ⓑ Ask the students some questions
    - Ⓒ Explain an economic problem
    - Ⓓ Show a graph to the students

TOEFL Listening
PART 2. Passage 3

ART HISTORY

Note-taking

1667

The _____ _____
- Open to the certain people from the _____ _____.
- Showed only artwork of graduates from the Royal Academy

19th Century

Private _____ and salons
- Creative and _____ artists e.g. Monet, Van Gogh
- Development of new art _____ like Impressionism

Questions 12-17 of 17

12. What is the main purpose of the lecture?
    - (A) To show the importance of art in France
    - (B) To describe a certain French art style
    - (C) To illustrate the history of an art exhibition
    - (D) To explain the origin of independent artists

13. What does the professor say about the French word *salon*?
    - (A) It was invented in the 1600s.
    - (B) Its meaning changed over time.
    - (C) Its origin is a French word for "space."
    - (D) It refers to the smallest room in a house.

14. What does the professor say about the Paris Salon in the beginning?
    - (A) It was open to all members of the art community.
    - (B) It focused on the art of Royal Academy graduates.
    - (C) It was an art school for members of the royal family.
    - (D) It closed all of its art exhibits in the 1600s.

15. What is the professor's attitude toward the judges of the Paris Salon?
    - (A) They should have received support from the royal family.
    - (B) They should have accepted more creative artists.
    - (C) They were too modern in their artistic taste.
    - (D) They did not appreciate traditional artists enough.

16. What does the professor imply about Monet and Van Gogh?
    - (A) Their works were shown in the Paris Salon.
    - (B) They were opposed to traditional art.
    - (C) Their art was not popular during their lifetimes.
    - (D) They graduated from the same art school.

17. Why does the professor mention Impressionism in the lecture?
    - (A) To show that the Paris Salon was interested in new art
    - (B) To highlight the importance of the Royal Academy
    - (C) To give an example of a new art movement
    - (D) To emphasize that earlier art styles were unpopular

Actual Test 2

Answer Book p. 62

TOEFL Listening

PART 1. Passage 1

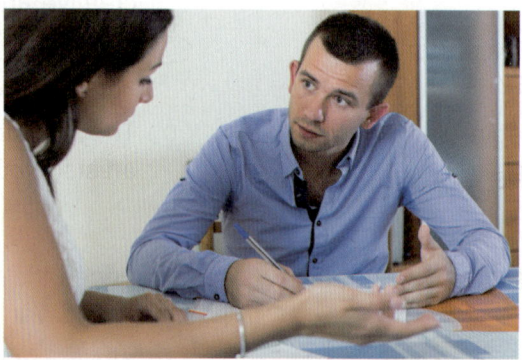

Note-taking

Student's Problem
Here to pick up a letter of recommendation
→ Can't submit my _____ without the letter

Assistant's Suggestion
Visit the _____ office and explain your _____
→ Might be able to _____ the date of the _____

Questions 1-5 of 11

1. What is the man's problem?
   - (A) He is unable to join a work trip.
   - (B) He has not received a document.
   - (C) He did not go to an earlier appointment.
   - (D) He forgot about a deadline.

2. According to the woman, what did Professor Miller do before his work trip?
   - (A) Approve several requests
   - (B) Prepare a presentation
   - (C) Leave some papers
   - (D) Cancel some appointments

3. Why does the woman mention the professor's research location?
   - (A) To give the reason for a delay
   - (B) To show what kind of work he is doing
   - (C) To indicate that a work trip will last long
   - (D) To explain why a task may be difficult

4. What is the man's attitude toward the woman's suggestion?
   - (A) He is not sure that it will work.
   - (B) He thinks it is similar to his idea.
   - (C) He agrees that it is the only solution.
   - (D) He believes it will take too much time.

5. What will the man probably do next?
   - (A) Check his e-mail
   - (B) Sign a letter of recommendation
   - (C) Give his contact information
   - (D) Call another professor on the campus

PHYSICS

Note-taking

Fahrenheit
- The _____ system developed in 1724
- Used a _____ thermometer _____
- Based on the melting and boiling points of water
- Almost _____ countries in the world use this.

Kelvin
- The _____ scale in science
- Most detailed and _____
- Based on the concept of _____ zero

6. What is the main topic of the lecture?
   Ⓐ The invention of the first thermometer
   Ⓑ Various ways to measure temperature
   Ⓒ Environmental factors that affect temperature
   Ⓓ Historical changes in temperature

7. According to the professor, why was mercury used in a thermometer?
   Ⓐ It never freezes.
   Ⓑ It is easy to find.
   Ⓒ It is sensitive to changes.
   Ⓓ It boils slowly.

8. Why does the professor mention the United States and Liberia?
   Ⓐ To highlight the origins of temperature measurement
   Ⓑ To show that few countries use a particular system
   Ⓒ To identify the countries that developed Celsius
   Ⓓ To compare the accuracy of different scales

9. What is the professor's opinion about the Celsius system?
   Ⓐ He thinks it is too confusing.
   Ⓑ He wishes more countries used it.
   Ⓒ He feels it was a big improvement.
   Ⓓ He believes it is less accurate than other systems.

10. The professor discusses different measurement scales. Indicate which type of scale the following phrases describe.

    Click in the correct box for each phrase.

	Fahrenheit	Celsius	Kelvin
Ⓐ Has no negative numbers			
Ⓑ Is the most used around the world			
Ⓒ Measures temperature of stars			
Ⓓ Is the oldest system			

Listen again to part of the lecture. Then answer the question.

11. What does the professor mean when he says this:
    Ⓐ Absolute zero is not the coldest possible temperature.
    Ⓑ The students do not need to know all the details yet.
    Ⓒ The professor cannot explain a complex concept.
    Ⓓ Scientists are still studying absolute zero.

TOEFL Listening
PART 2. Passage 1

Note-taking

Student's Question
Can't find a copy of the book
→ Is it possible to _____ the date of the _____ ?

Professor's Suggestion
- Try _____ on the Internet
- Check the campus _____
- Try a different university _____
- Borrow my _____ copy

Questions 1-5 of 17

1. Why does the student go to see the professor?
   - (A) To discuss the results of a quiz
   - (B) To ask for advice about a project
   - (C) To recommend a book for class
   - (D) To get help with preparation for a test

2. Why can't the professor change the date of a quiz?
   - (A) He needs to follow school rules.
   - (B) He wants to be fair to the other students.
   - (C) He does not have time to prepare a lecture.
   - (D) He thinks it will affect class schedules.

3. The professor gives several suggestions to help the student. Indicate whether each of the following is a suggestion.

   Click in the correct box for each phrase.

	Suggested	Not Suggested
(A) Go to a nearby bookstore		
(B) Sign up on a website		
(C) Visit a public library		
(D) Borrow a professor's book		

4. What is the professor's opinion of a website?
   - (A) He disagrees with its rules.
   - (B) He has used it before.
   - (C) He is surprised about its popularity.
   - (D) He is impressed with its collection.

5. What will the student probably do next?
   - (A) Visit the campus bookstore
   - (B) Apply for a library card
   - (C) Talk to the school librarian
   - (D) Meet with another professor

TOEFL Listening
PART 2. Passage 2

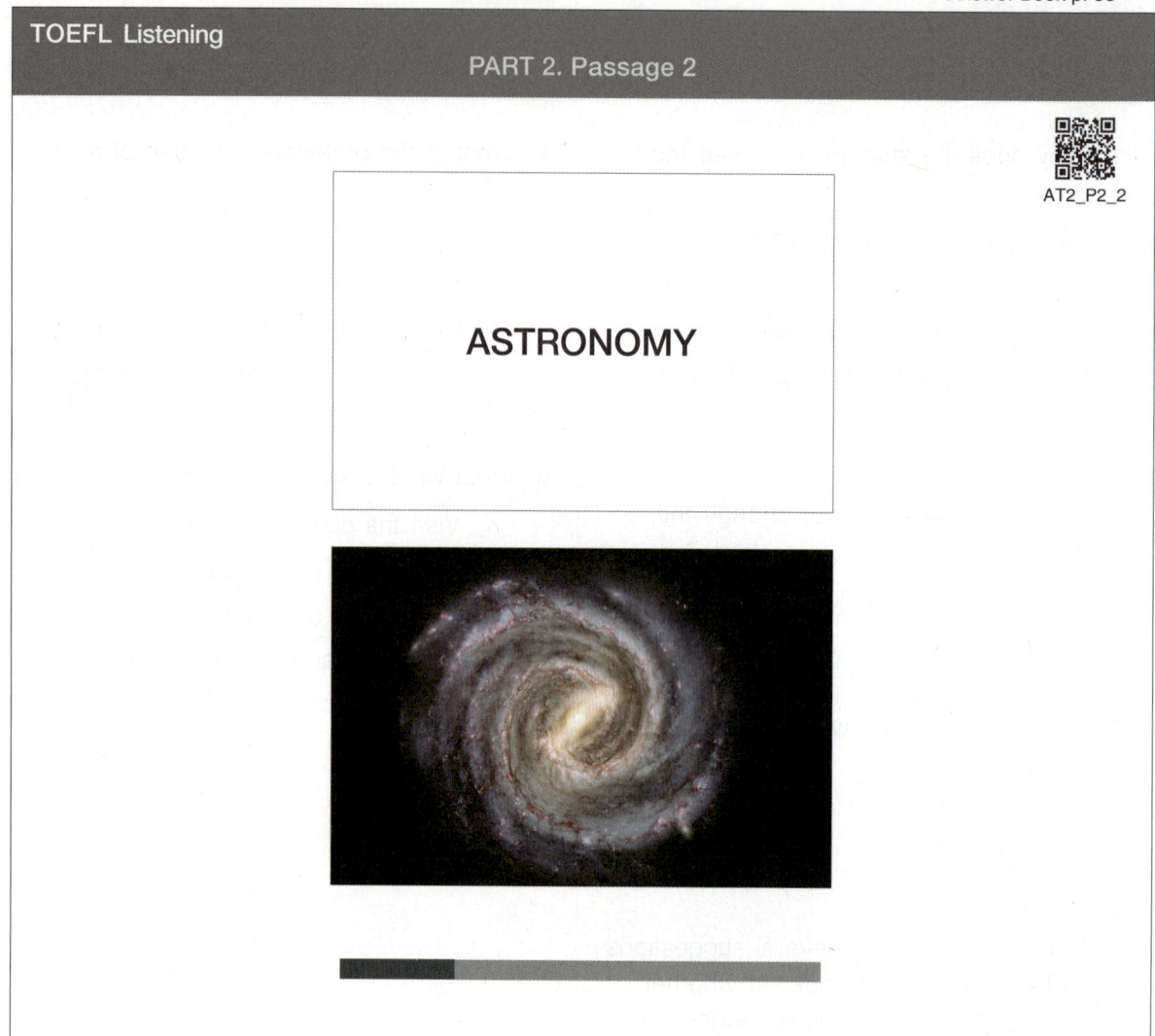

Note-taking

The _____ Way Galaxy
: A _____ of stars, dust, gas, and other objects held together by _____

- Name: From an ancient _____
- Shape: A _____
- Size: Only an _____ size, compared to other galaxies

6. What is the lecture mainly about?
   - Ⓐ The characteristics of a galaxy
   - Ⓑ How the Sun was formed
   - Ⓒ The size of the universe
   - Ⓓ What stars are made of

7. According to the professor, how is the Milky Way similar to our solar system?
   - Ⓐ They have unique shapes.
   - Ⓑ They both have planets and stars.
   - Ⓒ They stay together through gravity.
   - Ⓓ They are easier to study at night.

8. Where did the Milky Way Galaxy get its name?
   - Ⓐ From an old story
   - Ⓑ From a Greek word
   - Ⓒ From a famous astronomer
   - Ⓓ From a Chinese folktale

9. How does the professor explain the shape of the Milky Way?
   - Ⓐ By showing a photograph
   - Ⓑ By describing familiar objects
   - Ⓒ By introducing an experiment
   - Ⓓ By comparing different shapes

10. What is the professor's opinion of the solar system?
    - Ⓐ It is an important part of the galaxy.
    - Ⓑ It has qualities that are special.
    - Ⓒ It is difficult to notice.
    - Ⓓ It has an unusual shape and size.

11. What does the professor imply about the Milky Way?
    - Ⓐ Its gravity is spread out evenly.
    - Ⓑ It will become smaller over time.
    - Ⓒ Its stars are brighter than others.
    - Ⓓ It is not one of the biggest galaxies.

TOEFL Listening
PART 2. Passage 3

Note-taking

_____ **Limit Laws**
- 1910: Connecticut, the first state to set a limit for _____ _____
- 1974: A _____ _____ limit law for all states

Alcohol Laws
Made and _____ _____ by states

_____ _____ **Laws**
Helped drivers avoid accidents in intersections

Seatbelt and Airbag Laws
_____ use of seatbelts and airbags reduced accident _____.

Questions 12-17 of 17

12. What is the main topic of the lecture?
    - Ⓐ The history of automobile production in America
    - Ⓑ The development of American car safety regulations
    - Ⓒ The importance of reducing car crashes
    - Ⓓ The factors that cause car accidents

13. What does the professor say about Connecticut?
    - Ⓐ It produced the first automobile in America.
    - Ⓑ It had the most car accidents in 1910.
    - Ⓒ It was the first state to have speed limits.
    - Ⓓ It helped create a national driving law.

14. What are two characteristics of the national speed limit law?

    Choose 2 answers.
    - Ⓐ It was made after states introduced their own speed limits.
    - Ⓑ It reduced the death rate from accidents.
    - Ⓒ Its speed limit was lower than most state limits.
    - Ⓓ It did not help solve an oil crisis.

15. Why does the professor mention professional drivers like truck drivers?
    - Ⓐ To show that some drivers are safer than others
    - Ⓑ To highlight the cause of the worst car accidents
    - Ⓒ To explain how laws were applied differently
    - Ⓓ To give an example of how a law created more jobs

16. What is the professor's attitude toward traffic lights?
    - Ⓐ He believes that their colors need to be changed.
    - Ⓑ He thinks they are an easy system to follow.
    - Ⓒ He feels that they took a long time to develop.
    - Ⓓ He wants to use them at all intersections.

17. What does the professor imply about seatbelts and airbags?
    - Ⓐ They are not a requirement in some states.
    - Ⓑ They are useful for preventing accidents.
    - Ⓒ They were invented at the same time.
    - Ⓓ They are most effective when used together.

Photo Credits

www.shutterstock.com
p. 139   "Social Spider (Anelosimus eximius)" by Bernard DUPONT / CC BY-SA 2.0
p. 170   "Milky way" by Pablo Carlos Budassi / CC BY-SA 4.0

MEMO

MEMO

|H|A|C|K|E|R|S|
APEX
LISTENING
for the
TOEFL iBT® Intermediate

COPYRIGHT © 2022, by Hackers Language Research Institute

July 21, 2022

All rights reserved. No part of this publication may be reproduced, stored in a retrieval system, or transmitted, in any form or by any means, electronic, mechanical, photocopying, recording, or otherwise, without the prior written permission of the author and the publisher.

Hackers Language Research Institute
23, Gangnam-daero 61-gil, Seocho-gu, Seoul, Korea
Inquiries publishing@hackers.com

ISBN 978-89-6542-127-6 (53740)

Printed in South Korea

3 4 5 6 7 8 9 10   28 27 26 25 24

The Most Preferred Education Brand in Korea,
HACKERS BOOK (www.HackersBook.com)
- Free supplementary study materials

No. 1 in Hankyung Business' Most Preferred Brand Rankings 2019, Education Group category

HACKERS

APEX
LISTENING
for the TOEFL iBT
Intermediate

Answer Book

H|A|C|K|E|R|S

APEX
LISTENING
for the
TOEFL iBT® Intermediate

Answer Book

* Underlined words in the script are the answers to the Dictation exercise.

CHAPTER 01
Main Purpose/Topic

Example
본문 p. 15

A. (C) **B.** (B)

A.

Note-taking

Student's Problem
Can't find a book for my <u>economics</u> class

Librarian's Solution
Copies were just <u>returned</u> this morning.
→ Grab it from the <u>cart</u>

Listen to a conversation between a student and a librarian.

W: Hi. I have a question... Um, I can't <u>find a book</u> that I need for my economics class. Could you tell me where to find it?

M: Have you checked our online system? It will show whether there are <u>any</u> <u>available</u> <u>copies</u> or not. Other students may have checked out the book.

W: I have, and it showed that there are two copies right now. And they should be in the Economics and Business Section, but I couldn't find any of them...

M: OK. Let me have a look... Which book are you <u>looking for</u>?

W: Um, *Modern Economics and Business*, by Jack Harvey. I really need it today.

M: It looks like they were just returned this morning. They're probably not <u>back</u> <u>on</u> <u>the</u> <u>shelves</u> yet.

W: Oh, I see. Then when can I <u>check</u> <u>out</u> the book?

M: It's available now. You'll just need to grab it from the cart.

학생과 사서 사이의 대화를 들으시오.

W: 안녕하세요. 질문이 있는데요... 음, 제 경제학 수업에 필요한 책을 못 찾겠어서요. 어디서 찾을 수 있는지 알려주시겠어요?

M: 저희 온라인 시스템을 확인해 보셨나요? 그것은 이용할 수 있는 책들이 있는지 없는지 보여줄 거예요. 다른 학생들이 그 책을 대출했을지도 몰라요.

W: 확인해봤는데, 지금 두 권이 있다고 보여줬어요. 그리고 그것들이 경제학 및 비즈니스 구역에 있어야 하는데, 저는 그것들 중 어느 것도 찾지 못했어요...

M: 알겠습니다. 제가 한번 볼게요... 어떤 책을 찾고 계시나요?

W: 음, 잭 하비의 '현대 경제학과 비즈니스'에요. 저는 오늘 그것이 정말 필요해요.

M: 그것들이 오늘 아침에 막 반납된 것 같네요. 아마 아직 책꽂이에 안 꽂혀있는 것 같아요.

W: 오, 그렇군요. 그럼 그 책을 언제 대출할 수 있나요?

M: 지금 이용할 수 있어요. 카트에서 그냥 꺼내기만 하면 됩니다.

economics 뗑 경제학 available 쪵 이용할 수 있는; 시간이 있는
copy 뗑 (같은 책·신문 등의) 책, 한 부   check out 대출하다
look for ~을 찾다   return 동 반납하다; 돌아오다
shelf 뗑 책꽂이, 선반   grab 동 꺼내다; 붙잡다

학생은 왜 도서관을 찾아가는가?
(A) 책 추천을 받기 위해
(B) 어떤 책을 대출할지 결정하기 위해
(C) 책의 위치에 대해 물어보기 위해
(D) 책에 대한 주문을 넣기 위해

B.

Note-taking

The Czechs and Puppet Shows
The Czechs who performed <u>puppet</u> <u>shows</u> continued to use Czech.
→ To preserve their <u>language</u> and culture
→ Helped them <u>maintain</u> their cultural identity

Listen to part of a lecture in a history class.

P: From the 15th to 20th centuries, the Habsburg Empire ruled central Europe. The Czech lands were among the areas <u>ruled</u> <u>by</u> the Habsburgs. And interestingly, puppet shows <u>played</u> <u>an</u> <u>important</u> <u>role</u> here at that time. We'll talk about this today.

In the early 1600s, the Habsburg Empire <u>gained</u> <u>power</u> <u>over</u> the Czech lands. The Habsburg rulers forced Czech people to use only German. So, the Czech people were <u>required</u> <u>to</u> <u>use</u> German in official documents, laws, and even plays.

However, the laws did not apply to puppet shows. So, uh, people who performed puppet shows <u>continued</u> <u>to</u> <u>use</u> Czech. And Czech people <u>told</u> <u>traditional</u> <u>stories</u> in their native language through the puppets. Thus, puppet shows allowed the Czechs to <u>preserve</u> <u>their</u> <u>language</u> and culture. This led the Czechs to maintain their cultural identity even under Habsburg rule.

역사학 강의의 일부를 들으시오.

M: 15세기부터 20세기까지, 합스부르크 제국은 중부 유럽을 지배했습니다. 체코 땅은 합스부르크 왕가가 통치하는 지역 중 하나였죠. 그리고 흥미롭게도, 당시 여기서는 인형극이 중요한 역할을 했는데요. 오늘은 이것에 대해 이야기할 것입니다.

1600년대 초, 합스부르크 제국은 체코 땅에 대한 권력을 얻었습니다. 합스부르크 통치자들은 체코 사람들에게 독일어만 사용하도록 강요했어요. 그래서, 체코 사람들은 공문서, 법, 그리고 심지

어 연극에서까지 독일어를 사용해야 했습니다.

하지만, 이 법은 인형극에는 적용되지 않았어요. 그래서, 어, 인형극을 하는 사람들은 계속해서 체코어를 사용했어요. 그리고 체코 사람들은 인형을 통해 그들의 모국어로 전통적인 이야기들을 전했습니다. 따라서, 인형극은 체코인들이 그들의 언어와 문화를 보존할 수 있도록 해주었죠. 이것이 체코인들이 합스부르크 통치하에서도 문화적 정체성을 유지하도록 이끌었습니다.

Habsburg Empire 합스부르크 제국(중부 유럽을 중심으로 최대의 세력을 가졌던 합스부르크 왕가가 지배한 영지를 통칭하는 말)
rule 동 지배하다, 통치하다   Czech 형 체코의; 명 체코어
puppet show 인형극   power 명 권력, 힘   ruler 명 통치자, 지배자
force 동 ~을 강요하다; 명 물리력   German 명 독일어, 독일인
official document 공문서   apply to ~에 적용되다
traditional 형 전통적인   native language 모국어
preserve 동 보존하다, 지키다   identity 명 정체성, 신원

강의는 주로 무엇에 관한 것인가?
(A) 합스부르크 왕가가 체코 공화국을 침략한 이유
(B) 체코인들에게 인형극의 중요성
(C) 체코어의 기원
(D) 전통 인형극이 어떻게 공연되었는지

Listening Practice 1

본문 p.17

1 (D)   2 (A)   3 (C)

Note-taking

Student's Suggestion
Have a discussion session in class

Professor's Answer
- Take an advanced course
- Join a study group for the class

Listen to a conversation between a student and a professor.

S: Professor Sherman, do you have a few minutes? I'm Jacob Harrington, and I was, uh, hoping to speak with you about our Introduction to Philosophy class.

P: Sure, of course. What can I do for you?

S: ¹Um, I'd like to suggest having a discussion session in class. I think it would encourage a deeper understanding.

P: I see... Um, am I not explaining things clearly?

S: No, no. Your explanations are great. Um, I just wanted to develop what I've learned in the class with others.

P: ²Well, this is a beginner course. So, students will learn the basic material in this class.

S: But it seems like we're just memorizing the information...

P: You see, memorization is important in learning because we cannot discuss anything without basic knowledge.

S: Yeah. That makes sense.

P: If you want a discussion in class, I suggest you take an advanced course. It will include a discussion and require deeper thinking.

S: Oh, I didn't know that. I'll take one next semester.

P: ³Also, I recommend you join a study group for this class. That would provide you with, uh, a similar experience. You can review class material and share opinions on related topics with your classmates.

S: That sounds like a great option. Thank you, Professor!

학생과 교수 사이의 대화를 들으시오.

S: Sherman 교수님, 잠깐 시간 있으신가요? 저는 Jacob Harrington인데요, 저는, 어, 저희 철학 입문 수업에 관해서 교수님과 이야기하고 싶습니다.

P: 그럼, 물론이지. 무엇을 도와줄까?

S: 음, 저는 수업 시간에 토론 시간을 갖는 것을 제안하고 싶어요. 그게 더 깊게 이해하는 데 도움이 될 것 같아서요.

P: 그래... 음, 내가 설명을 명확하게 하지 않고 있니?

S: 아뇨, 아닙니다. 교수님의 설명은 좋습니다. 음, 저는 단지 제가 수업에서 배운 것을 다른 사람들과 함께 발전시키고 싶었어요.

P: 음, 이건 초급 과정이란다. 그래서, 학생들은 이 수업에서 기본적인 내용을 배울 거야.

S: 하지만 저희는 그냥 정보를 암기하기만 하는 것 같아요...

P: 알다시피, 우리는 기본적인 지식 없이는 어떤 것에 대해서도 토론을 할 수 없기 때문에 암기는 학습에서 중요하단다.

S: 네, 일리 있는 말씀이네요.

P: 수업 시간 내 토론을 원한다면, 고급 과정을 수강하는 것을 추천해. 그것에는 토론이 포함될 거고 더 깊은 사고를 필요로 할 거야.

S: 아, 그건 몰랐네요. 다음 학기에 그것을 들을게요.

P: 또, 이 수업에 대한 스터디 그룹에 가입하는 것을 추천한단다. 그것은 너에게, 어, 비슷한 경험을 제공해줄 거야. 수업 자료를 복습할 수 있고 동급생들과 관련 주제에 대한 의견을 나눌 수 있을거야.

S: 좋은 선택지인 것 같아요. 감사합니다, 교수님!

philosophy 명 철학   discussion 명 토론, 논의
understanding 명 이해, 합의   clearly 부 명확하게, 뚜렷하게
explanation 명 설명   beginner course 초급 과정
basic 형 기본적인, 근본적인   memorization 명 암기, 기억
advanced course 고급 과정   review 동 복습하다; 명 검토
related 형 관련된   option 명 선택지, 선택

1 학생은 왜 교수를 찾아가는가?
  (A) 수업 내 변화에 대해 불평하기 위해
  (B) 보고서 과제에 대해 문의하기 위해

(C) 그의 수업 일정에 대해 논의하기 위해
(D) 수업에 개선 사항을 제안하기 위해

2 학생은 교수의 수업에 대해 무엇이라고 말하는가?
(A) 학생들은 몇몇 정보를 암기해야 한다.
(B) 읽을거리가 너무 많다.
(C) 조별 과제가 매우 어렵다.
(D) 학생들은 더 많은 설명을 필요로 한다.

3 학생은 무엇을 하기로 동의하는가?
(A) 수업 시간에 발표하기
(B) 다른 교수님의 수업으로 옮기기
(C) 동급생들이 있는 스터디 그룹에 가입하기
(D) 보고서에 대해 수준 높은 주제를 고르기

Listening Practice 2
본문 p.19

1 (B)   2 (C)   3 (B)   4 (A)

Note-taking
Freezing, Melting, and Boiling Points of Matter
- In a higher place, pressure decreases.
  → Boiling point of water is much lower than normal.
- In a lower place, pressure increases.
  → Boiling point of water will go up.

Listen to part of a lecture in a chemistry class.

P: We have already learned about the three states of matter: liquid, solid, and gas. For example, water can be a liquid, a solid as ice, or a gas as vapor. ¹You see, what causes the difference in states are environmental factors... uh, like temperature and pressure. Now, we're going to talk about them in more detail.

Temperature influences the freezing point, melting point, and boiling point of matter. Water's normal freezing point is 0°C, and water becomes ice at this point. Above 0°C, ice melts and becomes liquid. ²Um, its boiling point is 100°C, and water turns into water vapor at 100°C...

But, remember I mentioned temperature and pressure? Well, these conditions are true at normal pressure. What happens when the pressure is lower or higher? The temperatures of the freezing, melting, and boiling points can change under different pressures.

Before I explain this in more detail, there are some rules you need to remember. Pressure is affected by height. When you are in a higher place, pressure decreases. And when you are in a lower place, pressure increases. Imagine that you are climbing a mountain. As you go up the mountain, you're in a higher place. So, uh, if you are on top of Mt. Everest, for instance, the pressure will be very low. ³At lower pressure, the boiling point of water is also much lower than normal. On top of Mt. Everest, water will boil at around 70°C. Now, consider the opposite. As we go down to a lower place like the deep sea, the pressure increases. Then, the boiling point of water will go up, too. ⁴There are places in the deep sea where water will not boil even at very high temperatures. In extreme cases, water can remain liquid even at 400°C!

화학 강의의 일부를 들으시오.

P: 우리는 이미 액체, 고체, 그리고 기체라는 물질의 세 가지 상태에 대해 배웠죠. 예를 들면, 물은 액체일 수도 있고, 얼음으로서 고체일 수도 있고, 혹은 증기로서 기체일 수도 있어요. 보다시피, 상태의 차이를 만드는 것은 환경적인 요인입니다... 어, 온도와 압력 같은 것이죠. 이제, 우리는 그것들에 대해 더 자세히 이야기할 것입니다.

온도는 물질의 어는점, 녹는점, 그리고 끓는점에 영향을 미칩니다. 물의 정상적인 어는점은 0°C이고, 이때 물은 얼음이 됩니다. 0°C 이상에서는, 얼음이 녹아서 액체가 되죠. 음, 그것의 끓는점은 100°C이고, 물은 100°C에서 수증기로 변해요...

그런데, 제가 온도와 압력을 언급했던 것을 기억하시나요? 음, 이 조건들은 정상적인 압력일 때에 해당됩니다. 압력이 더 낮거나 높으면 어떻게 될까요? 어는점, 녹는점, 그리고 끓는점의 온도는 다른 압력에 따라 변할 수 있어요.

제가 이것을 더 자세히 설명하기 전에, 여러분이 기억해야 할 몇 가지 법칙들이 있습니다. 압력은 고도에 의해 영향을 받아요. 여러분이 높은 곳에 있을 때, 압력은 감소해요. 그리고 여러분이 낮은 곳에 있을 때에는, 압력이 증가합니다. 여러분이 산을 오르고 있다고 상상해 보세요. 산을 올라감에 따라, 여러분은 더 높은 곳에 있게 되죠. 그래서, 어, 예를 들어, 여러분이 에베레스트산 꼭대기에 있다면, 압력이 매우 낮을 거예요. 낮은 압력에서는, 물의 끓는점도 정상보다 훨씬 낮아요. 에베레스트산 꼭대기에서, 물은 약 70°C에서 끓을 것입니다. 이제, 그 반대를 생각해 보세요. 깊은 바다와 같이 더 낮은 곳으로 내려감에 따라, 압력은 높아집니다. 그러면, 물의 끓는점도 올라갈 거예요. 깊은 바다에는 매우 높은 온도에서조차도 물이 끓지 않는 곳들이 있답니다. 극단적인 경우, 물이 400°C에서도 액체 상태로 유지될 수 있어요!

state 몡 상태   matter 몡 물질; 문제   liquid 몡 액체
solid 몡 고체   gas 몡 기체   vapor 몡 증기
environmental 휑 환경적인, 환경의   factor 몡 요인
pressure 몡 압력, 압박   freezing point 어는점
melting point 녹는점   boiling point 끓는점   water vapor 수증기
condition 몡 조건; 상태   height 몡 고도, 높이
extreme 휑 극단적인, 극도의

1 강의는 주로 무엇에 관한 것인가?
(A) 다양한 액체의 어는점
(B) 물질의 상태를 변화시키는 요인들
(C) 물의 화학적 구조
(D) 물에 대한 압력의 영향

2 교수에 따르면, 물은 100°C에서 어떻게 되는가?
(A) 그것은 액체로 변한다.

(B) 그것은 녹기 시작한다.
(C) 그것은 증기로 변한다.
(D) 그것은 고체 상태가 된다.

3 교수는 에베레스트산에서의 물의 끓는점에 관해 무엇이라고 말하는가?
(A) 그것은 항상 70°C에서 120°C 사이이다.
(B) 그것은 일반적인 끓는점보다 훨씬 낮다.
(C) 그것은 얼음의 끓는점과 같다.
(D) 그것은 정상적인 끓는점보다 약간 높다.

4 교수에 따르면, 우리가 깊은 바다에서 물을 끓이면 어떤 일이 일어날 것인가?
(A) 물이 매우 높은 온도에서도 액체 상태를 유지할 것이다.
(B) 물이 70°C에서 기체가 될 것이다.
(C) 물이 보통 때보다 더 짧은 시간 안에 끓을 것이다.
(D) 물이 몇 분 후면 고체 상태가 될 것이다.

Listening Practice 3   본문 p.21

1 (C)   2 (D)   3 (C)

Note-taking
Student's Problem
Wants to find a room in a dormitory because of a research project

Employee's Suggestion
- Find a roommate to share a house
- There is an available room in a dormitory.

Listen to a conversation between a student and a housing office employee.

M: Hi. I was hoping you could help me with something.
W: Sure. What do you need?
M: ¹Uh, I want to find a room in a dormitory. ²I need to live on campus because of a research project. I have to come to school early in the morning to work on it.
W: Oh, but the registration period ended last week. The notice was on the board on campus and on the website.
M: I know it's a little late, but my parents' house is too far from here. It takes about two hours to get to school.
W: ³OK, but why don't you find a roommate to share a house near the campus?
M: Well, actually, I was going to live with my friend near the campus, but he got an internship in a different state... All my other friends have already found roommates or live in a dormitory.
W: I see... I'll have a look and see what I can find. If any student decided to leave a dormitory, then we can arrange a room for you.

M: I understand.
W: You're in luck! It looks like there is an available room. Do you have your student ID with you?
M: Yes, here you are. Thank you so much.

학생과 기숙사 사무실 직원 사이의 대화를 들으시오.

M: 안녕하세요. 저를 좀 도와주셨으면 하는데요.
W: 물론이죠. 무엇이 필요하신가요?
M: 어, 저는 기숙사에 방을 구하고 싶어요. 연구 프로젝트 때문에 캠퍼스에서 살아야 하거든요. 아침 일찍 학교에 와서 그것을 진행해야 해요.
W: 아, 그런데 등록 기간이 지난주에 끝났어요. 캠퍼스 내 게시판과 웹사이트에 그 공지가 있었어요.
M: 조금 늦은 건 알지만, 저희 부모님 집은 여기서 너무 멀어서요. 학교에 오는 데에 두 시간 정도 걸려요.
W: 알겠어요, 그런데 캠퍼스 근처에 있는 집을 같이 쓸 룸메이트를 찾아보는 건 어때요?
M: 음, 사실, 제가 제 친구와 캠퍼스 근처에서 살려고 했는데, 그 친구가 다른 주에서 인턴직을 얻게 됐어요... 다른 모든 친구들은 이미 룸메이트를 구했거나 기숙사에 살고 있고요.
W: 그렇군요... 제가 한번 볼테니 뭘 찾을 수 있는지 보죠. 만약 어떤 학생이 기숙사를 퇴실하기로 결정했다면, 저희가 학생을 위해 방을 배치해 줄 수도 있어요.
M: 알겠습니다.
W: 운이 좋으시네요! 이용할 수 있는 방이 있는 것 같아요. 학생증을 갖고 계시나요?
M: 네, 여기 있어요. 정말 감사합니다.

---

dormitory 명 기숙사   registration period 등록 기간
notice 명 공지   board 명 게시판   roommate 명 룸메이트
internship 명 인턴직, 인턴사원 근무 (기간)   state 명 주; 상태
arrange 동 배치하다   student ID 학생증

1 학생의 문제는 무엇인가?
(A) 그는 룸메이트를 구해야 한다.
(B) 그는 아침 일찍 수업이 있다.
(C) 그는 기숙사에 방을 구하고 싶어 한다.
(D) 그는 그의 프로젝트 마감 기한을 늦춰야 한다.

2 학생은 왜 캠퍼스에 더 가까이 살아야 하는가?
(A) 캠퍼스에서 아르바이트직을 구하기 위해
(B) 그의 부모님의 집 근처에 살기 위해
(C) 걸어서 학교에 갈 수 있기 위해
(D) 연구 프로젝트를 진행하기 위해

3 직원은 학생에게 무엇을 하라고 추천하는가?
(A) 학생증을 신청하기
(B) 아파트를 빌리기
(C) 룸메이트와 집을 같이 쓰기
(D) 그의 이름을 명단에 올리기

Listening Practice 4

본문 p. 23

1 (B)   2 (C)   3 (C)   4 (B)

Note-taking
Types of Characters in Literature
- Flat Characters: Shows only one part of their personality that doesn't change
  e.g. Dr. Watson in *Sherlock Holmes*
- Round Characters: More complex and more real
  e.g. Jay Gatsby in *The Great Gatsby*

Listen to part of a lecture in a literature class.

P: I know that all of you have read fiction. ¹But have you ever thought about the types of characters in novels? We're going to discuss two main categories of characters in literature.

First, there are flat characters. Flat characters are not complex. Imagine a photograph of a person. This can show only one part of his or her personality. If a person is smiling in a picture, then we might think that this person is nice. But we can't be sure about this because a person is more complex than just a picture, right? ²Flat characters are similar to what we see in a picture. We can only know one part of their personality, which doesn't change throughout the story. ³For instance, think about Dr. Watson in *Sherlock Holmes*. He is a good friend who helps Sherlock, the main character, solve crimes and mysteries. He is an intelligent and loyal person, and this personality doesn't change. He keeps showing us this one side of his personality. We also don't know much about his life... The author doesn't tell us every detail of his life in the novel.

Next, there are round characters. ⁴These are the opposite of flat characters, so they are more complex and, uh... more real. Since there is a lot of information about their lives, we can really know about their personalities. So, they seem more like real people. Um, Jay Gatsby in *The Great Gatsby* is one example. The novel is about Jay Gatsby's effort to gain love and wealth. Gatsby had a poor childhood. So when he fell in love with a girl from a wealthy family, he couldn't marry her. This made him have a strong desire to become rich. He even participated in crimes. But we cannot say he is just a bad criminal because we know about his childhood and love story. We can easily understand him and his desire to become rich with this background.

문학 강의의 일부를 들으시오.

P: 여러분 모두가 소설을 읽어봤다는 것을 알고 있습니다. 하지만 소설 속 등장인물들의 유형에 대해 생각해 본 적이 있나요? 우리는 문학 속 등장인물들의 두 가지 주요 유형에 대해 논의할 거예요.

먼저, 평면적 인물이 있습니다. 평면적 인물은 복잡하지 않습니다. 한 사람의 사진을 상상해 보세요. 이것은 그 또는 그녀의 성격의 한 부분만을 보여줄 수 있죠. 만약 사람이 사진 속에서 웃고 있다면, 우리는 이 사람이 착하다고 생각할 수 있습니다. 하지만 사람은 사진보다 더 복잡하기 때문에 우리는 이것에 대해 확신할 수 없어요, 그렇죠? 평면적 인물은 우리가 사진에서 보는 것과 비슷해요. 우리는 그들의 성격의 일부분만 알 수 있는데, 이것은 이야기 내내 변하지 않습니다. 예를 들어, '셜록 홈즈'의 왓슨 박사를 생각해보세요. 그는 주인공인 셜록이 범죄와 수수께끼를 해결하는 것을 돕는 좋은 친구입니다. 그는 지적이고 충성스러운 사람이고, 이 성격은 변하지 않아요. 그는 그의 성격의 이 한 면을 계속해서 보여줍니다. 우리가 그의 삶에 대해 많이 아는 것도 아니죠... 작가는 소설에서 그의 삶의 모든 세부 내용을 우리에게 말해주지 않습니다.

다음으로, 입체적 인물이 있습니다. 이들은 평면적 인물의 정반대여서, 더 복잡하고, 어... 더 현실적이죠. 그들의 삶에 대한 많은 정보가 있기 때문에, 우리는 그들의 성격에 대해 정말로 알 수 있죠. 그래서, 그들은 더 실제 인물처럼 느껴집니다. 음, '위대한 개츠비'의 제이 개츠비가 한 예입니다. 그 소설은 사랑과 부를 얻기 위한 제이 개츠비의 노력에 관한 것인데요. 개츠비는 가난한 어린 시절을 보냈어요. 그래서 그가 부유한 집안의 한 소녀와 사랑에 빠졌을 때, 그는 그녀와 결혼할 수 없었죠. 이것이 그가 부자가 되고 싶은 강한 열망을 갖도록 했습니다. 그는 심지어 범죄에도 가담했어요. 하지만 우리는 그의 어린 시절과 사랑 이야기에 대해 알고 있기 때문에 그를 단지 나쁜 범죄자라고 말할 수 없습니다. 우리는 이러한 배경을 통해 그와 그가 부자가 되고자 하는 열망을 쉽게 이해할 수 있어요.

fiction 똉 소설   character 똉 등장인물; 성격   novel 똉 소설
category 똉 유형, 범주   flat character 평면적 인물
complex 휑 복잡한   personality 똉 성격   crime 똉 범죄
intelligent 휑 지적인, 총명한   loyal 휑 충성스러운, 충실한
author 똉 작가   round character 입체적 인물   wealth 똉 부
childhood 똉 어린 시절   desire 똉 열망, 욕구
participate in ~에 가담하다, 참여하다   criminal 똉 범죄자

1 강의의 목적은 무엇인가?
  (A) 소설을 쓰는 데 도움이 되는 조언들을 제공하는 것
  (B) 소설 속 등장인물들의 두 가지 주요 유형을 설명하는 것
  (C) 소설 속 유명한 등장인물들의 예시를 제공하는 것
  (D) 다양한 유형의 문학을 소개하는 것

2 교수는 평면적 인물에 관해 무엇이라고 말하는가?
  (A) 그들은 생동감 넘치는 성격을 가지고 있다.
  (B) 그들은 보통 주인공이다.
  (C) 그들은 성격을 일부분을 보여준다.
  (D) 그들은 긍정적인 특성을 가지고 있다.

3 교수는 왓슨 박사에 관해 무엇이라고 말하는가?
  (A) 그는 원래 주인공으로 만들어졌다.
  (B) 그 인물은 실제 인물에 기반을 둔 것이다.
  (C) 그의 성격은 이야기 내내 변하지 않는다.
  (D) 그 소설에는 그의 삶에 관한 상세한 정보가 포함되어 있다.

강의의 일부를 다시 듣고 질문에 답하시오.
P: These are the opposite of flat characters, so they are more complex and, uh... more real. Since there is a lot of information about their lives, we can really know about their

personalities. So, they seem more like real people.

4 교수는 이렇게 말함으로써 무엇을 의미하는가:
P: So, they seem more like real people.

(A) 대부분의 소설 속 등장인물들은 복잡하지 않다.
(B) 그들의 성격이 그러한 이유는 이해할 수 없는 일이 아니다.
(C) 작가는 등장인물들에 실제 인물들의 이름을 사용한다.
(D) 독자들은 등장인물들이 마지막에는 변할 것이라고 예상한다.

iBT Listening Test 1   본문 p.25

1 (C)   2 (B)   3 (D)   4 (A)

Note-taking
Student's Request
Asks for permission to change the topic of a paper
→ New topic: How climate change will cause many fish to die

Professor's Suggestion
- Will allow the change
- Talk about how fish loss can affect people
  → Add a few paragraphs at the end of a paper

Listen to a conversation between a student and a professor.

S: Excuse me, Professor Baker? ¹I want to ask for your permission to change the topic of my paper. It's the one about natural disasters.
P: Sure, David. The paper is due in four weeks. You have plenty of time to write about a new topic... Um, what is your new topic?
S: I want to write about how climate change will cause many fish to die.
P: I'll allow it. ²Um, why did you change your mind?
S: Well, uh, I was inspired by a documentary that I saw on TV.
P: Tell me more.
S: Well, according to the program, many kinds of fish will die because of climate change. The, um, ocean will become too hot for them to live. And, um, this could happen in the next 10 years.
P: That is terrible! ³And have you thought about what could happen if we lose a lot of fish in the next 10 years?
S: Um... No, I didn't think about it that much.
P: Well, billions of people around the world eat fish regularly... So, if we lose a lot of fish, many people won't have enough to eat.
S: Oh... That sounds like a big problem. ⁴Should I include that in my paper?
P: I think it will make your paper more interesting if you talk about how fish loss can affect people.
S: I see. Maybe more people will care about the problem if it affects them, right?
P: Exactly. But, um, to be clear, don't write too much about it. Just add a few paragraphs at the end of your paper.
S: I understand, Professor Baker. Thank you!

학생과 교수 사이의 대화를 들으시오.

S: 실례합니다, Baker 교수님? 제 보고서의 주제를 바꾸는 데 교수님의 허락을 구하고 싶습니다. 자연재해에 관한 것이에요.
P: 물론이지, David. 그 보고서는 4주 후가 마감이야. 새로운 주제에 대해 쓸 시간이 충분히 있단다... 음, 네 새로운 주제는 무엇이니?
S: 저는 기후 변화가 어떻게 많은 물고기들을 죽게 할지에 대해 쓰고 싶어요.
P: 허락하마. 음, 왜 마음을 바꿨니?
S: 그게, 어, 저는 TV에서 본 다큐멘터리에서 영감을 받았어요.
P: 자세히 말해보렴.
S: 음, 그 프로그램에 따르면, 많은 종류의 물고기들이 기후 변화 때문에 죽을 거예요. 음, 바다가 그것들이 살 수 없을 만큼 너무 뜨거워져서요. 그리고, 음, 이것은 향후 10년 안에 일어날 수 있어요.
P: 끔찍하구나! 그러면 향후 10년 안에 우리가 많은 물고기를 잃게 된다면 어떤 일이 일어날지에 대해 생각은 해봤니?
S: 음... 아니요, 그것에 대해 그 정도까지 생각해보지는 않았어요.
P: 음, 전 세계의 수십억 명의 사람들이 주기적으로 생선을 먹지... 그래서, 우리가 많은 생선을 잃게 되면, 많은 사람들이 먹을 것이 충분하지 않을 거야.
S: 오... 그것은 큰 문제 같네요. 제가 그것을 제 보고서에 포함해야 할까요?
P: 물고기 손실이 어떻게 사람들에게 영향을 미칠 수 있는지에 대해 이야기하면 보고서가 더 흥미로워질 것 같긴 하구나.
S: 알겠습니다. 그 문제가 사람들에게 영향을 준다면 더 많은 사람들이 그것에 관심을 가질 거예요, 그렇죠?
P: 그렇지. 그런데, 음, 확실히 하자면, 그것에 대해 너무 많이 쓰지는 말아라. 보고서 마지막에 몇 단락만 추가하렴.
S: 알겠습니다, Baker 교수님. 감사해요!

---

permission 명 허락, 허가   plenty of 충분한, 많은
climate change 기후 변화   allow 동 허락하다
inspire 동 영감을 주다   documentary 명 다큐멘터리
terrible 형 끔찍한   billion 명 10억   regularly 부 주기적으로
loss 명 손실, 분실   paragraph 명 단락

1 학생은 왜 교수를 찾아가는가?
(A) 강의에 대한 그의 생각을 전하기 위해
(B) 발표에 대해 다른 주제를 요청하기 위해
(C) 그가 새로운 주제에 대해 쓸 수 있는지 문의하기 위해
(D) 기후 변화에 대한 사실을 확인하기 위해

2 학생의 마음을 바꾸게 한 것은 무엇인가?
(A) 그가 참석한 강연
(B) 그가 본 프로그램

(C) 그가 방문한 웹사이트
(D) 그가 읽은 기사

3 교수에 따르면, 향후 10년 안에 무슨 일이 일어날 수 있는가?
(A) 과학자들이 기후 변화에 대한 해결책을 개발할 것이다.
(B) 많은 수원들이 물을 마시기에 안전하지 않을 것이다.
(C) 세계의 일부 지역은 동물들이 살기에 너무 더울 것이다.
(D) 많은 사람들이 먹을 생선이 충분하지 않을 것이다.

4 교수는 학생에게 보고서에 무엇을 추가하라고 하는가?
(A) 사람들과 관련 있는 가능한 결과
(B) 심각한 문제를 해결하기 위한 몇몇 방안들
(C) 기후 변화에 대한 자세한 설명
(D) 다큐멘터리에 대한 몇몇 단락들

iBT Listening Test 2
본문 p.28

1 (C)   **2** (C)   **3** (B)   **4** (D)   **5** (C)

Note-taking
Keystone Species

- Predators
  e.g. Tiger sharks maintain the population of sea turtles at a proper level.
- Ecosystem engineers
  e.g. Woodpeckers create holes in trees, which other animals depend on.
- Mutualists
  e.g. Flowers provide bees with honey, and the bees help flowers produce seeds.

Listen to part of a lecture in an ecology class.

P: In every environment, there are keystone species. Keystone species are very important for ecosystems. If they are removed, many other species may not exist. ¹Let's take a look at three types of keystone species.

First, there are predators. A good example is the tiger shark. The tiger shark is the main predator of sea turtles. When there are enough tiger sharks, the population of sea turtles is maintained at a proper level. Uh, sea turtles eat seagrass... and, um, seagrass is important for many kinds of wildlife. For example, many fish lay their eggs on seagrass, and, uh, young fish use seagrass as shelter while they grow up. ²So, um, if tiger sharks disappear, the sea turtles have no major predator. If this happens, sea turtles will eat all of the seagrass, and the other organisms will have no place to raise their babies.

Next, there are ecosystem engineers. Just like human engineers, these change the environment. ⁵An obvious example is the beaver. As you know, beavers build dams. Their dams turn streams into ponds, which, uh, other organisms depend on. But I really want to focus on woodpeckers. Um, woodpeckers create holes in trees. They use their beaks to search for insects under the tree bark. And, um, they also make larger holes. Then they build their nests in these holes. ³Once they have raised their babies, woodpeckers do not use the nesting holes anymore. But a wide variety of other animals do. For instance, squirrels, owls, and snakes sometimes use woodpecker holes for shelter or to raise their babies.

Finally, we have mutualists. ⁴Mutualists are two types of animals that benefit each other. Thus, they have closely related relationships. Bees and flowers are examples of mutualists. Flowers provide bees with honey. And in return, the bees help flowers produce seeds so that they can reproduce. So, uh, bees will starve without flowers. And the number of flowers will decrease without bees. But it also affects the entire ecosystem if one of these disappears. For example, many birds depend on flower seeds for food, and the number of these birds will be reduced. And other animals which eat these birds will decrease as well.

생태학 강의의 일부를 들으시오.

P: 모든 환경에는, 핵심종이 있습니다. 핵심종은 생태계에 매우 중요합니다. 그것들이 없어진다면, 다른 많은 종들이 존재하지 않을지도 모릅니다. 세 종류의 핵심종들을 살펴봅시다.

먼저, 포식자가 있습니다. 뱀상어가 좋은 예시죠. 뱀상어는 바다거북의 주요 포식자입니다. 뱀상어가 충분히 있을 때, 바다거북의 개체 수는 적절한 수준으로 유지됩니다. 어, 바다거북은 해초를 먹는데... 음, 해초는 많은 종류의 야생 동물들에게 중요해요. 예를 들어, 많은 물고기들이 해초 위에 알을 낳고, 어, 어린 물고기들은 자라는 동안 해초를 은신처로 사용합니다. 그래서, 음, 뱀상어가 사라진다면, 바다거북들은 주요 포식자가 없게 돼요. 이렇게 된다면, 바다거북들은 모든 해초를 다 먹을 것이고, 다른 유기체들이 새끼들을 키울 장소가 없을 것입니다.

다음으로, 생태계 공학자들이 있어요. 마치 인간 공학자들처럼, 이것들은 환경을 변화시킵니다. 분명한 예시가 비버입니다. 여러분도 알다시피, 비버는 댐을 짓습니다. 그것들의 댐은 개울을 연못으로 만드는데, 어, 다른 유기체들이 이것에 의존하죠. 하지만 제가 정말 집중하고 싶은 건 딱따구리에요. 음, 딱따구리는 나무에 구멍을 만들죠. 그것들은 부리를 사용해서 나무껍질 밑에 있는 곤충을 찾아요. 그리고, 음, 그것들은 더 큰 구멍도 만들어요. 그러고 나서 그것들은 이 구멍들에 둥지를 지어요. 새끼들을 기르고 나면, 딱따구리는 더 이상 둥지 구멍을 사용하지 않습니다. 하지만 다른 다양한 동물들이 사용을 해요. 예를 들어, 다람쥐, 올빼미, 그리고 뱀은 때때로 딱따구리 구멍을 은신처나 새끼들을 기르기 위해 사용합니다.

마지막으로, 상리 공생 생물이 있습니다. 상리 공생 생물은 서로에게 이익을 주는 두 종류의 동물입니다. 따라서, 그들은 밀접하게 연결된 관계를 갖고 있어요. 벌과 꽃이 상리 공생 생물의 예시입니다. 꽃은 벌에게 꿀을 제공하죠. 그리고 대신, 벌들은 꽃들이 씨앗을 생산하는 것을 도와서 그것들이 번식할 수 있도록 합니다. 그래서, 어, 벌들은 꽃이 없으면 굶어 죽을 겁니다. 그리고 벌이 없으면 꽃의 수가 줄어들 것이고요. 하지만 이것들 중 하나가 사라진다면 이것은 전체 생태계에도 영향을 미칩니다. 예를 들어, 많은 새들이 먹이로 꽃씨에 의존하는데, 이 새들의 수가 줄어들겠죠. 그리고 이 새들을 잡아먹는 다른 동물들 또한 줄어들 거예요.

keystone species 핵심종   tiger shark 뱀상어   sea turtle 바다거북
population 명 개체 수, 인구   seagrass 명 해초
wildlife 명 야생 동물   shelter 명 은신처   organism 명 유기체
ecosystem engineer 생태계 공학자   obvious 형 분명한, 명확한
depend on ~에 의존하다, 의지하다   woodpecker 명 딱따구리
focus on ~에 집중하다, ~에 주력하다   beak 명 (새의) 부리
bark 명 나무껍질   nest 명 (새의) 둥지
mutualist 명 상리 공생 생물   in return 대신에, 보답으로
reproduce 동 번식하다; 복사하다   starve 동 굶어 죽다, 굶주리다

1 강의의 주된 주제는 무엇인가?
  (A) 생태계에서의 상어의 역할들
  (B) 멸종위기에 처한 종의 몇몇 예시들
  (C) 몇몇 종류의 핵심종
  (D) 포식자와 피식자 간의 관계

2 교수에 따르면, 만약 뱀상어가 사라진다면 무슨 일이 일어나는가?
  (A) 바다거북의 수가 줄어들 것이다.
  (B) 물고기가 해초 위에 알을 낳기 시작할 것이다.
  (C) 바다거북이 모든 해초를 다 먹을 것이다.
  (D) 물고기는 어떠한 주요 포식자도 없을 것이다.

3 교수는 딱따구리의 둥지 구멍에 관해 무엇이라고 말하는가?
  (A) 그것들은 나무의 건강을 해칠 수 있다.
  (B) 다른 많은 동물들도 그것들을 사용한다.
  (C) 딱따구리는 매년 그것들을 재사용한다.
  (D) 그것들은 다양한 곤충들을 끌어들인다.

4 교수는 상리 공생 생물들에 관해 무엇이라고 말하는가?
  (A) 그것들은 천적이 거의 없다.
  (B) 그것들은 큰 숲에 가장 흔히 있다.
  (C) 그것들은 포식자와 피식자 간의 균형을 만든다.
  (D) 그것들은 서로에게 이익을 주는 두 유기체이다.

강의의 일부를 다시 듣고 질문에 답하시오.
P: An obvious example is the beaver. As you know, beavers build dams. Their dams turn streams into ponds, which, uh, other organisms depend on. But I really want to focus on woodpeckers.

5 교수는 왜 이렇게 말하는가:
  P: But I really want to focus on woodpeckers.
  (A) 모든 사람이 비버에 대해 알았는지 확인하기 위해
  (B) 딱따구리가 비버보다 더 중요하다는 것을 나타내기 위해
  (C) 특정 종류의 생태계 공학자를 강조하기 위해
  (D) 비버와 딱따구리 간의 관계를 설명하기 위해

Vocabulary Review   본문 p. 32

1 grab   2 fiction   3 available
4 starve   5 population   6 wealth
7 intelligent   8 inspire   9 traditional
10 (C)   11 (B)   12 (A)
13 (D)   14 (B)

CHAPTER 02
Detail

Example   본문 p. 35

A. (C)   **B.** (A), (C)

A.

Note-taking
Student's Problem
An online advertisement is not on school website.

Director's Solution
Ask any professor for a signature

Listen to a conversation between a student and the director of campus activities.
W: Hi. I'm looking for the director of campus activities.
M: That's me. What can I do for you?
W: I'm the head of the Literature Club. We applied to have an online advertisement on our school website, but it's not there.
M: Um, did you submit all of the forms?
W: I did. I checked them twice. We really need an advertisement to promote a special lecture. A famous writer, Katherine Oliver, will be here to talk about her recent novel.
M: That sounds interesting. Let me take a look and find out what the problem is... Hmm... Did you get a signature from a professor?
W: No, we don't have an advisor... Is there anything I can do?
M: You can ask any professor for a signature. I'm sure that one of the literature professors would be happy to help you.
W: OK, I'll do that.

학생과 캠퍼스 활동 책임자 사이의 대화를 들으시오.
W: 안녕하세요. 저는 캠퍼스 활동 책임자를 찾고 있는데요.
M: 바로 접니다. 무엇을 도와 드릴까요?
W: 저는 문학 동아리의 회장이에요. 저희가 학교 웹사이트에 온라인

광고를 싣는 것을 신청했는데, 그게 거기에 없어서요.
M: 음, 모든 서류를 제출하셨나요?
W: 했어요. 제가 두 번이나 확인했고요. 저희가 특강을 홍보하기 위해서 광고가 정말 필요해요. 유명한 작가인 Katherine Oliver가 그녀의 최신 소설에 대해 이야기하러 이곳에 올 거예요.
M: 그거 재미있겠는데요. 제가 한번 보고 무엇이 문제인지 알아볼게요... 흠... 교수님께 서명은 받으셨나요?
W: 아니요, 저희는 지도 교수님이 없어요... 제가 할 수 있는 일이 있을까요?
M: 아무 교수님께 서명을 부탁드려도 돼요. 문학 교수님들 중 한 분께서 기꺼이 도와주실 거라고 확신해요.
W: 좋아요, 그렇게 할게요.

director 명 책임자   head 명 회장; 머리   Literature 명 문학
apply to ~에 신청하다   advertisement 명 광고
submit 동 제출하다   form 명 서류; 종류   promote 동 홍보하다
find out 알아보다, 알아내다   signature 명 서명
advisor 명 지도 교수

광고 신청을 위한 서류들에서 빠진 것은 무엇인가?

(A) 광고를 위한 비용
(B) 학생증 번호
(C) 교수의 서명
(D) 강의에 대한 설명

B.

Note-taking
Jupiter's Great Red Spot
Why is it red?
→ The leading theory
: It comes from a combination of ammonia in the clouds and solar energy.

Listen to part of a lecture in an astronomy class.

P: If you look at the surface of Jupiter, you will see many unique patterns. Um, these patterns are made by clouds. Jupiter is covered with giant gas clouds that are much bigger than the clouds on Earth. Among them, there is a giant red storm called the Great Red Spot. Why is it red, though?
No one knows exactly what creates this red color. But the leading theory suggests that the storm's color comes from a combination of two factors: ammonia in the clouds and solar energy. Um, ammonia forms the top layer of Jupiter's atmosphere, and it doesn't have any color. However, when it meets powerful light from the Sun, a material is created that has a red color. Still, the theory has a weak point... So now, let's talk about what the weak point is.

천문학 강의의 일부를 들으시오.

P: 목성의 표면을 보면, 많은 독특한 무늬들을 보게될 거예요. 음, 이 무늬들은 구름에 의해 만들어진 것입니다. 목성은 지구의 구름보다 훨씬 더 큰 거대한 가스 구름으로 덮여 있어요. 그것들 중에, 대적점이라고 불리는 거대한 붉은 폭풍이 있습니다. 그런데, 그것이 왜 붉은 걸까요?

정확히 무엇이 이 붉은색을 만드는지는 아무도 알지 못합니다. 하지만 유력한 이론은 폭풍의 색이 구름 속의 암모니아와 태양 에너지라는 두 가지 요소가 결합한 것에서 나온 것이라고 제시합니다. 음, 암모니아는 목성의 대기의 맨 위층을 형성하는데, 그것은 어떠한 색도 가지고 있지 않아요. 하지만, 그것이 태양의 강력한 빛을 만나면, 붉은색을 가진 물질이 만들어집니다. 그렇지만, 이 이론에도 약점이 있죠... 자 이제, 이 약점이 무엇인지에 대해 이야기해 봅시다.

surface 명 표면   Jupiter 명 목성   unique 형 독특한
storm 명 폭풍   Great Red Spot (목성의) 대적점
leading 형 유력한; 이끄는   theory 명 이론
combination 명 결합, 조합   ammonia 명 암모니아
solar energy 태양 에너지   layer 명 층   atmosphere 명 대기
material 명 물질; 직물   weak point 약점

교수에 따르면, 대적점의 색의 원인이 되는 두 가지 요소는 무엇인가? 2개의 답을 고르시오.

(A) 구름 속의 암모니아
(B) 표면의 독특한 무늬들
(C) 태양 에너지
(D) 대기 중의 붉은 먼지

Listening Practice 1

본문 p.37

1 (A)   2 (B)   3 (C)

Note-taking
Student's Problem
Cannot take the test because of a debate contest

Professor's Suggestion
- Can double the student's midterm score
- Can give extra points in class

Listen to a conversation between a student and a professor.

S: Hi, Professor Anderson. I hope you aren't too busy. ¹Do you have a moment to talk about next week's test? Uh, I don't think I can take the test.
P: Oh? Is there a problem?
S: Um... ²I was chosen by the debate club to participate in a debate contest next week. One of the other team members can't make it.
P: I see. Well, it's important to participate in school activities, so congratulations to you. Um, is this a big contest?
S: It's a college championship. Our team will be representing the school.
P: That's amazing! I hope you do well... But you'll

need to submit a letter from the debate club to prove that first.
S: Yes, I have the letter right here, actually... But, um, what about the test? I could write a paper on the topic instead.
P: Well, I can double your midterm score to make up for missing the final.
S: Um, I got a low grade on my midterm. It may not be high enough... Is there any other way to increase my score?
P: Well, you can get extra points in class, too. ³If you participate more in discussions, then I can give you extra points for that.
S: All right, Professor Anderson. That sounds fine.

학생과 교수 사이의 대화를 들으시오.

S: 안녕하세요, Anderson 교수님. 너무 바쁘시지 않길 바라요. 다음 주 시험에 대해 이야기할 시간이 있으신가요? 어, 제가 시험을 못 볼 것 같아서요.
P: 오? 무슨 문제라도 있니?
S: 음... 제가 토론 동아리에서 다음 주 토론 대회에 참가하는 것으로 선정되었어요. 다른 팀원들 중 한 명이 참가하지 못하게 되어서요.
P: 그렇구나. 음, 학교 활동에 참여하는 것은 중요하니까, 축하한다. 음, 큰 대회니?
S: 대학 결승전이에요. 저희 팀이 학교를 대표할 거예요.
P: 정말 놀랍구나! 네가 잘하길 바란다... 하지만 먼저 그것을 증명하기 위해서 토론 동아리에서 받은 증서를 제출해야 할 거야.
S: 네, 사실, 증서가 바로 여기 있어요... 하지만, 음, 시험은요? 제가 주제에 대한 보고서를 대신 쓸 수도 있을 것 같은데요.
P: 음, 기말고사를 놓친 것을 만회하기 위해 중간고사 점수를 두 배로 만들 수도 있단다.
S: 음, 제가 중간고사에서 낮은 점수를 받았어요. 충분히 높지 않을지도 몰라요. 제 점수를 올릴 수 있는 다른 방법이 있을까요?
P: 음, 수업 시간에 가산점을 받을 수도 있지. 만약 네가 토론에 더 참여한다면, 그것에 대해 가산점을 줄 수 있어.
S: 좋아요, Anderson 교수님. 그거 괜찮네요.

debate 뗭 토론   contest 뗭 대회   make it 참가하다; 성공하다
championship 뗭 결승전, 선수권 대회   represent 동 대표하다
prove 동 증명하다, 입증하다   double 동 두 배로 만들다; 두 배가 되다
midterm 뗭 중간고사   score 뗭 점수, 득점
make up for ~을 만회하다   final 뗭 기말고사; 형 마지막의
extra points 가산점

1 학생은 왜 교수를 찾아가는가?
(A) 시험을 못 보게 되는 것에 대한 조언을 구하기 위해
(B) 다가오는 학교 행사에 그를 초대하기 위해
(C) 학교 공부의 양에 대해 불평하기 위해
(D) 토론을 준비하는 것에 대한 도움을 요청하기 위해

2 교수는 왜 학생을 축하해 주는가?
(A) 그녀가 해외 유학을 하는 것이 받아들여졌다.
(B) 그녀는 학교 활동에 참여해달라는 요청을 받았다.
(C) 그녀는 시험에서 가장 높은 점수를 받았다.
(D) 그녀는 그녀의 팀과 함께 지역 대회에서 우승을 했다.

3 교수에 따르면, 학생은 어떻게 가산점을 받을 수 있는가?
(A) 특별 보고서를 작성함으로써
(B) 수업 시 발표를 함으로써
(C) 수업 시 토론에 참여함으로써
(D) 재시험을 치름으로써

Listening Practice 2   본문 p.39

1 (B)   **2** (C)   **3** (A), (D)   **4** (C)

Note-taking
A Theory of a Black Swan
Conditions for a Black Swan
• Outside of our regular knowledge
• Creates a huge impact on our society
  e.g. 'Earth is flat' → 'Earth is round',
       Paper and pens → Internet

Listen to part of a lecture in a psychology class.

P: Who has heard of the Black Swan Theory? Well, as you might expect, it is related to a black swan. ¹The Black Swan Theory is about a fact or event that seems impossible. But, the impossible becomes real with new information. And, uh, this changes people's psychology. In fact, it changes their whole view of reality.

In the old days, Europeans thought that all swans were white. Imagine that you have seen thousands of swans, and all of them were white. You might think that all swans are white. ²Well, this belief continued for many years because there were no black swans in Europe. But, uh, when European explorers traveled to Australia in the 17th century, they saw black swans for the first time. This changed their view about what a swan could be.

The theory was later developed by Nassim Nicholas Taleb in 2001. In his book, he suggests some conditions for a Black Swan. ³ᴬAt first, a Black Swan is outside of our regular knowledge. We can never expect that it is real until we discover it. ³ᴰBut once it is known, it has a huge impact on our society. Imagine that one day we find out something that turns our knowledge upside down. Everyone will be shocked and confused.

⁴So, uh, here are some good examples. Once, people thought Earth was flat. But when they learned it was round, it changed their thinking completely. ⁴Similarly, most people could not imagine communication without paper and pens. But the Internet changed all of that. It

even changed the way we live. Um, think of how often you use the Internet every day. Before the Internet, no one knew how important it would become. It, uh, surprised everyone. A Black Swan will only have value after it is discovered, but its value will be very high.

심리학 강의의 일부를 들으시오.

P: 흑조 이론에 대해 들어본 사람이 있나요? 음, 여러분이 예상할 수 있듯이, 그것은 흑조와 관련이 있는데요. 흑조 이론은 불가능해 보이는 사실 혹은 사건에 관한 것입니다. 하지만, 불가능한 것은 새로운 정보를 통해 현실이 돼요. 그리고, 어, 이것은 사람들의 심리를 바꾸어 놓습니다. 사실, 그것은 그들의 현실에 대한 견해 전체를 바꾸죠.

옛날에는, 유럽인들은 모든 백조가 흰색이라고 생각했어요. 여러분이 수천 마리의 백조들을 봤는데, 그것들 모두가 흰색이었다고 상상해보세요. 여러분은 모든 백조가 흰색이라고 생각할지도 모릅니다. 음, 유럽에는 흑조가 없었기 때문에 이 생각은 수년 동안 지속되었어요. 하지만, 어, 17세기에 유럽인 탐험가들이 호주를 여행했을 때, 그들은 처음으로 흑조를 봤습니다. 이것은 백조가 무엇이 될 수 있는지에 대한 그들의 견해를 바꾸었죠.

후에 이 이론은 2001년에 나심 니콜라스 탈레브에 의해 발전되었어요. 그의 책에서, 그는 흑조에 대한 몇 가지 조건들을 제시합니다. 처음에, 흑조는 우리의 일반적인 지식의 밖에 있습니다. 우리는 그것을 발견하기 전까지는 그것이 진짜라고 결코 예상할 수 없죠. 하지만 그것이 알려지고 나면, 그것은 우리 사회에 큰 영향을 미칩니다. 어느날 우리의 지식을 거꾸로 뒤집는 무언가를 발견한다고 상상해보세요. 모두가 충격을 받고 혼란스러워할 것입니다.

그래서, 어, 여기 좋은 예시들이 있습니다. 한때, 사람들은 지구가 평평하다고 생각했습니다. 하지만 그들이 그것이 둥글다는 것을 알았을 때, 그것은 그들의 생각을 완전히 바꾸었죠. 마찬가지로, 대부분의 사람들은 종이와 펜이 없는 의사소통을 상상할 수 없었습니다. 하지만 인터넷은 이 모든 것을 바꾸어 놓았죠. 그것은 우리가 사는 방식조차도 바꿨습니다. 음, 여러분이 매일 인터넷을 얼마나 자주 사용하는지 생각해보세요. 인터넷이 있기 전에는, 아무도 그것이 얼마나 중요해질지 몰랐습니다. 그것은, 어, 모두를 놀라게 했죠. 흑조는 발견된 후에야 가치가 생기겠지만, 그 가치는 매우 높을 것입니다.

---

psychology 명 심리, 심리학 view 명 견해
thousands of 수천의 belief 명 생각, 믿음 knowledge 명 지식
impact 명 영향 upside down 거꾸로
confused 형 혼란스러워하는 flat 형 평평한
completely 부 완전히 similarly 부 마찬가지로, 비슷하게
communication 명 의사소통 value 명 가치

1 강의의 주된 주제는 무엇인가?

(A) 새로운 종의 새
(B) 예상치 못한 사건에 대한 이론
(C) 문화에 따른 현실에 대한 견해
(D) 오래된 믿음에 대한 새로운 증거

2 교수는 17세기의 유럽인 탐험가들에 대해 무엇이라고 말하는가?

(A) 그들은 지리학에 대해 한정된 지식을 가지고 있었다.
(B) 그들은 백조를 그들과 함께 호주로 데려왔다.
(C) 그들은 이전에 흑조를 본 적이 없었다.
(D) 그들은 호주에 도착한 최초의 외국인이었다.

3 탈레브에 따르면, 흑조의 두 가지 조건은 무엇인가? 2개의 답을 고르시오.

(A) 그것은 일반적인 지식 밖에 있다.
(B) 그것은 현실적이기보다 상상의 것이다.
(C) 그것은 대부분의 사람들에게 받아들여지지 않는다.
(D) 그것은 사회에 큰 영향을 끼친다.

4 교수는 왜 인터넷을 언급하는가?

(A) 의사소통의 중요성을 강조하기 위해
(B) 사람들이 한때 새로운 지식을 거부한 이유를 설명하기 위해
(C) 극적인 변화의 예시를 제공하기 위해
(D) 새로운 기술이 어떻게 빠르게 가치를 만들어낼 수 있는지 보여주기 위해

Listening Practice 3   본문 p.41

1 (C)   2 (B)   3 (D)

Note-taking
Student's Problem
Won't be available to work at night

Manager's Answer
Lunchtime shift: Full
→ Morning shift: A position is available.

Listen to a conversation between a student and a food service manager.

M: Hi, are you Ms. Stewart, the food service manager? I was told to come and speak to you about a question I had.

W: That's right. Uh, are you one of our student staff members? How can I help you?

M: Yes. My name is Ryan, and I work on the nighttime shift from 6 to 8 p.m. ¹But I was wondering if I could ask for a change of shift.

W: Are you having problems with other staff members on the nighttime shift?

M: No... ²Um, you see, I won't be available to work at night. I joined a band and, um, I need to practice in the evenings.

W: I see. So which shift are you interested in?

M: I want to move to the lunchtime shift if it's possible.

W: Well, the lunchtime shift is full. It's the most popular shift among the student staff.

M: Well, what about the morning shift? ³I was worried about waking up so early, but if there's no other option...

W: One of the students on the morning shift just quit, so we have a position.

M: I guess I'll have to take that one, then. Thank you for your help, Ms. Stewart.

학생과 급식 관리자 사이의 대화를 들으시오.

M: 안녕하세요, 급식 관리자이신 Stewart씨인가요? 제가 궁금한 게 있는데 Stewart씨께 가서 얘기하면 된다는 말을 들어서요.

W: 맞아요. 어, 우리 학생 직원 중 한 명인가요? 무엇을 도와드릴까요?

M: 네. 제 이름은 Ryan이고, 저는 6시부터 8시까지 야간 근무를 해요. 그런데 제가 교대 근무 변경을 요청할 수 있을지 궁금합니다.

W: 야간 근무 조의 다른 직원들과 문제가 있나요?

M: 아니요... 음, 그러니까, 제가 밤에 일을 할 수 없게 돼서요. 제가 밴드에 가입을 했는데, 음, 저녁마다 연습을 해야 해요.

W: 그렇군요. 그래서 어떤 교대 조에 관심이 있나요?

M: 가능하다면 점심시간 근무 조로 옮기고 싶어요.

W: 음, 점심시간 근무 조는 꽉 찼어요. 학생 직원들 사이에서 가장 인기 있는 조거든요.

M: 음, 오전 근무 조는 어때요? 너무 일찍 일어나는 게 걱정이었는데, 다른 선택지가 없다면...

W: 오전 근무 조 학생 중 한 명이 막 그만둬서, 자리가 있어요.

M: 그럼, 그것으로 해야겠네요. 도움을 주셔서 감사해요, Stewart씨.

staff 명 직원 shift 명 (교대) 근무, 교대 조
wonder 동 궁금하다 position 명 자리, 위치

1 대화의 주된 주제는 무엇인가?

(A) 새로운 직원을 찾는 것
(B) 직원들 사이의 문제를 해결하는 것
(C) 일부 근무 시간을 변경하는 것
(D) 교내식당 메뉴에 품목들을 추가하는 것

2 학생은 왜 밤에 시간이 안 되는가?

(A) 그는 음악 경연대회를 준비하고 있다.
(B) 그는 밴드 연습에 참여해야 한다.
(C) 그는 보통 밤늦게 공부를 한다.
(D) 그는 졸업하기 위해 추가 수업을 들어야 한다.

3 학생은 무엇을 걱정했는가?

(A) 연습 시간에 빠지는 것
(B) 직원들과 사이 좋게 지내는 것
(C) 더 짧은 시간을 근무하는 것
(D) 아침 일찍 일어나는 것

Listening Practice 4   본문 p.43

1 (B)   2 (A)   3 (C)   4 (C)

Note-taking
Sediment
: Loose rocks and minerals that are broken down over time

Sediment Transport
- By wind   e.g. Sand hills called dunes
- By water   e.g. At the bottom of a waterfall

Listen to part of a lecture in a geology class.

P: People don't think about sediment, but it's very important. Sediment is rocky material that is moved from one place to another. It can be found everywhere... in the mountains, the desert, and even the sea. It helps us grow food and contributes to a healthy environment... [1]But, what exactly is sediment, and how does it move from one place to another?

So, first of all, sediment is made up of loose rocks and minerals that are broken down over time. However, it also contains tiny parts of plants and animals that, uh, are left behind after they die... [2]Individual sediments come in many sizes, too. Sometimes, they are as small as a grain of sand. Other times, they can be as big as a large rock or stone.

Because sediment is made up of loose material, it is easily moved around... The way that this happens, um, scientists call this process sediment transport... It occurs mainly through wind and water.

First, there is wind. Strong wind breaks down rocks and moves soil, sand, and dirt across long distances. [3]As sediments are blown by the wind, they hit each other and break down into smaller pieces. Eventually, they collect into large piles or are moved across a wide area. In fact, wind is the main cause of sediment transport in the desert. Wind mostly moves away sand. This sometimes creates large sand hills called dunes.

Second, we have water. Heavy rains, ocean waves, and fast-moving rivers can cause rocks to become loose and transport sediment to other places... Um, you'll often find lots of sediment at the bottom of a waterfall. You know, the power of a waterfall is very strong, so it makes sediment fall to the ground. [4]But the largest amount of sediment is collected, um, where rivers enter the sea.

지질학 강의의 일부를 들으시오.

P: 사람들은 퇴적물에 대해 생각하지 않지만, 그것은 매우 중요합니다. 퇴적물은 한 곳에서 다른 곳으로 이동하는 암석 물질인데요. 그것은 어디서든 찾을 수 있어요... 산, 사막, 심지어 바다에서요. 그것은 우리가 식량을 재배하는 데 도움이 되고 건강한 환경에 기여하죠... 그런데, 퇴적물은 정확히 무엇이고 어떻게 한 곳에서 다른 곳으로 이동할까요?

자, 우선, 퇴적물은 시간이 지나면서 분해된 무른 암석과 광물로 이루어져 있습니다. 그런데, 그것에는, 어, 식물들과 동물들이 죽

은 후에 남겨진 아주 작은 부분들도 포함되어 있죠... 각각의 퇴적물은 크기도 다양합니다. 때때로, 그것들은 모래알만큼 작습니다. 다른 때에는, 그것들이 큰 암석이나 돌만큼 클 수도 있죠.

퇴적물은 무른 물질로 이루어져 있기 때문에, 쉽게 옮겨집니다... 이것이 일어나는 방식을, 음, 과학자들이 이 과정을 퇴적물 운반이라고 합니다... 그것은 주로 바람과 물을 통해 일어나죠.

먼저, 바람이 있습니다. 강한 바람은 암석을 부수고 먼 거리를 가로질러 토양, 모래, 그리고 흙을 옮깁니다. 퇴적물이 바람에 날리면서, 그것들은 서로 부딪히며 더 작은 조각들로 부서져요. 결국, 그것들은 큰 더미로 모이거나 넓은 지역을 가로질러 옮겨집니다. 실제로, 바람은 사막에서 퇴적물 운반의 주요 원인이에요. 바람은 대부분 모래를 이동시키죠. 이것은 때때로 사구라고 불리는 큰 모래 언덕을 만듭니다.

둘째로, 물이 있습니다. 폭우, 바다의 파도, 그리고 빠르게 흐르는 강물은 암석을 무르게 만들고 퇴적물을 다른 곳으로 운반할 수 있어요... 음, 여러분은 종종 폭포 아래에서 많은 퇴적물을 발견할 거예요. 알다시피, 폭포의 세기가 매우 강하기 때문에, 퇴적물이 바닥으로 떨어지게 만들죠. 하지만 가장 많은 양의 퇴적물이 모이는 곳은, 음, 강이 바다로 유입되는 곳입니다.

sediment 명 퇴적물   rocky 형 암석의
contribute to ~에 기여하다, 원인이 되다   loose 형 무른, 풀린
mineral 명 광물   tiny 형 아주 작은
transport 명 운반; 동 운반하다   occur 동 일어나다, 발생하다
break down ~을 부수다   soil 명 토양   dirt 명 흙; 먼지
eventually 부 결국   collect 동 모이다; 모으다
pile 명 더미, 포개 놓은 것   heavy rain 폭우   waterfall 명 폭포

1 강의의 주된 주제는 무엇인가?

(A) 퇴적물이 발견되는 장소
(B) 퇴적물이 무엇이고 어떻게 움직이는지
(C) 식량 재배에 있어서 퇴적물의 중요성
(D) 퇴적물이 어떻게 환경을 건강하게 만드는지

2 퇴적물의 주요 특징은 무엇인가?

(A) 그것은 크기가 다양하다.
(B) 그것은 동물들에게 먹이를 제공한다.
(C) 그것은 대부분 식물로 이루어져 있다.
(D) 그것은 곡물 더미이다.

3 퇴적물이 바람에 날리면 무슨 일이 일어나는가?

(A) 그것은 공기를 오염시킨다.
(B) 그것은 물리적인 손상을 야기한다.
(C) 그것은 더 작은 조각들로 부서진다.
(D) 그것은 큰 암석들로 형성된다.

4 교수에 따르면, 물속에서는 많은 양의 퇴적물이 어디에서 발견될 수 있는가?

(A) 해안가에서
(B) 호숫가 근처에서
(C) 강과 바다 사이에서
(D) 산꼭대기에서

iBT Listening Test 1

본문 p.45

1 (C) **2** (D) **3** (B) **4** (A)

Note-taking

Student's Question
Wants to study psychology as another major
→ Can you tell me how to apply?

Application Process
- Complete basic requirements
- Meet with the head of each department
- Write a letter stating you will complete your majors

Listen to part of a conversation between a student and a professor.

S: Hello, Professor Morris. Can I talk to you? I was in some of your classes before. My name is Alice.

P: Of course, Alice. I remember... You're majoring in business management, right?

S: Yes, that's right. [1]I'm here to ask for your advice... As I said, I took a few of your psychology classes before. Um, but now I want to study psychology as another major.

P: Oh, is that so? I'm happy to hear that. [2]But why do you want to study psychology as a second major?

S: Well, I want to be a marketing professional after college. I, um, think understanding human behavior will help in that field. You know, marketers need to know how consumers think.

P: You're right, it will be helpful! In that case, majoring in both business management and psychology will be perfect for you. That way you can become a professional in both areas.

S: [4]Yes, but I'm worried too because it sounds difficult. Do you think I can do it?

P: I am sure of it. You're intelligent and you work hard. Um, how are your grades? Are they good?

S: Thank you, yes. I'm doing well in all of my classes. Um, can I ask one more thing? [3]Can you tell me how to apply?

P: Well, first, you have to complete all of the basic requirements for each major. Then, you should meet with the head of each department. Lastly, you should write a letter stating that you promise to complete your double major.

S: Thank you for that detailed information, Professor Morris. I'll give it a try.

학생과 교수 사이의 대화를 들으시오.

S: 안녕하세요, Morris 교수님. 이야기 좀 할 수 있을까요? 저는 전에 교수님 수업을 몇 개 들었어요. 제 이름은 Alice예요.

P: 물론이지, Alice. 기억한단다... 경영학을 전공하고 있지, 그렇지?

S: 네, 맞아요. 저는 교수님의 조언을 구하러 왔어요... 말씀 드렸듯이, 저는 전에 교수님의 심리학 수업 몇 개를 들었어요. 음, 그런데 이

제는 심리학을 또 다른 전공으로 공부하고 싶어요.
P: 아, 그래? 그 말을 들으니 기쁘구나. 그런데 왜 심리학을 두 번째 전공으로 공부하려고 하니?
S: 음, 저는 대학 졸업 후 마케팅 전문가가 되고 싶은데요. 저는, 음, 사람의 행동을 이해하는 것이 그 분야에서 도움이 될 것이라고 생각해요. 아시다시피, 마케터들은 소비자들이 어떻게 생각하는지 알아야 하잖아요.
P: 맞아, 도움이 될 거야! 그렇다면, 경영학과 심리학을 모두 전공하는 것이 너에게 딱 맞을 것 같구나. 그렇게 하면 두 분야에서 모두 전문가가 될 수 있지.
S: 네, 하지만 어려울 것 같아서 걱정도 돼요. 제가 할 수 있을 것 같으신가요?
P: 나는 확신한단다. 너는 똑똑하고 열심히 하잖아. 음, 네 성적은 어떠니? 괜찮니?
S: 감사합니다, 네. 저는 모든 수업에서 잘하고 있어요. 음, 한 가지만 더 여쭤봐도 될까요? 어떻게 지원하는지 알려주실 수 있나요?
P: 음, 먼저, 각 전공의 기본적인 필요조건을 모두 충족해야 해. 그러고 나서, 각 학과장을 만나야 한단다. 마지막으로, 복수전공을 이수하겠다고 약속하는 증서를 써야 해.
S: 상세한 정보 감사합니다, Morris 교수님. 한번 해볼게요.

major in ~을 전공하다   business management 경영학
psychology 명 심리학   marketing 명 마케팅
professional 명 전문가   field 명 분야; 들판
consumer 명 소비자   area 명 분야; 지역
requirement 명 필요조건, 요건   head of department 학과장

1 대화의 주된 주제는 무엇인가?
   (A) 수업에 늦게 등록하는 것
   (B) 몇몇 과정들을 이수하는 것
   (C) 또 다른 분야를 전공으로 공부하는 것
   (D) 소규모 사업을 시작하는 것

2 학생은 왜 심리학을 공부하고 싶어 하는가?
   (A) 졸업을 위한 필요조건을 충족하기 위해
   (B) 그녀의 성적을 올리기 위해
   (C) 마케팅 과제를 준비하기 위해
   (D) 더 나은 마케터가 되기 위해

3 교수는 어떻게 학생을 돕는가?
   (A) 요청을 승인함으로써
   (B) 상세한 조언을 제공함으로써
   (C) 추천서를 써줌으로써
   (D) 학생을 가르치겠다고 제안함으로써

대화의 일부를 다시 듣고 질문에 답하시오.
S: Yes, but I'm worried too because it sounds difficult. Do you think I can do it?
P: I am sure of it. You're intelligent and you work hard.

4 교수는 왜 이렇게 말하는가:
   P: I am sure of it.
   (A) 그는 학생이 두 개의 전공을 동시에 공부할 수 있다고 생각한다.
   (B) 그는 복수전공이 학생의 진로에 도움이 될 것이라고 믿는다.
   (C) 그는 복수전공에 지원하는 방법에 대해 확신한다.
   (D) 그는 학생의 요청이 받아들여질 것임을 알고 있다.

iBT Listening Test 2   본문 p. 48

1 (C)   2 (B)   3 (D)   4 (A), (B)   5 (C)

Note-taking
Sustainability
: Natural resources can be used today and in the future.

Natural Resources
• Renewable Sources: Can easily reproduce themselves
            e.g. Most plants and animals
• Non-renewable Sources: Cannot be created easily and
            take millions of years to form
            e.g. Gold, silver, coal, natural gas, and oil

Listen to part of a lecture in an environmental science class.

P: Sustainability means that we can continue to do or use something in the future. ¹When we talk about natural resources, sustainability means we can use these resources today and in the future... possibly forever. But we must manage our use of natural resources properly to keep them sustainable.

Generally, there are two kinds of natural resources. The first is renewable, and the second is non-renewable. ²Renewable resources easily reproduce themselves. For example, most plants and animals can reproduce, so they are naturally renewable... This allows us to use them without limitation. On the other hand, the amount of gold and silver on Earth is fixed. This means that these resources are not renewable. Once we use all of them, they cannot be created easily. Similarly, coal, natural gas, and oil take millions of years to form. They may be produced someday, but not in one lifetime, so we can say that they are non-renewable.

So, uh, obviously we must be very careful with non-renewable resources. But, um, we must also pay attention to how we use renewable ones. Renewable resources are only sustainable if we use them wisely. Well, let's look at the example of forests. We know that trees naturally reproduce. But did you know that forests can disappear? Humans have always used wood for many things like paper and buildings. ³We also cut down trees for agriculture, which happens on a large scale. A recent study found that 18 million acres of forests are removed each year. If we keep cutting this number of trees, forests will not be sustainable. For example, already 20 percent of the Amazon rainforest has been lost forever.

So why is the sustainability of natural resources important? Well, let me continue explaining this with forests. They provide many organisms with a home. [4A]When we misuse the forest, many species can disappear forever as well. You know, living things are connected to each other, so this will eventually affect us, too. [4B]Also, misuse can make climate change worse. Trees take in carbon dioxide from the air and release oxygen, right? [5]Global warming will happen much faster without enough trees. So, um, protecting our forests is not just an option anymore... We cannot wait any longer.

환경 과학 강의의 일부를 들으시오.
P: 지속 가능성은 우리가 미래에 무언가를 계속하거나 사용할 수 있다는 것을 의미합니다. 우리가 천연자원에 대해 이야기할 때, 지속 가능성은 우리가 현재와 미래에 이 자원들을 사용할 수 있다는 것을 의미하죠... 어쩌면 영원히요. 그러나 우리가 천연자원을 지속 가능하게 유지하기 위해서는 천연자원의 사용을 적절하게 관리해야 합니다.

일반적으로, 천연자원은 두 종류가 있습니다. 첫 번째는 재생 가능한 것이고, 두 번째는 재생 불가능한 것입니다. 재생 가능한 자원은 그것들 스스로 재생산을 합니다. 예를 들어, 대부분의 식물과 동물은 번식을 할 수 있어서, 자연적으로 재생 가능하죠... 이는 우리가 그것들을 제한 없이 사용할 수 있도록 합니다. 반면에, 지구상의 금과 은의 양은 정해져 있어요. 이는 이 자원들이 재생 가능하지 않다는 것을 의미하죠. 우리가 그것들을 모두 사용하고 나면, 그것들은 쉽게 만들어질 수 없어요. 마찬가지로, 석탄, 천연가스, 그리고 석유는 만들어지려면 수백만 년이 걸립니다. 그것들은 언젠가는 생산될 수 있겠지만, 한 사람의 일생 동안은 아니기 때문에, 우리는 그것들이 재생 불가능한 것이라고 말할 수 있어요.

그래서, 어, 우리는 분명히 재생 불가능한 자원에 대해 매우 신중해야 해요. 하지만, 음, 우리는 재생 가능한 것을 어떻게 사용하는지에도 유의해야 합니다. 재생 가능한 자원은 우리가 현명하게 사용할 때만 지속 가능하거든요. 자, 산림을 예로 살펴봅시다. 우리는 나무가 자연적으로 재생한다는 것을 알고 있죠. 그런데 여러분은 산림이 사라질 수 있다는 것을 알고 있었나요? 인간은 항상 종이와 건물과 같이 많은 것들을 위해 나무를 사용해왔습니다. 우리는 농업을 위해 나무를 베기도 하는데, 이것은 대규모로 일어나죠. 최근 한 연구에서는 매년 1,800만 에이커의 산림이 없어지고 있다는 것을 발견했습니다. 만약 우리가 이만큼의 나무를 계속 벤다면, 산림은 지속 가능하지 않을 거예요. 예를 들어, 이미 아마존 열대 우림의 20%가 영원히 사라졌습니다.

그렇다면 왜 천연자원의 지속 가능성이 중요할까요? 자, 이것을 계속해서 산림을 가지고 설명해볼게요. 그것들은 많은 유기체들에게 서식지를 제공합니다. 우리가 산림을 남용하면, 많은 종 또한 영원히 사라질 수 있습니다. 알다시피, 생물들은 서로 연결되어 있기 때문에, 이것은 결국 우리에게도 영향을 미칠 것입니다. 또한, 남용은 기후 변화를 더 악화시킬 수 있어요. 나무가 공기 중의 이산화탄소를 흡수하고 산소를 방출하잖아요, 그렇죠? 나무가 충분히 없으면 지구 온난화가 훨씬 더 빠르게 일어날 거예요. 그래서, 음, 산림을 보호하는 것은 더 이상 선택사항이 아닙니다... 우리는 더 이상 기다리고 있을 수만은 없어요.

sustainability 명 지속 가능성 natural resource 천연자원
manage 동 관리하다; 간신히 해내다 renewable 형 재생 가능한
non-renewable 형 재생 불가능한
reproduce 동 재생산하다, 재생하다; 번식하다
limitation 명 제한 coal 명 석탄 natural gas 천연가스
agriculture 명 농업
acre 명 에이커(토지 면적의 단위, 1 acre = 약 4,046.71m²)
rainforest 명 열대 우림 misuse 동 남용하다; 명 남용
take in ~을 흡수하다, 섭취하다 release 동 방출하다; 풀어 주다

1 강의의 주된 주제는 무엇인가?
 (A) 가장 가치가 있는 천연자원
 (B) 전 세계의 산림에 대한 위협
 (C) 지속 가능성의 중요성
 (D) 재생 가능한 에너지 자원의 종류

2 교수는 대부분의 식물과 동물에 관해 무엇이라고 말하는가?
 (A) 그것들의 수가 한정되어 있다.
 (B) 그것들은 재생 가능한 자원이다.
 (C) 그것들이 재생산하는 데에는 수년이 걸린다.
 (D) 그것들은 다양한 실용적인 용도를 가지고 있다.

3 교수는 나무를 베는 것에 관해 무엇이라고 말하는가?
 (A) 그것은 전보다 덜 빠르게 일어나고 있다.
 (B) 그것은 기계로 인해 하는 것이 더 쉬워졌다.
 (C) 그것은 사람들이 더 많은 나무를 심는 것을 필요로 하게끔 한다.
 (D) 그것은 재생 가능한 자원을 지속 불가능하게 만들 것이다.

4 산림 남용의 두 가지 가능한 결과는 무엇인가?
 2개의 답을 고르시오.
 (A) 생물 종들이 영원히 사라질 수 있다.
 (B) 기후 변화가 더 심각해질 것이다.
 (C) 나무가 질병을 앓을 수 있다.
 (D) 이산화탄소가 산소를 감소시킬 것이다.

강의의 일부를 다시 듣고 질문에 답하시오.
P: Global warming will happen much faster without enough trees. So, um, protecting our forests is not just an option anymore... We cannot wait any longer.

5 교수는 왜 이렇게 말하는가:
 P: So, um, protecting our forests is not just an option anymore...
 (A) 지구 온난화의 인적 원인을 강조하기 위해
 (B) 몇몇 산림이 성공적으로 복구되었음을 보여주기 위해
 (C) 산림을 보호하는 것의 중요성을 강조하기 위해
 (D) 사람들이 어떻게 산림을 보호할 수 있는지 설명하기 위해

Vocabulary Review
본문 p.52

1 misuse
2 promote
3 communication
4 prove
5 find out
6 belief
7 value
8 renewable
9 contribute to
10 (D)
11 (C)
12 (B)
13 (B)
14 (A)

CHAPTER 03
Function

Example
본문 p.55

A. (C)   B. (B)

A.

Note-taking

Student's Question
Would like to ask for some advice about my paper

Professor's Answer
A paragraph is not related to the topic.
→ Compare the outline and the draft

Listen to a conversation between a student and a professor.

S: Professor Ross, I'd like to ask for some advice about my paper. Here's my paper...
P: We were supposed to meet 30 minutes ago... Why are you so late?
S: Uh, I had a problem with the printer. I finished writing the paper yesterday, but the library printer had an error this morning.
P: Oh, I know about that printer. I've had the same experience myself... Well, it's fine. We can discuss your paper now.
S: Thank you for understanding.
P: Let's see... Overall, it seems fine, but the third paragraph is not exactly related to the topic.
S: Oh, I didn't realize that. I think I made the same mistakes in my last paper, too.
P: After writing a draft, you should compare the outline and the draft to make sure everything is related to the topic.

학생과 교수 사이의 대화를 들으시오.

S: Ross 교수님, 제 보고서에 대한 조언을 구하고 싶습니다. 제 보고서는 여기 있어요...
P: 30분 전에 만나기로 했는데... 왜 이렇게 늦었니?
S: 어, 프린터에 문제가 있었어요. 제가 어제 보고서를 다 썼는데, 오늘 아침에 도서관 프린터에 오류가 있었거든요.
P: 아, 그 프린터에 대해 알고 있지. 나도 같은 경험을 했거든... 음, 괜찮아. 지금 네 보고서에 대해 논의하면 되니까.
S: 이해해 주셔서 감사합니다.
P: 어디 보자... 전체적으로, 괜찮은 것 같은데, 세 번째 단락이 주제와 꼭 관련이 있는 것은 아니구나.
S: 아, 그건 몰랐네요. 제가 저번 보고서에서도 같은 실수를 한 것 같아요.
P: 초안을 작성한 후에, 개요와 초안을 비교해서 모든 것이 주제와 관련이 있는지 확인하렴.

paper 명 보고서   error 명 오류, 실수
overall 부 전체적으로, 종합적으로   be related to ~과 관련 있는
draft 명 초안, 원고   outline 명 개요

대화의 일부를 다시 듣고 질문에 답하시오.
S: I finished writing the paper yesterday, but the library printer had an error this morning.
P: Oh, I know about that printer. I've had the same experience myself...

교수는 왜 이렇게 말하는가:
P: Oh, I know about that printer.

(A) 다른 프린터를 추천하기 위해
(B) 보고서가 인쇄되어야 함을 확실히 하기 위해
(C) 그녀가 상황을 이해한다고 말하기 위해
(D) 다른 학생들도 같은 문제를 겪었음을 나타내기 위해

B.

Note-taking

How Antelope Squirrels Control Their Body Temperature

Sweating is not a good way to cool down.
→ Instead, they dig deep holes and go inside them.

Listen to part of a lecture in a biology class.

P: Many animals can naturally control their body temperature through sweating. But not all animals have this ability. Instead, some animals depend on the environment around them. An example of this is antelope squirrels.
Antelope squirrels live in very hot, dry places like deserts. They look for food during the day under extreme heat, so their body temperature increases. But because of their small size, sweating is not a good way for them to cool down. If they sweat to reduce their body heat, they will lose too much moisture. You know what happens when you lose moisture in dry places... It becomes hard to survive. So, instead, these squirrels use the environment. They dig deep holes that are cool and dark inside. Once they go inside the holes, their body temperature drops very quickly.

생물학 강의의 일부를 들으시오.

P: 많은 동물들은 땀을 흘리는 것을 통해 자연스럽게 체온을 조절할 수 있습니다. 하지만 모든 동물이 이러한 능력을 지닌 것은 아닙니다. 대신에, 어떤 동물들은 그것들 주변의 환경에 의존합니다. 이것의 예시로 영양 다람쥐가 있어요.

영양 다람쥐는 사막과 같은 매우 덥고 건조한 곳에서 삽니다. 그것들은 낮 동안 극심한 더위 속에서 먹이를 찾기 때문에, 체온이 올라가요. 하지만 그것들은 크기가 작아서, 땀을 흘리는 것은 더위를 식히는 좋은 방법이 아닙니다. 그것들이 몸의 열을 줄이기 위해 땀을 흘린다면, 너무 많은 수분을 잃게 돼요. 건조한 곳에서 수분을 잃으면 어떻게 되는지 알죠... 살아남기 힘들어집니다. 그래서, 대신에, 이 다람쥐들은 환경을 이용해요. 그것들은 내부가 시원하고 어두운 깊은 구멍을 팝니다. 그것들이 그 구멍 안으로 들어가면, 체온이 매우 빠르게 떨어집니다.

naturally 〔부〕 자연스럽게, 물론   control 〔동〕 조절하다; 지배하다
body temperature 체온   sweat 〔명〕 땀; 〔동〕 땀을 흘리다
antelope squirrel 영양 다람쥐   extreme 〔형〕 극심한, 극도의
heat 〔명〕 더위, 열   cool down (더위를) 식히다   reduce 〔동〕 줄이다
moisture 〔명〕 수분

강의의 일부를 다시 듣고 질문에 답하시오.

P: If they sweat to reduce their body heat, they will lose too much moisture. You know what happens when you lose moisture in dry places... It becomes hard to survive.

교수는 이렇게 말함으로써 무엇을 의미하는가:

P: You know what happens when you lose moisture in dry places...

(A) 체온을 조절하는 능력은 중요하다.
(B) 건조한 곳에서 수분의 중요성은 명백하다.
(C) 영양 다람쥐는 수분이 많이 없어도 살 수 있다.
(D) 건조한 곳에 있는 동물들은 땀을 많이 흘려서 살아남는다.

Listening Practice 1   본문 p.57

1 (C)   2 (B)   3 (C)

Note-taking
Student's Problem
<u>Failed</u> a class and received a <u>letter</u> from the school

Employee's Suggestion
- Stay in a <u>dormitory</u> on campus
- Take the class <u>again</u> next semester

Listen to a conversation between a student and a registrar's office employee.

M: Excuse me. ¹I received a letter from the school last week. It says that I, uh, failed one of my classes. Does the school usually send letters like this?

W: Yes, a letter is automatically sent to students' homes when they fail a class.

M: Oh, I didn't know that... This is the first time that it has happened to me. Um, do you know why I failed the class? It wasn't explained in the letter.

W: You should ask your professor for details. But, the system shows that you were often late for the class and missed it several times.

M: That's true... I, uh, thought it would be easy to attend a 9 a.m. class. But, it was difficult to get to the campus on time.

W: What seems to be the problem?

M: Um, I live more than an hour away from campus. So, I have to wake up very early to get to school on time.

W: I see. ²Perhaps you could stay in a dormitory on campus. It would be much more convenient.

M: I will definitely consider that. ³But, what about the class? I need to pass it in order to graduate.

W: Don't worry. There's always another chance. The class will be offered again next semester.

M: All right. I'll sign up for it then. Thanks!

학생과 학적과 직원 사이의 대화를 들으시오.

M: 실례합니다. 제가 지난주에 학교로부터 우편을 받았는데요. 제가, 어, 수업 중 하나에서 낙제했다고 나와 있어서요. 학교에서 보통 이런 우편들을 보내나요?

W: 네, 학생들이 수업에서 낙제했을 때 우편이 학생들의 집으로 자동으로 보내집니다.

M: 오, 그건 몰랐네요... 저한테 이런 일이 일어난 건 이번이 처음이라서요. 음, 제가 왜 그 수업에 낙제했는지 아시나요? 그건 우편에 설명되어 있지 않았어요.

W: 자세한 사항은 교수님께 여쭤보셔야 해요. 하지만, 시스템상에서 학생이 종종 수업에 늦고 몇 번 빠진 것으로 나오네요.

M: 맞아요... 제가, 어, 오전 9시 수업에 가는 게 쉬울 거라고 생각했거든요. 그런데, 제시간에 캠퍼스에 도착하는 게 어려웠어요.

W: 뭐가 문제인 것 같으세요?

M: 음, 저는 캠퍼스에서 한 시간 이상 떨어진 곳에 살아요. 그래서, 저는 학교에 제시간에 도착하려면 아주 일찍 일어나야 해요.

W: 그렇군요. 어쩌면 캠퍼스 내 기숙사에서 지내볼 수도 있겠어요. 그게 훨씬 더 편리할 거예요.

M: 그걸 꼭 고려해볼게요. 하지만, 수업은 어떻게 해야 할까요? 저는 졸업하기 위해서는 그것을 통과해야만 해요.

W: 걱정하지 마세요. 기회는 항상 있어요. 그 수업은 다음 학기에도 다시 개설될 예정이거든요.

M: 좋아요. 그때 신청할게요. 감사합니다!

fail 〔동〕 낙제하다, 실패하다   automatically 〔부〕 자동으로
miss 〔동〕 빠지다; 놓치다   attend 〔동〕 (학교 등에) 가다, 참석하다
convenient 〔형〕 편리한   pass 〔동〕 통과하다; 지나가다

1 대화의 주된 주제는 무엇인가?

(A) 우편에 있는 잘못된 정보
(B) 학생들을 시험하는 것에 대한 학교의 시스템

(C) 학생의 수업에 대한 걱정
(D) 다음 학기에 학생이 가질 선택지들

2 직원은 학생에게 무엇을 하라고 제안하는가?

(A) 캠퍼스에 다른 버스를 타고 다니기
(B) 학교 기숙사에서 살기
(C) 그의 수업 일정을 변경하기
(D) 그의 교수에게 조언을 요청하기

대화의 일부를 다시 듣고 질문에 답하시오.

M: But, what about the class? I need to pass it in order to graduate.
W: Don't worry. There's always another chance. The class will be offered again next semester.

3 직원은 왜 이렇게 말하는가:

W: There's always another chance.

(A) 학생에게 시험에 대해 상기시키기 위해
(B) 학생의 이름이 목록에 있는 것을 확실히 하기 위해
(C) 학생에게 수업을 다시 들을 수 있다고 말하기 위해
(D) 학생이 졸업할 수 있다는 것을 확인시켜 주기 위해

Listening Practice 2 본문 p.59

1 (D) 2 (C) 3 (D) 4 (B)

Note-taking
The Design of Sagrada Familia
- Gothic style
- Art Nouveau: Lots of curved lines and complicated decorations
- Catalan Modernism: Shapes copied from nature
- Playful designs from Gaudi's own imagination

Listen to part of a lecture in an architecture class.

P: Recently, we were discussing the architecture of famous churches around the world. ¹One of the most famous churches is the one in Barcelona, Spain. It's called Sagrada Familia, and it attracts millions of tourists a year. Let's talk about its design.

So, the construction of Sagrada Familia started in 1882. Its original architect was, uh, Francisco del Villar. He designed the church in the Gothic style, which includes pointed windows and sharp towers. Unfortunately, del Villar had a disagreement with the builders of the church. So, he was replaced by Antoni Gaudi in 1883. ²Gaudi was only 31 years old when he took over Sagrada Familia's construction, which was, uh, quite unusual. However, Gaudi was already known for his creative designs at this age.

Gaudi decided to keep some of the original Gothic ideas, like, uh, the building plan in the shape of a cross. But Gaudi also changed many other features... ³He combined the Gothic style with Art Nouveau, which features lots of curved lines and complicated decorations. So, um, you'll notice other characteristics of Art Nouveau throughout the building. There are lots of dramatic shapes and decorations... And, uh, he also included features of Catalan Modernism, such as shapes copied from nature, as well as playful designs from his own imagination. Gaudi's idea was to have a church that was full of light and color. ⁴He was careful about every detail.

S: Um, is that why its construction was never finished?

P: Well, that's probably one reason. Gaudi worked on Sagrada Familia for over 40 years! What else can I say? Only a small part of it was complete by the time he died in 1926. After his death, other architects were hired to finish the building based on Gaudi's ideas.

건축학 강의의 일부를 들으시오.

P: 최근에, 우리는 전 세계의 유명한 교회들의 건축 양식에 대해 논의하고 있었어요. 가장 유명한 교회들 중 하나는 스페인의 바르셀로나에 있는 것입니다. 그것은 사그라다 파밀리아라고 불리는데, 매년 수백만 명의 관광객을 끌어 모으죠. 그것의 디자인에 관해 이야기해 봅시다.

자, 사그라다 파밀리아의 건축은 1882년에 시작되었는데요. 원래 건축가는, 어, 프란시스코 델 비야르였어요. 그는 교회를 고딕 양식으로 디자인했는데, 이것에는 뾰족한 창문과 뾰족한 탑이 포함됐죠. 안타깝게도, 델 비야르는 교회의 건축가들과 의견 충돌이 있었어요. 그래서, 그는 1883년에 안토니 가우디로 대체되었어요. 가우디는 사그라다 파밀리아의 건축을 이어 받았을 때 겨우 31살이었는데, 이것은, 어, 꽤 이례적이었죠. 하지만, 가우디는 이 나이에 이미 창의적인 디자인으로 알려져 있었어요.

가우디는 원래의 고딕 아이디어들 중 일부를 유지하기로 결심했는데요, 예를 들면, 어, 십자가 모양의 건축 계획 같은 것이었어요. 하지만 가우디는 다른 많은 부분들을 바꾸기도 했습니다... 그는 고딕 양식을 아르 누보와 결합시켰는데, 이는 수많은 곡선과 복잡한 장식이 특징이에요. 그래서, 음, 여러분은 건물 전체에 걸쳐 아르 누보의 다른 특징들을 볼 수 있을 겁니다. 수많은 과장된 모양과 장식들이 있죠... 그리고, 어, 그는 또한 자신의 상상에서 나온 장난스러운 디자인들뿐만 아니라, 자연에서 모방한 모양들과 같이 카탈루냐 모더니즘의 특징들도 포함시켰어요. 가우디의 계획은 빛과 색으로 가득한 교회를 만드는 것이었습니다. 그는 모든 세부 사항에 대해 신중했어요.

S: 음, 그게 그것의 건축이 끝나지 못했던 이유인가요?

P: 음, 그게 어쩌면 한 가지 이유일 수 있어요. 가우디는 사그라다 파밀리아를 40년 넘게 작업을 했거든요! 무슨 말을 더 할 수 있겠어요? 그가 1926년에 사망했을 때까지 그것의 아주 일부분만이 완성되었어요. 그의 죽음 이후, 다른 건축가들이 가우디의 계획을 바탕으로 그 건물을 완성하기 위해 고용되었죠.

architecture 명 건축 (양식), 건축학
attract 동 끌어 모으다, 마음을 끌다   tourist 명 관광객
construction 명 건축, 건설   Gothic 형 고딕의   pointed 형 뾰족한
unfortunately 부 안타깝게도, 불행하게도
disagreement 명 의견 충돌   take over 이어 받다, 인수하다

cross 명 십자가　　feature 명 특징, 특색; 동 ~을 특징으로 포함하다
Art Nouveau 아르 누보('새로운 예술'을 뜻하는 프랑스어로, 19~20세기에 국제적으로 유행한 예술 양식)　　dramatic 형 과장된, 극적인
Catalan Modernism 카탈루냐 모더니즘(19세기 말부터 20세기 초 스페인의 카탈루냐에서 일어난 예술부흥운동을 말하며, 이는 건축 분야에서는 고딕, 이슬람 등 여러 양식이 혼합된 형태로 나타남)
playful 형 장난스러운, 장난기 많은

1 강의는 주로 무엇에 관한 것인가?

(A) 스페인 건축의 역사
(B) 유명한 건축가의 이력
(C) 한 도시의 가장 큰 명소들
(D) 유명한 교회의 디자인

2 교수에 따르면, 가우디의 어떤 점이 이례적이었는가?

(A) 그가 뾰족한 탑을 사용한 것
(B) 고딕 건축 양식에 대한 그의 애정
(C) 그가 프로젝트를 시작한 나이
(D) 다른 건축가들과의 의견 충돌

3 교수가 아르 누보 양식의 특징으로 언급하는 것은 무엇인가?

(A) 십자가 모양의 건물
(B) 뾰족한 창문과 탑
(C) 장난스럽고 화려한 디자인
(D) 곡선과 장식

강의의 일부를 다시 듣고 질문에 답하시오.

P: He was careful about every detail.
S: Um, is that why its construction was never finished?
P: Well, that's probably one reason. Gaudi worked on Sagrada Familia for over 40 years! What else can I say? Only a small part of it was complete by the time he died in 1926.

4 교수는 이렇게 말함으로써 무엇을 의미하는가:

P: What else can I say?

(A) 사그라다 파밀리아의 디자인은 건축하기에 어려웠다.
(B) 가우디의 신중함이 아마도 긴 건축 시간을 야기했을 것이다.
(C) 교회 건축가들이 가우디에게 너무 많은 변경사항을 요청했다.
(D) 사그라다 파밀리아의 최종 디자인은 알려지지 않았다.

Listening Practice 3　　본문 p.61

1 (D)　　2 (B)　　3 (A)

Note-taking
Student's Question
A class is full. → What are my options?

Advantages of Online Courses
• Can save time on your commute
• Can replay the course videos to review lessons

Listen to a conversation between a student and a registrar's office employee.

W: Hello. My name is Victoria, and I have a question to ask you about a course.
M: Sure, Victoria. How can I help you?
W: ¹Well, I wanted to sign up for Professor Wilson's course on Russian history, but, um, I found out that the class is full. I'm wondering what my options are.
M: ²Let me check on my computer to see if there are similar courses... Hmm... That course is offered online. Does that interest you?
W: Um, I think that taking a course in person would be better... I can meet the professor and ask questions right away.
M: I understand, but it is the only class about Russian history for this semester. Also, I recommend you take it. ³You see, online courses offer several advantages.
W: What do you mean?
M: Well, you don't need to come to school, so you can save time on your commute... Um, you can even replay the course videos if you need to review class material.
W: I like that I can review lessons easily.
M: And even though it's online, all the lessons from the class will be the same. Your assignments will still be checked by Professor Wilson, too.
W: That's true. I'll sign up for the online course, then.

학생과 학적과 직원 사이의 대화를 들으시오.

W: 안녕하세요. 제 이름은 Victoria인데, 강의에 대해 여쭤볼 것이 있어요.
M: 물론이죠, Victoria. 어떻게 도와드릴까요?
W: 음, 제가 Wilson 교수님의 러시아 역사 강의를 신청하고 싶었는데, 음, 그 수업이 꽉 찼다는 걸 알게 됐어요. 제게 어떤 선택지가 있는지 궁금해요.
M: 제 컴퓨터로 비슷한 강의들이 있는지 확인해 볼게요... 흠... 그 강의는 온라인으로 제공되네요. 관심 있으신가요?
W: 음, 저는 강의를 직접 듣는 게 더 나을 것 같아요... 교수님을 만나서 바로 질문할 수 있잖아요.
M: 이해는 하지만, 이게 이번 학기 러시아 역사에 대한 유일한 수업이에요. 또, 저는 학생이 그것을 수강하는 것을 추천해요. 그러니까, 온라인 강의들은 여러 장점들을 제공하거든요.
W: 무슨 말씀이세요?
M: 음, 학교에 오지 않아도 되니, 통학하는 시간을 절약할 수 있죠... 음, 수업 자료를 복습해야 할 경우 강의 영상을 다시 볼 수도 있고요.
W: 강의 내용을 쉽게 복습할 수 있는 건 좋네요.
M: 그리고 그게 온라인이기는 해도, 수업의 모든 강의 내용은 같을 거예요. 과제물도 똑같이 Wilson 교수님께서 확인하실 거고요.
W: 그러네요. 그럼, 온라인 강의를 신청할게요.

course 명 강의, 수업　　sign up for ~을 신청하다, 등록하다
find out 알게 되다　　in person 직접　　right away 바로, 즉시

recommend 동 추천하다
commute 명 통학, 통근; 동 통학하다, 통근하다   material 명 자료

1 학생은 왜 학적과를 찾아가는가?

  (A) 교수에 대한 정보를 얻기 위해
  (B) 새로운 대학으로 옮기는 것에 대해 알아보기 위해
  (C) 몇몇 등록된 정보를 변경하기 위해
  (D) 강의를 듣는 것에 대한 선택지에 대해 알아보기 위해

2 직원은 어떻게 학생을 돕는가?

  (A) 교수의 전화번호를 알려줌으로써
  (B) 컴퓨터로 강의들을 확인함으로써
  (C) 학생에게 사무실로 가라고 말해줌으로써
  (D) 학생의 정보를 기록함으로써

대화의 일부를 다시 듣고 질문에 답하시오.
M: You see, online courses offer several advantages.
W: What do you mean?
M: Well, you don't need to come to school, so you can save time on your commute... Um, you can even replay the course videos if you need to review class material.

3 학생은 이렇게 말함으로써 무엇을 의미하는가:
  W: What do you mean?

  (A) 그녀는 몇몇 장점들에 대한 설명이 필요하다.
  (B) 그녀는 직원의 생각에 동의하지 않는다.
  (C) 그녀는 몇몇 강의의 필요조건을 이해하지 못한다.
  (D) 그녀는 온라인 강의를 듣고 싶지 않다.

Listening Practice 4 본문 p. 63

1 (C)   2 (D)   3 (B)   4 (C)

Note-taking
Wetlands
: Land areas that are <u>covered</u> <u>in</u> water for a long time
- Types: <u>Freshwater</u> wetlands and <u>tidal</u> wetlands
- <u>Homes</u> for a variety of plants and animals

Listen to part of a lecture in an ecology class.

P: The natural world has many <u>physical</u> <u>environments</u> with, uh, different characteristics... For example, you have deserts that are very dry and hot, or uh, forests that are very green and cool... ¹Well, today I'm going to focus on another environment called a wetland and talk about its features.

Wetlands are land areas that are <u>covered</u> <u>in</u> <u>water</u> for a long time. They mainly form when water is <u>unable</u> <u>to</u> <u>drain</u> fast enough. So, a large amount of water collects in one area. In general, there are <u>two</u> <u>types</u> <u>of</u> <u>wetlands</u>. The first are freshwater wetlands. Fresh water is water that is <u>low</u> <u>in</u> <u>salt</u>, so you'll find freshwater wetlands near rivers, lakes, and other <u>sources</u> <u>of</u> <u>fresh</u> <u>water</u>. As you move near the coast, on the other hand, you'll find another kind called tidal wetlands. ²You know, tides are when ocean water <u>rises</u> <u>and</u> <u>falls</u>. Every time this happens, some water from the ocean flows toward land and <u>mixes</u> <u>with</u> <u>fresh</u> <u>water</u>, which creates tidal wetlands.

Now, wetlands are <u>homes</u> <u>for</u> a wide variety of plants and animals, especially birds. ⁴Many birds spend their lives in wetlands because they find <u>shelter</u> <u>and</u> <u>food</u> there. Let me explain it in more detail. In the Chesapeake Bay, which is on the east coast of Maryland, you can find <u>both</u> <u>kinds</u> <u>of</u> <u>wetlands</u>. And more than 250 species of birds live there. Wood ducks are one of them. They're commonly found in freshwater wetlands near trees. They are the only ducks to <u>make</u> <u>nests</u> in the holes of trees in this region. In the Chesapeake Bay's tidal wetlands, you will find American oystercatchers. ³The Chesapeake Bay produces about 14 million oysters every year along its muddy beaches. So, over 50 percent of the oystercatchers in Maryland come here to eat oysters.

생태학 강의의 일부를 들으시오.

P: 자연계에는 다양한 특성을 가진, 어, 여러 물리적 환경이 있습니다. 예를 들어, 매우 건조하고 더운 사막이 있고, 혹은 어, 매우 푸르고 시원한 산림도 있죠... 음, 오늘 저는 습지라고 불리는 또 다른 환경에 초점을 맞추고 그것의 특징에 대해 이야기할 겁니다.

습지는 오랜 시간을 물로 덮여 있는 육지 지역입니다. 그것들은 주로 물이 충분히 빠르게 배수되지 않을 때 형성돼요. 그래서, 많은 양의 물이 한 곳에 모이게 되죠. 일반적으로, 습지는 두 가지 종류가 있습니다. 첫 번째는 담수성 습지입니다. 담수는 염분이 적은 물인데, 그래서 강, 호수, 그리고 담수의 다른 수원 근처에서 담수성 습지를 발견할 수 있어요. 반면에, 해안 근처로 이동하면, 조수성 습지라고 불리는 또 다른 종류의 습지를 발견할 겁니다. 알다시피, 조수는 바닷물이 높아졌다 낮아졌다 하는 것이죠. 이런 일이 일어날 때마다, 일부 바닷물이 육지를 향해 흘러가서 담수와 섞이게 되는데, 이것이 조수성 습지를 만듭니다.

자, 습지는 다양한 식물과 동물들, 특히 새들에게는 서식지입니다. 많은 새들이 습지에서 은신처와 먹이를 구하기 때문에 그곳에서 일생을 보내죠. 좀 더 자세히 설명해 볼게요. 메릴랜드주의 동쪽 해안에 있는 체서피크만에서 여러분은 두 종류의 습지를 발견할 수 있습니다. 그리고 250종 이상의 새들이 그곳에 살고 있어요. 아메리카원앙이 그것들 중 하나입니다. 그것들은 나무 근처의 담수성 습지에서 흔히 발견됩니다. 그것들은 이 지역에서 나무 구멍에 둥지를 만드는 유일한 오리들이죠. 체서피크만의 조수성 습지에서는 아메리카검은물떼새를 볼 수 있을 것입니다. 체서피크만은 갯벌에서 매년 약 1,400만 개의 굴을 생산해요. 그래서, 메릴랜드주의 아메리카검은물떼새들의 50% 이상이 굴을 먹기 위해 이곳으로 옵니다.

physical environment 물리적 환경(비생물적 환경)   wetland 명 습지
drain 동 배수되다, 물이 빠지다   fresh water 담수
coast 명 해안   tidal 형 조수의   tide 명 조수
flow 동 흐르다; 명 흐름   Chesapeake Bay 체서피크만
Maryland 메릴랜드주   species 명 종
wood duck 아메리카원앙   region 명 지역, 지방

American oystercatcher 아메리카검은물떼새
oyster 명 굴　muddy beach 갯벌, 진흙 해변

1 강의는 주로 무엇에 관한 것인가?

   (A) 다양한 종류의 환경
   (B) 물이 습지에 미치는 영향
   (C) 습지의 특징
   (D) 습한 기후와 건조한 기후의 차이점

2 교수에 따르면, 조수성 습지는 언제 형성되는가?

   (A) 강한 파도가 일부 해안에 부딪힐 때
   (B) 얕은 지역에 비가 내릴 때
   (C) 담수가 땅 속에 있는 염분과 섞일 때
   (D) 바다의 물이 담수와 결합할 때

3 교수는 체서피크만의 아메리카검은물떼새들에 관해 무엇이라고 말하는가?

   (A) 그것들은 매년 다른 지역에 둥지를 만든다.
   (B) 그것들은 해변에서 먹이를 구한다.
   (C) 그것들은 빠른 속도로 감소하고 있다.
   (D) 그것들은 담수 근처에서 사는 것을 선호한다.

강의의 일부를 다시 듣고 질문에 답하시오.

P: Many birds spend their lives in wetlands because they find shelter and food there. Let me explain it in more detail.

4 교수는 왜 이렇게 말하는가:

P: Let me explain it in more detail.

   (A) 동물의 중요성을 보여주기 위해
   (B) 습지의 역할을 강조하기 위해
   (C) 보다 구체적인 정보를 소개하기 위해
   (D) 다른 요점을 꺼내기 위해

iBT Listening　Test 1　　본문 p. 65

1 (C)　**2** (B)　**3** (D)　**4** (C)

Note-taking

Student's Question
Can I join the group for the science fair?
→ Any advice for activities outside the classroom?

Professor's Suggestion
Talk to Professor Foster about his new experiment on artificial intelligence
→ Wait for him or come back tomorrow

Listen to a conversation between a student and a professor.

S: Hi, Professor Greene. Here's my assignment. Um, I know it's late, but I had a car accident yesterday.

P: I'm sorry to hear that, Ben, but I'll need an official document as proof.

S: OK, uh, I'll bring the accident report tomorrow...

¹But anyway, um, I'm also wondering if I can join the group you've organized for the science fair.

P: Well, I'm afraid the group is already full... Many students wanted to join.

S: Oh, no... Um, I really need to do activities outside the classroom. ⁴I don't have much time left because it's my last year here at school. Um, do you have any advice?

P: Sure. Those activities will help with your career after graduation... Perhaps you could talk to Professor Foster. ²He is looking for students who can help him with his new experiment on artificial intelligence.

S: Oh, really? I took one of his classes about artificial intelligence last year, and I found it interesting. Do you know what kind of work I'll be doing?

P: You will probably gather data and organize the results of the experiment.

S: I think I can do that. I'll go to talk to Professor Foster right away.

P: I heard that he has a meeting this afternoon, so he will not be in his office right now. ³But he should be back soon. You can either wait for him or come back tomorrow. I'll let him know that you stopped by.

S: Thanks, Professor Greene. I'll go wait outside. I don't have any more classes today, anyway.

P: That's fine. Good luck!

학생과 교수 사이의 대화를 들으시오.

S: 안녕하세요, Greene 교수님. 여기 제 과제물입니다. 음, 늦은 건 알지만, 제가 어제 교통사고를 당해서요.

P: 유감이구나, Ben, 하지만 공문서가 증거로 필요하단다.

S: 알겠습니다, 어, 제가 내일 사고 보고서를 가져올게요... 하지만 어쨌든, 음, 저는 교수님께서 과학 박람회를 위해 조직하신 조에 합류할 수 있을지도 궁금합니다.

P: 음, 유감스럽게도 그 조는 이미 꽉 찼단다... 많은 학생들이 참여하고 싶어했어서 말이야.

S: 오, 이런... 음, 전 정말 교외 활동을 해야 해요. 여기 학교에서의 마지막 해이기 때문에 시간이 얼마 남지 않았거든요. 음, 조언을 좀 해주실 수 있나요?

P: 물론이지. 그러한 활동들은 졸업 후 네 진로에 도움이 될 거란다... 어쩌면 Foster 교수님과 얘기해 볼 수 있겠구나. 그가 인공 지능에 대한 새로운 실험을 도와줄 수 있는 학생들을 찾고 있거든.

S: 오, 정말요? 작년에 인공 지능에 대한 그 교수님의 수업 중 하나를 들었는데, 흥미로웠거든요. 제가 어떤 일을 하게 될지 아시나요?

P: 아마 데이터를 수집하고 실험 결과를 정리하게 될 거야.

S: 그건 할 수 있을 것 같은데요. Foster 교수님께 바로 말씀드리러 갈게요.

P: 그가 오늘 오후에 회의가 있다고 들어서, 지금 사무실에 안 계실 거야. 하지만 곧 돌아오실 거란다. 그를 기다려도 되고 내일 다시 와도 돼. 네가 들렀다고 전해드릴게.

S: 감사해요, Greene 교수님. 밖에서 기다릴게요. 어차피, 오늘은 수업도 더 이상 없어서요.
P: 그렇게 하렴. 행운을 빌어!

assignment 몡 과제(물)   car accident 교통사고
proof 몡 증거 (서류); 증명   report 몡 보고서; 보도
join 통 합류하다, 참여하다   organize 통 조직하다, 준비하다
science fair 과학 박람회   career 몡 진로; 직업
graduation 몡 졸업   experiment 몡 실험
artificial intelligence 인공 지능   gather 통 수집하다, 모으다
stop by ~에 들르다

1 대화의 주된 주제는 무엇인가?
  (A) 제시간에 과제를 제출하는 것
  (B) 어떤 수업을 들을지에 대한 조언을 구하는 것
  (C) 참여할 학교 활동을 찾는 것
  (D) 새로운 과목에 대해 배우는 것

2 학생은 왜 교수의 제안에 놀라는가?
  (A) 그는 동아리에 참여하는 것에 대해 들떴다.
  (B) 그는 프로젝트 주제에 대한 강의를 들었다.
  (C) 그는 요청에 대한 어떠한 도움도 기대하지 않았다.
  (D) 그는 일을 수행할 수 있을지 자신이 없다.

3 학생은 다음에 무엇을 할 것인가?
  (A) 내일로 약속을 잡기
  (B) 벽에 게시된 공지 확인하기
  (C) 수업이 끝나면 다시 오기
  (D) 교수가 돌아올 때까지 기다리기

대화의 일부를 다시 듣고 질문에 답하시오.
S: I don't have much time left because it's my last year here at school. Um, do you have any advice?
P: Sure. Those activities will help with your career after graduation...

4 교수는 왜 이렇게 말하는가:
  P: Those activities will help with your career after graduation...
  (A) 학생에게 진로를 선택하는 것에 대해 조언하기 위해
  (B) 최근에 일어난 사고에 대해 도움을 주기 위해
  (C) 그녀가 학생의 우려를 이해한다는 것을 보여주기 위해
  (D) 학생이 성적을 향상시켜야 한다는 것을 암시하기 위해

iBT Listening Test 2   본문 p. 68

1 (D)   2 (A)   3 (B)   4 (C)   5 (C)

Note-taking
In 1688
A Roman Catholic king James II had a baby boy.
→ Some powerful Protestants formed a plan.
→ William and Mary agreed to invade England.

In 1689
William and Mary made many important decisions:
− More power to the people in government
− The right to have free elections

Listen to part of a lecture in a history class.

P: OK, where were we last time? Oh, we were talking about the late 17th century in England. ¹Well, then, let's start with the Glorious Revolution.
The Glorious Revolution happened from 1688 to 1689. At the time, England was ruled by a Roman Catholic king called James II, but England's people were mostly Protestant. Protestants are Christians who separated from the Roman Catholic Church. The two groups, uh, disagreed about some Christian beliefs and did not have a good relationship. ²James II made many Protestants angry by trying to introduce policies that benefited Catholics. He also wanted to change England's system of government to give more power to the king. Despite these concerns, many Protestants thought they could wait until James II died. And, uh, after he died, his daughter Mary—who was Protestant—would take over.

³Unfortunately, in 1688, James had a baby boy. This meant that the boy would become the ruler of England after James II died, not Mary. That is when some powerful Protestants formed a plan. They did not want England to be ruled by another Catholic and asked Mary and her husband William, the ruler of the Netherlands, to invade England. William and Mary agreed. They, uh, sailed on ships from the Netherlands to England. James II tried to stop William and Mary, but he didn't have many supporters. So, he ran away to France, where he eventually died. After James II ran away, William and Mary became the rulers of England without a war. ¹Um, this is why it is called the Glorious Revolution. It happened without much blood.

Now, William and Mary agreed to rule the country together, and they made many important decisions... The biggest one was that William and Mary promised to follow the laws created by politicians. ⁴This decision gave less power to the king and queen and more power to the people in government. Isn't that incredible?

This decision changed England's history forever. ⁵Because of the Glorious Revolution, England became a country ruled by politicians instead of kings... And that's not all. William and Mary also gave people the right to have free elections. So, you can see that they had a big influence on England's way of life.

역사학 강의의 일부를 들으시오.
P: 자, 지난 시간에 어디까지 했죠? 아, 17세기 후반의 영국에 대해 이야기하고 있었죠. 음, 그럼, 명예혁명부터 시작해 봅시다.
명예혁명은 1688년부터 1689년까지 일어났습니다. 그 당시에, 영국은 제임스 2세라는 로마 가톨릭 왕에 의해 통치되었지만, 영

국의 사람들은 대부분 개신교도였어요. 개신교도는 로마 가톨릭 교회에서 분리된 기독교도입니다. 그 두 집단은, 어, 일부 기독교 신앙에 대해 의견이 달랐고 사이가 좋지 않았습니다. 제임스 2세는 가톨릭교도들에게 이득이 되는 정책들을 도입하려고 해서 많은 개신교도들을 화나게 했죠. 그는 또한 왕에게 더 많은 권력을 주기 위해 영국 정부의 시스템을 바꾸고 싶어 했어요. 이러한 걱정거리에도 불구하고, 많은 개신교도들은 제임스 2세가 죽을 때까지 기다릴 수 있다고 생각했답니다. 그러면, 어, 그가 죽은 후에는, 개신교도였던 그의 딸 메리가 이어받을 테니까요.

불행히도, 1688년에, 제임스는 아들을 낳았어요. 이것은 메리가 아닌, 그 소년이 제임스 2세가 죽은 후에 영국의 통치자가 될 것임을 의미했죠. 이때가 바로 몇몇 영향력 있는 개신교도들이 계획을 세운 때였어요. 그들은 영국이 또 다른 가톨릭교도에 의해 통치되기를 원하지 않았고, 메리와 네덜란드의 통치자인 그녀의 남편 윌리엄에게 영국을 침략할 것을 부탁했습니다. 윌리엄과 메리는 동의했고요. 그들은, 어, 네덜란드에서 영국으로 가는 배에 탔어요. 제임스 2세는 윌리엄과 메리를 막으려고 해봤지만, 그에게는 많은 지지자가 없었죠. 그래서, 그는 프랑스로 도망쳤는데, 그는 결국 이곳에서 죽게 됐습니다. 제임스 2세가 도망친 후, 윌리엄과 메리는 전쟁 없이 영국의 통치자가 되었죠. 음, 이게 그것이 명예혁명이라고 불리는 이유입니다. 그것은 많은 피를 흘리지 않고 일어났으니까요.

자, 윌리엄과 메리는 나라를 함께 통치하기로 동의했고, 그들은 여러 중요한 결정을 내렸어요... 가장 큰 것은 윌리엄과 메리가 정치인들이 만든 법을 따르겠다고 약속했다는 것입니다. 이 결정은 왕과 왕비에게 더 적은 권력을, 정부에 있는 사람들에게는 더 많은 권력을 주었어요. 놀랍지 않나요?

이 결정은 영국의 역사를 영원히 바꾸어 놓았습니다. 명예혁명 때문에, 영국은 왕 대신 정치인에 의해 통치되는 나라가 되었거든요... 그리고 그게 다가 아닙니다. 윌리엄과 메리는 또한 사람들에게 자유선거를 할 수 있는 권리를 주었어요. 그래서, 그들이 영국의 삶의 방식에 큰 영향을 미쳤다는 것을 알 수 있죠.

Catholic 형 가톨릭의; 명 가톨릭교도
Protestant 명 개신교도; 형 개신교의
Christian 명 기독교도; 형 기독교의   policy 명 정책
benefit 동 이득이 되다, 유익하다   powerful 형 영향력 있는
Netherlands 명 네덜란드   invade 동 침략하다, 침입하다
supporter 명 지지자   run away 도망치다   politician 명 정치인
right 명 권리; 형 옳은   free election 명 자유선거

1 강의는 주로 무엇에 관한 것인가?
   (A) 두 개의 다른 종교 간의 전쟁의 원인
   (B) 로마 가톨릭 교회의 흥망성쇠
   (C) 유럽에서 일어난 일련의 혁명들
   (D) 전투 없이 일어난 영국의 혁명

2 교수에 따르면, 개신교도들은 왜 제임스 2세에게 화가 났는가?
   (A) 그는 자신이 더 많은 권력을 가지려고 했다.
   (B) 그는 정부에 개신교도들을 금지했다.
   (C) 그는 그의 딸을 다른 나라로 보냈다.
   (D) 그는 일부 사람들에게 가톨릭교도가 되라고 강요했다.

3 교수에 따르면, 영국의 영향력 있는 개신교도들이 계획을 세우게 된 원인은 무엇인가?
   (A) 제임스 2세의 죽음
   (B) 제임스 2세의 아들의 출생
   (C) 네덜란드의 침략
   (D) 윌리엄과 메리의 귀환

4 윌리엄과 메리의 결정에 대한 교수의 태도는 무엇인가?
   (A) 그녀는 그것이 더 일찍 이뤄졌어야 한다고 생각한다.
   (B) 그녀는 그들의 평화로운 행동에 감동했다.
   (C) 그녀는 그것의 장기적인 영향력에 깊은 인상을 받았다.
   (D) 그녀는 그들이 그것을 하도록 강요 받았다고 생각한다.

강의의 일부를 다시 듣고 질문에 답하시오.
P: Because of the Glorious Revolution, England became a country ruled by politicians instead of kings... And that's not all. William and Mary also gave people the right to have free elections. So, you can see that they had a big influence on England's way of life.

5 교수는 왜 이렇게 말하는가:
   P: And that's not all.
   (A) 한 나라의 통치자가 되는 것이 얼마나 힘든 것인지 보여주기 위해
   (B) 몇몇 정치인들이 왜 윌리엄과 메리를 좋아하지 않았는지 설명하기 위해
   (C) 윌리엄과 메리가 가졌던 영향력을 강조하기 위해
   (D) 영국의 많은 사람들이 여전히 가톨릭교도였다는 것을 나타내기 위해

Vocabulary Review   본문 p.72

1 architecture   2 playful   3 experiment
4 drain   5 moisture   6 supporter
7 recommend   8 take over   9 automatically
10 (C)   11 (B)   12 (B)
13 (A)   14 (D)

CHAPTER 04
Attitude

Example   본문 p.75

A. (B)   B. (C)

A.
Note-taking
Student's Problem
Doesn't know where to start with a project

Steps to Make an Outline
1. Write down everything to include
2. Find the main point[idea] to focus on

Listen to a conversation between a student and a professor.

S: Hello, Professor Bailey. I need your advice on my research project.
P: Sure. What's the problem?
S: Uh, I searched for information online about my topic, but there was too much of it. I don't know where to start... I feel like I'm lost.
P: I know the feeling. You always get more than what you ask for on the Internet, right? Well, how about making an outline first?
S: Um, how do I make an outline? Can you give me more details?
P: Of course. First, write down everything you want to include in your project. And then find the main point that you want to focus on. Once you find it, you'll know what you need to support the main idea.
S: I can do that. It will make it easier to search for information, too. Thank you for your help, Professor.

학생과 교수 사이의 대화를 들으시오.

S: 안녕하세요, Bailey 교수님. 제 연구 프로젝트에 대한 교수님의 조언이 필요합니다.
P: 그래. 무엇이 문제니?
S: 어, 제 주제에 대한 정보를 온라인에서 검색해봤는데, 너무 많았어요. 어디서부터 시작해야 할지 모르겠어요... 길을 잃은 것 같아요.
P: 나도 그 기분을 알지. 인터넷에서는 항상 원하는 것보다 더 많은 것을 얻게 돼, 그렇지? 음, 우선 개요를 만드는 게 어떠니?
S: 음, 개요를 어떻게 만드나요? 좀 더 자세히 말씀해 주시겠어요?
P: 물론이야. 먼저, 프로젝트에 포함하고 싶은 모든 것을 적어. 그리고 네가 집중하고 싶은 요점을 찾으렴. 그것을 찾고 나면, 네 주된 주제를 뒷받침하기 위해 무엇이 필요한지 알게 될 거란다.
S: 그건 할 수 있겠어요. 정보도 더 쉽게 검색할 수 있게 할 것 같아요. 도와주셔서 감사합니다, 교수님.

search 동 검색하다, 찾아보다　lost 형 길을 잃은
feeling 명 기분, 느낌　main point 요점
support 동 뒷받침하다, 지지하다

인터넷에 대한 교수의 의견은 무엇인가?
(A) 그것은 보통 시간 낭비이다.
(B) 그것에는 너무 많은 정보가 있다.
(C) 그것은 개요를 만드는 데 유용하다.
(D) 그것은 연구 주제가 되어야 한다.

B.
Note-taking
Causes of Waves
- Wind
  : Blows on the surface of the ocean and waves form
- Events like earthquakes
  : Can create a large sea wave called a tsunami

Listen to part of a lecture in an oceanography class.

P: So, let's talk about what causes waves... The most common cause is wind. When wind blows on the surface of the ocean, waves form. These are called wind-driven waves. They're also called surface waves because they only happen near the surface of the water. These kinds of small waves usually aren't dangerous.

However, big waves are... Um, they start at sea and grow stronger as they move toward land. Many times, they're caused by powerful storms. But they can also be caused by other events like earthquakes... Now, I know what you're thinking. Yes, these events don't happen only on land, but they also happen underwater... Earthquakes underwater cause the ground to move. This movement makes large amounts of water move as well. The movement can be so strong that it creates a large sea wave called a tsunami.

해양학 강의의 일부를 들으시오.

P: 자, 무엇이 파도를 일으키는지에 대해 얘기해 보죠. 가장 흔한 원인은 바람입니다. 바다의 표면에 바람이 불 때, 파도가 형성되는데요. 이것들을 풍파라고 부릅니다. 그것들은 물의 표면 근처에서만 발생하기 때문에 표면파라고도 불려요. 이러한 유형의 작은 파도들은 보통 위험하지 않죠.

하지만, 큰 파도는 그래요... 음, 그것들은 바다에서 시작해서 육지로 이동할수록 더 강력해집니다. 많은 경우, 그것들은 강력한 폭풍으로 인해 발생해요. 하지만 그것들은 지진과 같은 다른 현상들에 의해서도 발생할 수 있어요... 자, 여러분이 무슨 생각을 하고 있는지 알아요. 네, 이 현상들은 육지에서만 일어나는 것이 아니라, 물속에서 일어나기도 합니다... 해저 지진은 땅이 움직이게 하는데요. 이 움직임은 많은 양의 물도 움직이게 하죠. 그 움직임은 너무 강력해서 쓰나미라고 불리는 큰 파도를 만들 수 있습니다.

wind-driven wave 풍파(바람에 의해 생긴 파도)　earthquake 명 지진
underwater 형 물속의, 해저의　tsunami 명 쓰나미

강의의 일부를 다시 듣고 질문에 답하시오.
P: But they can also be caused by other events like earthquakes... Now, I know what you're thinking. Yes, these events don't happen only on land, but they also happen underwater...

교수는 이렇게 말함으로써 무엇을 의미하는가:
P: Now, I know what you're thinking.

(A) 그녀는 전에 수업 시간에 주제에 관해 이야기한 적이 있다.
(B) 그녀는 학생들에게 문제에 대해 상기시키고 싶어 한다.

(C) 그녀는 학생들이 혼란스러워할 수도 있다는 것을 안다.
(D) 그녀는 학생들에게 주제에 관해 읽어보도록 했다.

Listening Practice 1   본문 p.77

1 (D)   2 (B)   3 (A)

Note-taking
Student's Problem
The group is not making good progress.

Professor's Solution
- Choose a leader who can make decisions
- Brainstorm for topics
- Give a specific task to every member

Listen to a conversation between a student and a professor.

S: Hello, Professor Stephens. Do you have time to see me now?
P: Hi, Oliver. Yes. How is your group assignment going?
S: That's what I want to talk about. ¹Uh, our group is not making good progress. All the other groups have chosen topics and started their research, but...
P: ³Are you the team leader?
S: Uh, we don't have one, actually.
P: Well, that makes sense... It's difficult to make progress without a leader. You know, a leader can make decisions on things like, uh, what to do next.
S: I see. Uh, maybe I could volunteer for the job.
P: I believe you'll make a good leader. ²Um, also, I recommend that all of you brainstorm for topics. It's important that everyone is involved at this stage. That way, you can be sure that everyone agrees with the final topic.
S: That's true... Um, is there anything else we should do after choosing a topic?
P: Well, lastly, I would make sure every member is given a specific task. They should know exactly what they have to work on.
S: You're right. I'll tell them what you've told me. I hope it makes things go faster.
P: It should... If you still have problems, let me know. I can speak to the group as a whole.

학생과 교수 사이의 대화를 들으시오.

S: 안녕하세요, Stephens 교수님. 지금 잠깐 시간 있으신가요?
P: 안녕, Oliver. 그래. 조별 과제는 어떻게 되어가고 있니?
S: 그게 바로 제가 말씀드리고 싶은 거예요. 어, 저희 조가 진전이 잘 없어서요. 다른 모든 조들은 주제를 정해서 조사를 시작했는데...
P: 네가 조장이니?
S: 어, 사실, 저희는 조장이 없어요.
P: 음, 이해가 되는구나... 조장 없이는 진전이 있기가 어려워. 그러니까, 조장은 결정을 내릴 수 있거든, 어, 다음에 무엇을 할지와 같이 말이야.
S: 그렇군요. 어, 어쩌면 제가 자원해서 그 일을 할 수도 있겠어요.
P: 네가 좋은 조장이 될 거라고 생각해. 음, 또, 너희 모두가 주제에 대해 브레인스토밍 하는 것을 추천한다. 이 단계에서 모든 사람이 참여하는 게 중요하지. 그렇게 하면, 모든 사람이 최종 주제에 동의한다는 것을 확실히 할 수 있거든.
S: 그렇네요... 음, 주제를 정하고 난 후에 저희가 해야 할 일이 또 있을까요?
P: 음, 마지막으로, 모든 조원이 구체적인 할 일이 있는지 확실히 해야겠지. 그들이 자신이 해야 하는 것이 정확히 무엇인지 알아야 해.
S: 맞아요. 교수님께서 제게 말씀하신 것을 그들에게 전할게요. 그게 일이 더 빨리 진행되게 하길 바라요.
P: 그럴 거야... 만약 그래도 문제가 있다면, 나에게 알려주렴. 내가 조 전체에 이야기하면 되니까 말이야.

progress 명 진전   team leader 조장   decision 명 결정
brainstorm 동 브레인스토밍하다(자유롭게 아이디어를 내놓는 회의 방식)
involved 형 참여하는, 관여하는   agree with ~에 동의하다
specific 형 구체적인

1 학생의 문제는 무엇인가?
 (A) 그는 과제를 제때 제출하지 않았다.
 (B) 그는 조원들과 의견 충돌이 있다.
 (C) 그는 몇몇 수업에 빠져야 한다.
 (D) 그는 조의 진전에 대해 걱정하고 있다.

2 교수에 따르면, 주제에 대한 브레인스토밍을 왜 모든 사람이 해야 하는가?
 (A) 다수의 의견을 얻기 위해
 (B) 동의된 것임을 확실히 하기 위해
 (C) 좋은 점수를 받기 위해
 (D) 조사를 더 빠르게 진행하기 위해

대화의 일부를 다시 듣고 질문에 답하시오.
P: Are you the team leader?
S: Uh, we don't have one, actually.
P: Well, that makes sense... It's difficult to make progress without a leader.

3 교수는 이렇게 말함으로써 무엇을 의미하는가:
 P: Well, that makes sense...
 (A) 그녀는 문제의 이유를 이해했다.
 (B) 그녀는 조장의 선택에 동의하지 않는다.
 (C) 그녀는 자신의 의견이 학생의 의견보다 낫다고 생각한다.
 (D) 그녀는 조장이 왜 조를 떠났는지 확신할 수 없다.

Listening Practice 2

본문 p.79

1 (C)   2 (B)   3 (A), (B)   4 (D)

Note-taking
Abiotic Factors
e.g. Temperature, light, water, and minerals

Biotic Factors
- Producers: Change abiotic factors into other things
- Consumers: Plant eaters, predators, or eat both
- Decomposers: Break down the materials

Listen to part of a lecture in an ecology class.

P: Now let's talk about ecosystems in more detail. [1]I want you to understand the major factors in ecosystems. Uh, these are called abiotic and biotic factors.

First, the word *abiotic* refers to non-living things. So, uh, these factors include things like temperature, light, and water. [2]Even though these are not alive, organisms depend on abiotic factors to survive, grow, and reproduce. [4]Can anyone think about a specific example that illustrates this relationship?

S: Uh, how about soil and plants? If the soil does not have the right nutrients, then plants will not grow as well.

P: That's exactly what I was looking for... A good example is the minerals in the soil. Minerals are abiotic. They are not alive, but they are essential for healthy plants. Minerals help plants stay green so that they can create energy and grow.

Now, let's consider the biotic factors of ecosystems. These are the living things, such as plants, animals, and fungi. There are several types of biotic elements in every ecosystem, and each of these has a unique and important role in the environment. Firstly, there are producers. They change abiotic factors into something else for organisms. For example, plants use abiotic factors like sunlight, water, and carbon dioxide to create oxygen, which is essential for many organisms. [3]Next, there are consumers, uh, like animals. Some consumers are plant eaters, while others are predators that get their nutrition only from hunting prey. And, some consumers eat both plants and animals. Finally, there are decomposers. Decomposers break down the materials created by producers and consumers. For instance, when a tree dies, it will start to rot. This is because decomposers, like mushrooms or earthworms, break down the dead tree into smaller pieces. Gradually, it will turn into dirt.

생태학 강의의 일부를 들으시오.

P: 이제 생태계에 대해 좀 더 자세히 이야기해 봅시다. 저는 여러분이 생태계의 주요 요인들을 이해했으면 좋겠는데요. 어, 이것들은 무생물적 그리고 생물적 요인이라고 불립니다.

먼저, '무생물'이라는 단어는 생명이 없는 것들을 의미해요. 그래서, 어, 이 요인들에는 온도, 빛, 그리고 물과 같은 것들이 포함되죠. 비록 이것들이 살아있는 것은 아니어도, 유기체들은 생존하고, 자라고, 번식하기 위해 무생물적 요인에 의존합니다. 이 관계를 나타내는 구체적인 예시에 대해 생각할 수 있는 사람이 있을까요?

S: 어, 토양과 식물은 어떤가요? 만약 토양이 적절한 영양소를 가지고 있지 않다면, 식물도 자라지 못할 거예요.

P: 그게 바로 제가 찾고 있던 거예요... 좋은 예시가 토양에 있는 무기물이거든요. 무기물은 무생물적이죠. 그것들은 살아있는 것은 아니지만, 건강한 식물을 위해 필수적이에요. 무기물은 식물들이 에너지를 생성하고 자랄 수 있도록 그것들이 푸른 상태를 유지하는 데 도움이 됩니다.

이제, 생태계의 생물적 요인을 생각해 봅시다. 이것들은 식물, 동물, 그리고 곰팡이류와 같은 생물들이죠. 모든 생태계에는 몇 가지 유형의 생물적 요인들이 있는데, 각각 환경에서 특별하고 중요한 역할을 합니다. 먼저, 생산자들이 있습니다. 그것들은 유기체를 위해 무생물적 요인들을 다른 것들로 바꾸는데요. 예를 들어, 식물들은 햇빛, 물, 그리고 이산화탄소와 같은 무생물적 요인들을 활용해서 많은 유기체들에게 필수적인 산소를 만들죠. 다음으로, 동물과 같이, 어, 소비자들이 있어요. 어떤 소비자들은 식물을 먹는 반면, 다른 것들은 먹이를 사냥하는 것에서만 영양분을 얻는 포식자입니다. 그리고, 어떤 소비자들은 식물과 동물 모두를 먹죠. 마지막으로, 분해자가 있어요. 분해자는 생산자와 소비자에 의해 만들어진 물질을 분해해요. 예를 들어, 나무가 죽으면, 그것은 썩기 시작할 거예요. 이것은 버섯이나 지렁이와 같은 분해자들이 죽은 나무를 더 작은 조각들로 분해하기 때문이죠. 점차, 그것은 흙으로 변할 것입니다.

abiotic 〔형〕 무생물적   biotic 〔형〕 생물적   organism 〔명〕 유기체
illustrate 〔동〕 나타내다, 설명하다   nutrient 〔명〕 영양소
mineral 〔명〕 무기물; 광물   essential 〔형〕 필수적인
fungus 〔명〕 곰팡이류, 균류   producer 〔명〕 생산자
consumer 〔명〕 소비자   predator 〔명〕 포식자
decomposer 〔명〕 분해자   break down ~을 분해하다, ~을 부수다
rot 〔동〕 썩다   mushroom 〔명〕 버섯   earthworm 〔명〕 지렁이
gradually 〔부〕 점차, 서서히

1 강의의 주된 주제는 무엇인가?
- (A) 다양한 종류의 생물들
- (B) 특정 유기체들이 어떻게 서로를 돕는지
- (C) 생태계의 두 가지 주요 요인들
- (D) 무기물이 환경에서 중요한 이유

2 교수는 생태계의 무생물적 요인에 관해 무엇이라고 말하는가?
- (A) 건강한 식물은 성장을 위해 그것들을 필요로 하지 않는다.
- (B) 유기체는 생존을 위해 그것들에 의존한다.
- (C) 그것들은 대부분의 생태계에서 희귀하다.
- (D) 그것들은 몇몇 생물들에게 해로울 수 있다.

3 교수에 따르면, 소비자의 두 가지 유형은 무엇인가? 2개의 답을 고르시오.
- (A) 먹이를 사냥하는 포식자
- (B) 식물을 먹는 동물
- (C) 산소를 만드는 식물

(D) 죽은 식물을 분해하는 곰팡이류

강의의 일부를 다시 듣고 질문에 답하시오.
P: Can anyone think about a specific example that illustrates this relationship?
S: Uh, how about soil and plants? If the soil does not have the right nutrients, then plants will not grow as well.
P: That's exactly what I was looking for...

4 교수는 이렇게 말함으로써 무엇을 의미하는가:
P: That's exactly what I was looking for...

(A) 그녀는 자신이 올바른 정보를 찾았다고 생각한다.
(B) 그녀는 중요한 점을 언급하는 것을 잊었다.
(C) 그녀는 학생이 설명을 해주기를 기대한다.
(D) 그녀는 학생의 대답에 감명을 받았다.

Listening Practice 3 본문 p. 81

1 (D)   **2** (C)   **3** (C)

Note-taking
Student's Request
Needs advice about studying abroad

Professor's Suggestion
Go somewhere that challenges you to learn new skills, like another language

> Listen to a conversation between a student and a professor.
>
> S: Good morning, Professor Parks. Are you busy? I want to get your advice about something.
> P: Sure, Riley. How can I help you?
> S: ¹Uh, you know that I'm planning to study abroad, right? Well, what do you think about studying in Scotland?
> P: That's an interesting choice. Why there?
> S: Um, I guess it would be a nice place to visit, and they speak English too.
> P: I see... I would discourage you from going there...
> S: Oh? May I ask why? I thought Scotland would be an interesting place to visit.
> P: That's true. But like you said, people there speak English like we do. ²It would be better to go somewhere that challenges you to learn new skills, like another language. That's one of the advantages of going to a new country.
> S: I don't know many languages. I mean, I learned some German and French in high school.
> P: Then you should go to Switzerland. They speak both German and French over there.
> S: ³Oh, I get it... I can improve both languages in Switzerland.
> P: And, if you go there, you can still visit Scotland. It only takes a few hours by plane.
> S: That's true! I think you've changed my mind, Professor!

학생과 교수 사이의 대화를 들으시오.
S: 좋은 아침이에요, Parks 교수님. 바쁘신가요? 제가 조언을 듣고 싶은 것이 있어서요.
P: 물론이지, Riley. 어떻게 도와주면 될까?
S: 어, 제가 해외 유학을 할 계획인 것은 아시죠, 그렇죠? 음, 스코틀랜드에서 공부하는 것에 대해 어떻게 생각하세요?
P: 흥미로운 선택이구나. 왜 거기니?
S: 음, 방문하기에 좋은 곳일 것 같고, 사람들이 영어를 사용하기도 해서요.
P: 그렇구나... 나는 네가 거기에 가는 것을 말리고 싶구나...
S: 오? 이유를 여쭤봐도 될까요? 스코틀랜드는 방문해볼 만한 흥미로운 곳이라고 생각했거든요.
P: 그건 맞지. 하지만 네가 말했듯이, 그곳 사람들은 우리처럼 영어를 사용해. 다른 언어와 같이 새로운 능력을 배우도록 도전 의식을 북돋우는 곳으로 가는 것이 더 좋을 거란다. 그게 새로운 나라에 가는 것의 장점 중 하나지.
S: 저는 많은 언어를 몰라요. 그러니까, 저는 고등학교에서 독일어와 프랑스어를 조금 배웠어요.
P: 그렇다면 스위스에 가보렴. 그곳에서는 독일어와 프랑스어를 모두 사용해.
S: 오, 알겠어요... 스위스에서 저는 두 언어를 모두 향상시킬 수 있겠네요.
P: 그리고, 만약 네가 그곳에 가면, 스코틀랜드도 방문할 수 있어. 비행기로 몇 시간밖에 안 걸리거든.
S: 그렇네요! 제 마음을 바꾸신 것 같아요, 교수님!

study abroad 해외 유학을 하다   Scotland 명 스코틀랜드
discourage 동 말리다, 막다   challenge 동 도전 의식을 북돋우다
advantage 명 장점   German 명 독일어   French 명 프랑스어
Switzerland 명 스위스   improve 동 향상시키다   mind 명 마음

1 학생은 왜 교수를 찾아가는가?
(A) 수업 프로젝트를 논의하기 위해
(B) 입사 지원서에 대한 도움을 받기 위해
(C) 어학 프로그램에 신청하기 위해
(D) 해외 유학에 관해 문의하기 위해

2 교수에 따르면, 새로운 나라에 가는 것의 장점은 무엇인가?
(A) 새로운 친구를 사귀는 것
(B) 다양한 직업을 탐색하는 것
(C) 새로운 능력을 배우는 것
(D) 다양한 볼거리를 보는 것

3 스위스에 가는 것에 대한 학생의 의견은 무엇인가?
(A) 그녀는 이동 거리에 대해 걱정하고 있다.
(B) 그녀는 여전히 스코틀랜드에 가는 것을 선호한다.

(C) 그녀는 그것이 도움이 될 것이라고 생각한다.
(D) 그녀는 그곳이 방문하기에 지루한 장소라고 생각한다.

Listening Practice 4 본문 p. 83

1 (B) 2 (C) 3 (C) 4 (C)

Note-taking

1850 Fugitive Slave Act
: Required all escaped slaves to return to their owners even in free states

From 1850 to 1865, the Underground Railroad
: A network[group] of people who offered food and shelter to slaves

Listen to part of a lecture in a history class.

P: OK, so we previously discussed the 1850 Fugitive Slave Act in the US. ¹Now, we are going to talk about the unexpected outcome of this act. This is one of the most dramatic parts of American history: the Underground Railroad.

But before we move on to today's topic, let me refresh your memories... So, there were about five million slaves in the US at that time, mostly in the South. The South needed slaves for farms, especially cotton farms. However, about a thousand slaves escaped from the South every year. ²The Fugitive Slave Act required all escaped slaves to return to their owners if they were caught. And it was required even in free states in the north. You know, slavery was not allowed in free states, so we can see how strict the law was. So, uh, this was a challenge for slaves who escaped to free states like Pennsylvania.

Now, uh, some people ignored the law. These people disagreed with slavery, so they developed the Underground Railroad. The Underground Railroad was a network that existed from 1850 to 1865. ¹/⁴When you hear the name, you might think that it was a railroad located underground. But that's not what it was. It was simply a group of people who offered food and shelter to escaping slaves... um, along escape routes. Surprised, right? People communicated in person instead of writing things down. They also used secret codes to, uh, avoid slave catchers. About 100,000 people escaped this way. That may seem small compared to the millions of remaining slaves. ³However, the movement was still a successful effort by ordinary people who wanted justice.

역사학 강의의 일부를 들으시오.

P: 자, 그래서 우리는 이전에 미국의 1850년도 도망노예법에 대해 논의했죠. 이제, 우리는 이 법의 예상치 못한 결과에 대해 이야기할 거예요. 이는 미국 역사의 가장 극적인 부분 중 하나인, 지하 철도 조직입니다.

하지만 오늘의 주제로 넘어가기 전에, 여러분의 기억을 되살려 보겠습니다... 그래서, 그 당시 미국에는 약 5백만 명의 노예가 있었는데, 대부분 남부에 있었죠. 남부에서는 농장, 특히 목화 농장을 위한 노예가 필요했습니다. 그러나, 매년 약 천 명의 노예들이 남쪽에서 탈출을 했어요. 도망노예법은 모든 탈출한 노예들이 잡힐 경우 주인에게 돌아가도록 요구했습니다. 그리고 그것은 심지어 북부의 자유주에서도 요구되었죠. 알다시피, 노예제도는 자유주에서 허용되지 않았기 때문에, 그 법이 얼마나 엄격했는지 알 수 있어요. 그래서, 어, 이것은 펜실베이니아와 같은 자유주로 도망친 노예들에게 난제였어요.

자, 어, 일부 사람들은 그 법을 무시했어요. 이 사람들은 노예제도에 반대했기 때문에, 지하 철도 조직을 만들었죠. 지하 철도 조직은 1850년부터 1865년까지 존재했던 네트워크였어요. 그 이름을 들으면, 여러분은 그것이 지하에 위치한 철도였다고 생각할지도 몰라요. 하지만 그게 아니었어요. 그것은 단순히 도망치는 노예들에게 음식과 은신처를 제공했던 한 무리의 사람들이었죠... 음, 탈출 경로를 따라서요. 놀랐죠, 그렇죠? 사람들은 무언가를 적는 대신 직접 의사소통을 했습니다. 그들은 또한 노예를 잡는 사람들을 피하기 위해, 어, 비밀 암호를 사용했어요. 이와 같은 방식으로 약 10만 명이 탈출을 했습니다. 수백만 명의 남아 있던 노예들에 비하면 그것은 적어 보일지도 모르죠. 하지만, 그래도 이 운동은 정의를 원하는 평범한 사람들에 의한 성공적인 노력이었습니다.

Fugitive Slave Act 도망노예법
unexpected 혱 예상치 못한, 예기치 않은 outcome 몡 결과
act 몡 법(률); 행동 Underground Railroad 지하 철도 조직
cotton 몡 목화, 솜 escaped 혱 탈출한 free state 자유주
strict 혱 엄격한 challenge 몡 난제, 어려움; 도전
Pennsylvania 몡 펜실베이니아주(미국 동부의 주) ignore 동 무시하다
shelter 몡 은신처 route 몡 경로, 길 remaining 혱 남아 있는
movement 몡 운동; 움직임 justice 몡 정의, 공평성

1 강의는 주로 무엇에 관한 것인가?

(A) 주의 법들 간의 차이점
(B) 노예들이 탈출하도록 도운 사람들의 네트워크
(C) 사람들이 철도를 만든 이유들
(D) 노예를 구출하기 위한 정부의 노력

2 교수에 따르면, 도망노예법에 대한 설명으로 옳은 것은?

(A) 그것은 특정 주에서만 요구되었다.
(B) 그것은 노예들에게 음식과 은신처를 제공했다.
(C) 그것은 노예제도가 불법인 곳에서도 적용되었다.
(D) 그것은 철도 노동자들에 의해 무시되었다.

3 지하 철도 조직에 대한 교수의 태도는 무엇인가?

(A) 그것은 역사적 가치가 적다.
(B) 그것은 개선되어야 했다.
(C) 그것은 의미 있는 노력이었다.
(D) 그것은 더 많은 관심을 받아야 한다.

강의의 일부를 다시 듣고 질문에 답하시오.

P: When you hear the name, you might think that it was a railroad located underground. But that's not what it was. It was simply a group of people who offered food and shelter to escaping slaves... um, along escape routes. Surprised, right?

4 교수는 왜 이렇게 말하는가:

P: Surprised, right?

(A) 주제가 이해하기 어렵다는 것을 암시하기 위해
(B) 행위의 결과가 예상치 못한 것임을 암시하기 위해
(C) 이름과 현실의 차이를 강조하기 위해
(D) 비밀 암호의 용도를 설명하기 위해

iBT Listening Test 1
본문 p. 85

1 (B)   2 (D)   3 (B)   4 (A)

Note-taking

Student's Problem
Wants to return a textbook to get money back
→ Won't have time to get the receipt today

Employee's Suggestion
Could process the return today
→ Bring the receipt tomorrow

Listen to a conversation between a student and an employee in the university bookstore.

W: Hi. ¹I want to return this textbook. But, uh, I wonder if I will get my money back if I do.

M: Um, it depends. Could you show me your receipt?

W: Um, I left it in my room at the dormitory...

M: I need to know when you bought the book. You see, we only accept returns when it's within two weeks. There should be a date on the receipt.

W: But I paid for the book with a credit card. I think you have a record of the sale.

M: I will still need the receipt, though. It's a store policy... ²And we're closing in 20 minutes.

W: Oh, no, I won't have time to go to my room and get the receipt today...

M: Is there a reason why you have to get a refund today?

W: ⁴Uh, I bought the book two weeks ago. It will be past the deadline if I come back tomorrow...

M: Hmm... Well, this is a new policy, and the manager is really strict about it. But it doesn't seem fair in your case...

W: Is there anything you can do? I really need the money to buy a textbook for another class. The class starts next Monday.

M: I guess I could process the return today. But you need to bring the receipt tomorrow morning. I could get in trouble if you don't... ³Um, actually, leave your student ID with me so that I know you're coming back.

W: Thanks so much! I can do that. Let me get it out of my purse for you.

대학 서점에서 학생과 직원 사이의 대화를 들으시오.

W: 안녕하세요. 저는 이 교재를 반품하고 싶은데요. 그런데, 어, 그렇게 하면 제 돈을 돌려받을 수 있을지 궁금해요.

M: 음, 상황에 따라 다르죠. 영수증을 보여주시겠어요?

W: 음, 제가 그것을 기숙사 방에 두고 왔어요...

M: 제가 학생이 그 책을 언제 구매했는지 알아야 해요. 그러니까, 저희가 2주 이내의 건만 반품을 받거든요. 영수증에 날짜가 있을 거예요.

W: 하지만 제가 책값을 신용카드로 지불했어요. 판매 기록이 있을 것 같은데요.

M: 그래도 영수증이 필요해요. 가게 규정이거든요... 그리고 저희가 20분 후면 문을 닫아요.

W: 오, 이런, 오늘은 방에 가서 영수증을 가져올 시간이 없겠네요...

M: 오늘 환불을 받아야 하는 이유가 있나요?

W: 어, 제가 그 책을 2주 전에 샀거든요. 내일 다시 오면 기한이 지나 있을 거예요...

M: 흠... 음, 이게 새로운 규정인데, 관리자가 그것에 대해 정말 엄격해요. 하지만 학생의 경우에는 타당한 것 같지 않네요...

W: 당신이 해주실 수 있는게 있을까요? 저는 다른 수업의 교재를 살 돈이 꼭 필요해요. 그 수업이 다음 주 월요일이면 시작해요.

M: 제가 오늘 반품 처리를 할 수 있을 것 같아요. 하지만 내일 아침에 영수증을 가져오셔야 해요. 안 그러면 제가 곤란해질 수도 있어요... 음, 아예, 학생이 돌아올 거라는 걸 제가 알 수 있도록 학생증을 제게 남겨놓고 가주세요.

W: 정말 고마워요! 그렇게 할 수 있어요. 제가 지갑에서 꺼내서 드릴게요.

return 통 반품하다; 돌아오다; 명 반품   textbook 명 교재, 교과서
receipt 명 영수증   record 명 기록   sale 명 판매
refund 명 환불   deadline 명 기한   fair 형 타당한; 공평한
get in trouble 곤란에 처하다   purse 명 지갑

1 대화는 주로 무엇에 관한 것인가?
   (A) 신용카드에 관한 문제
   (B) 환불을 받는 것에 대한 절차
   (C) 제품 반품의 원인
   (D) 교재를 주문하는 것에 대한 규정

2 학생은 왜 오늘 영수증을 가져올 수 없는가?
   (A) 그녀의 신용카드가 없어졌다.
   (B) 그녀는 지금 수업에 참석해야 한다.
   (C) 그녀는 방에 들어갈 수 없다.
   (D) 서점이 곧 문을 닫을 것이다.

3 학생은 다음에 무엇을 할 것인가?
   (A) 추가로 구매하기
   (B) 신분증 제공하기
   (C) 학생 설문 조사지 작성하기
   (D) 작성한 불만 사항을 제출하기

대화의 일부를 다시 듣고 질문에 답하시오.
W: Uh, I bought the book two weeks ago. It will be past the deadline if I come back tomorrow...
M: Hmm... Well, this is a new policy, and the manager is really strict about it. But it doesn't seem fair in your case...

4 직원은 이렇게 말함으로써 무엇을 암시하는가:
   M: But it doesn't seem fair in your case...
   (A) 학생은 규정을 따를 필요가 없다.
   (B) 관리자가 도움을 제공할 수 없을 것이다.
   (C) 규정은 모든 사람에게 평등하게 적용되어야 한다.
   (D) 새로운 규정은 별로 효과적이지 않다.

iBT Listening Test 2   본문 p.88

1 (B)   2 (B)   3 (A)   4 (C)   5 (C)

Note-taking
Heinrich's Law
- First category: Accidents did not lead to an injury
- Second category: Accidents caused a minor injury
- Third category: Accidents resulted in a major injury
e.g. A company with 330 accidents
: 300 were in the first category, 29 in the second, and 1 in the third.

Listen to part of a lecture in a sociology class.

P: How many workplace accidents do you hear about on the news? Quite a few, right? It might sound like workplaces are dangerous. But, uh, it's important to consider this scientifically. ¹An industrial safety expert named Herbert Heinrich tried to analyze accidents in the 1930s. He made categories for different workplace accidents and discussed how they happen.

OK... So Heinrich first analyzed 75,000 workplace accidents. Then, he divided them into three categories. The first category was any accidents that did not lead to an injury. ²The second category was accidents that caused a minor injury, like hurting a finger. And can you guess the third category? It was accidents that resulted in a major injury, like breaking bones. This is Heinrich's Law, or Heinrich's Pyramid, and there are a couple of important points to remember about it.

Heinrich suggested that accidents happen at certain rates. Um, Heinrich used the example of a company with 330 accidents in total. ³According to him, 300 of those accidents were in the first category, 29 in the second, and 1 in the third. This means that the largest number of accidents did not cause any injury, but at least one of them was serious.

He also mentioned that each category of accidents is closely related... Uh, let's say that a painter falls off a ladder because the ladder is broken. He is lucky and does not have any injuries. So, his accident is in the first category. However, he does not fix the broken ladder and falls again. This time, he hurts his finger. Now he has an accident in the second category. Still, he does not fix the ladder, so he falls again and breaks his arm. He has a serious accident in the third category. What does this tell us? ⁴Well, I think it means the worker could have avoided the serious accident if he fixed the ladder.

⁵Heinrich concluded that employees are usually the cause of accidents. He said that almost 90 percent of work accidents happen because of employees' unsafe decisions. However, many people do not accept this today. They think that Heinrich blamed employees too much. They say that other factors like poor management systems and working too long can also cause accidents... not just employees' mistakes.

사회학 강의의 일부를 들으시오.

P: 여러분은 뉴스에서 얼마나 많은 작업장 사고에 대해 듣나요? 꽤 많아요, 그렇죠? 작업장들이 위험한 것처럼 들릴 수도 있어요. 하지만, 어, 이것을 과학적으로 고찰하는 것이 중요합니다. 허버트 하인리히라는 이름의 산업 안전 전문가는 1930년대에 일어난 사고들을 분석하려고 했어요. 그는 다양한 작업장 사고들에 대한 범주를 만들고 그것들이 어떻게 발생하는지에 대해 얘기했죠.

자... 그래서 하인리히는 먼저 75,000건의 작업장 사고들을 분석했어요. 그러고 나서, 그는 그것들을 세 가지 범주로 나누었죠. 첫 번째 범주는 부상으로 이어지지 않은 사고들이었어요. 두 번째 범주는 손가락을 다치는 것과 같이 가벼운 부상을 초래한 사고들이었죠. 그러면 세 번째 범주를 추측할 수 있나요? 그것은 뼈가 부러지는 것과 같이 큰 부상을 초래한 사고들이었어요. 이것이 하인리히의 법칙, 즉 하인리히의 피라미드인데, 그것에 대해 기억해야 할 중요한 점이 두어 가지가 있습니다.

하인리히는 사고들이 특정 비율로 발생한다고 제시했어요. 음, 하인리히는 총 330건의 사고들이 있었던 한 회사의 예시를 사용했죠. 그에 따르면, 그 사고들 중 300건이 첫 번째 범주에, 29건이 두 번째에, 그리고 1건의 사고가 세 번째에 속했어요. 이는 대다수의 사고들은 부상을 야기하지는 않았지만, 그것들 중 최소 한 건은 심각했다는 것을 의미합니다.

그는 또한 각각의 사고 범주들이 밀접하게 연관되어 있다고 언급했어요... 어, 한 페인트공이 사다리가 부러져서 떨어졌다고 해봅시다. 그가 운이 좋아서 어떠한 부상도 입지 않아요. 그러면, 그의 사고는 첫 번째 범주에 속합니다. 하지만, 그는 부서진 사다리를 고치지 않아서 다시 떨어집니다. 이번에는, 그가 손가락을 다쳐요. 이제 그는 두 번째 범주에 속한 사고를 당한 거죠. 여전히, 그는 사다리를 고치지 않아서, 그는 다시 떨어졌고 팔이 부러져요. 그는 세 번째 범주에 속한 심각한 사고를 당합니다. 이것이 우리에게 무엇을 말해줄까요? 음, 저는 그 근로자가 사다리를 고쳤다면 심각한 사고를 피할 수 있었음을 의미한다고 생각합니다.

하인리히는 보통 직원들이 사고의 원인이라고 결론을 내렸어요. 그는 거의 90퍼센트의 작업 사고들이 직원들의 안전하지 못한 결정 때문에 일어난다고 말했죠. 하지만, 오늘날 많은 사람들은 이것을 받아들이지 않습니다. 그들은 하인리히가 지나치게 많이 직

CHAPTER 04 | Attitude   31

원들에게 책임을 돌렸다고 생각해요. 그들은 형편없는 경영 시스템과 너무 오랫동안 일을 하는 것과 같은 다른 요인들도 사고를 일으킬 수 있다고 말합니다... 직원들의 실수뿐만이 아니라요.

workplace 명 작업장, 일터   consider 동 고찰하다, 고려하다
scientifically 부 과학적으로   industrial 형 산업의
safety 명 안전   expert 명 전문가   analyze 동 분석하다
category 명 범주   injury 명 부상   rate 명 비율; 속도
serious 형 심각한   fall off 떨어지다   ladder 명 사다리
conclude 동 결론을 내리다   unsafe 형 안전하지 못한
blame 동 ~에게 책임을 돌리다, ~를 탓하다   poor 형 형편없는
management 명 경영, 관리

1 강의의 주된 주제는 무엇인가?
  (A) 작업장 안전을 개선할 방법
  (B) 작업장 사고들에 관한 연구
  (C) 다양한 산업 내 위험한 직업들
  (D) 작업장에서 가장 흔한 부상들

2 교수는 두 번째 범주에 관해 무엇이라고 말하는가?
  (A) 그것은 가장 흔한 사고 범주이다.
  (B) 그것에는 작은 부상을 야기한 사고들이 포함된다.
  (C) 그것은 보통 위험한 작업 환경 때문에 발생한다.
  (D) 그것은 사고 건수가 가장 높다.

3 교수에 따르면, 330건의 사고들 중 심각한 부상은 얼마나 많이 발생하는가?
  (A) 1건
  (B) 29건
  (C) 30건
  (D) 300건

4 하인리히 법칙에 대한 교수의 태도는 무엇인가?
  (A) 그녀는 그가 한 연구의 양에 감명받았다.
  (B) 그녀는 직원들이 사고의 원인이라는 것에 동의한다.
  (C) 그녀는 큰 부상들은 예방될 수 있다고 생각한다.
  (D) 그녀는 더 많은 회사들이 그 법칙을 가르쳐야 한다고 생각한다.

강의의 일부를 다시 듣고 질문에 답하시오.
P: Heinrich concluded that employees are usually the cause of accidents. He said that almost 90 percent of work accidents happen because of employees' unsafe decisions. However, many people do not accept this today. They think that Heinrich blamed employees too much.

5 교수는 이렇게 말함으로써 무엇을 의미하는가:
  P: However, many people do not accept this today.
  (A) 오늘날 작업장에서의 사고는 덜 흔하다.
  (B) 고용주들은 종종 직원들의 안전에 대해 신경 쓰지 않는다.
  (C) 직원들이 항상 사고의 책임이 있는 것은 아니다.
  (D) 많은 회사들이 안전하지 않은 경영 관행을 가지고 있다.

Vocabulary Review
본문 p. 92

1 support   2 brainstorm   3 discourage
4 blame   5 unexpected   6 gradually
7 fair   8 agree with   9 nutrient
10 (C)   11 (A)   12 (D)
13 (B)   14 (C)

CHAPTER 05
Organization

Example
본문 p. 95

A. (C)   **B.** (B)

A.

Note-taking
Student's Problem
Tried to register for a class, but it was full
Advisor's Suggestion
Add your name to the waiting list

Listen to a conversation between a student and an academic advisor.

W: Hi, I was wondering if you could help me. You see, one of the classes I tried to register for was full yesterday.
M: It was? What's your number on the waiting list?
W: What? Oh, uh, I didn't know there was a waiting list...
M: Yes, when a class is full, students can put their names on a waiting list. That way, if someone drops the class, students on the waiting list can get in. It's an option you can select when you register online.
W: Oh, that must be the problem... I actually registered in person at the registrar's office with, um, Mr. Hanlon, I believe?
M: Well, he should have let you know about that... Anyway, it's not too late. You can still add your name to the list.
W: OK, thanks. I'll do that right away.

학생과 지도 교수 사이의 대화를 들으시오.
W: 안녕하세요, 저를 도와주실 수 있을지 궁금합니다. 그러니까, 제가 등록하려고 했던 수업 중 하나가 어제 다 찼거든요.
M: 그랬나요? 대기자 명단에서 학생의 번호가 몇 번인가요?
W: 네? 오, 어, 대기자 명단이 있는 줄 몰랐네요...

M: 네, 수업이 다 차면, 학생들은 대기자 명단에 이름을 올릴 수 있어요. 그렇게 하면, 누군가가 수업을 취소할 경우, 대기자 명단에 있는 학생들이 들어갈 수 있죠. 온라인으로 등록할 때 고를 수 있는 선택지예요.

W: 오, 그게 문제였군요... 저는 사실 학적과에서 직접 등록했는데요, 음, 아마 Hanlon씨?에게 한 것 같아요.

M: 음, 그분이 학생에게 그것에 대해 알려줬어야 했는데... 어쨌든, 아직 늦지 않았어요. 여전히 명단에 학생의 이름을 추가할 수 있어요.

W: 네, 감사해요. 바로 할게요.

register 동 등록하다   waiting list 대기자 명단   drop 동 취소하다
select 동 고르다; 선발하다

학생은 왜 Hanlon씨를 언급하는가?

(A) 그녀가 어떤 수업을 듣는 것에 관심이 있는지 나타내기 위해
(B) 그녀가 어떻게 대기자 명단에 관해 들었는지 설명하기 위해
(C) 그녀가 어떤 정보를 얻지 못했다는 것을 보여주기 위해
(D) 그녀가 명단에 이름을 올렸다는 것을 증명하기 위해

B.

Note-taking

Ascribed Status

: Decided when you are <u>born</u>
 e.g. A <u>prince</u> has a high status.

Achieved Status

: Based on your <u>effort</u>
 e.g. Oprah Winfrey has a high status.

Listen to part of a lecture in a sociology class.

P: In sociology, there are <u>two kinds of status</u>. There is ascribed status and achieved status.

First, there is ascribed status. This is decided when you are born. It includes being male or female, upper-class or lower-class, and so on. It is determined by factors like gender, race, and <u>family background</u>. A prince, for instance, has a high ascribed status because he is born into a royal family.

Second, let's consider achieved status. Achieved status is <u>based on your effort</u>. Oprah Winfrey is a good example. She was born a poor, black woman in the American South. But, she <u>worked hard to succeed</u> as a broadcaster. Eventually, she became a popular talk show host and producer. Her ascribed status was low, but she later had high <u>achieved status</u>.

사회학 강의의 일부를 들으시오.

P: 사회학에서, 지위에는 두 가지 종류가 있습니다. 귀속 지위와 성취 지위가 있죠.

첫째로, 귀속 지위가 있습니다. 이것은 여러분이 태어날 때 결정돼요. 그것에는 남성 또는 여성, 상류층 또는 하류층 등이 포함됩니다. 그것은 성별, 인종, 그리고 가정 환경과 같은 요인들에 의해 결정되죠. 예를 들어, 왕자는 왕실에서 태어났기 때문에 높은 귀속 지위를 가져요.

두 번째로, 성취 지위를 생각해 봅시다. 성취 지위는 여러분의 노력에 기반을 둡니다. 오프라 윈프리가 좋은 예시예요. 그녀는 미국 남부에서 가난한 흑인 여성으로 태어났어요. 하지만, 그녀는 방송인으로 성공하기 위해 열심히 노력했습니다. 결국, 그녀는 인기 있는 토크쇼 진행자이자 제작자가 되었죠. 그녀의 귀속 지위는 낮았지만, 후에 높은 성취 지위를 가지게 됐습니다.

sociology 명 사회학   status 명 지위   ascribed status 귀속 지위
achieved status 성취 지위   gender 명 성별   race 명 인종
family background 가정 환경   royal family 왕실
effort 명 노력, 수고   succeed 동 성공하다, 출세하다
broadcaster 명 방송인   host 명 진행자; 주인
producer 명 제작자, 생산자

교수는 강의를 어떻게 구성하는가?

(A) 시간이 지남에 따라 사회적 지위가 어떻게 변했는지 이야기함으로써
(B) 개념들을 소개하고 예시들을 제공함으로써
(C) 세계적으로 유명한 사람들의 삶을 묘사함으로써
(D) 특정 개념의 중요성을 강조함으로써

Listening Practice 1   본문 p. 97

1 (C)   **2** (D)   **3** (B)

Note-taking

Student's Problem

Dr. Cooper can't give a <u>talk</u> at the dinner party.
→ Needs to find a <u>new</u> <u>person</u>

Professor's Solution

Professor Daniels will be able to do that.
→ Has been <u>teaching</u> for a long time

Listen to a conversation between a student and a professor.

S: Do you have a minute, Professor Taylor? I need your advice about <u>the department dinner party</u>.

P: Sure, Ellen, what's the problem?

S: ¹Well, Dr. Cooper <u>was supposed to give</u> a talk at the dinner, but now he can't come. He's, um, <u>attending a conference</u> that day.

P: I see. Have you found someone else yet?

S: No, and I only have three days left to find a new person.

P: Hmm... Have you considered <u>not having the talk</u> at all? That might be <u>the easiest solution</u>.

S: Well, I thought of that, but I'm worried that the students will be disappointed. They're <u>expecting to hear</u> a talk.

P: I understand. What about Professor Daniels? She

might be available.

S: Do you think she can prepare a talk in the next three days?

P: That depends... Um, what's the talk about, anyway?

S: ²Um, Dr. Cooper was going to talk about his experience as a teacher.

P: Professor Daniels will be able to do that, don't you think? She's been teaching for a long time... Would you like me to ask her for you?

S: Thank you, Professor. But, uh, maybe I should ask her myself.

P: Very good. I believe she's in her office right now... ³Do you know where her office is?

S: Yes, uh, I actually took one of her classes last semester. So, I know where it is. Thank you again, Professor.

학생과 교수 사이의 대화를 들으시오.

S: 잠깐 시간 있으신가요, Taylor 교수님? 학과 만찬회에 관해 교수님의 조언이 필요해서요.

P: 물론이지, Ellen, 무엇이 문제니?

S: 음, Cooper 박사님께서 만찬회 때 강연을 하시기로 되어 있었는데, 이제 오실 수 없게 되었어요. 그분이, 음, 그날 학회에 참석하시거든요.

P: 그렇구나. 다른 사람을 아직 못 찾았니?

S: 네, 그리고 저는 새로운 분을 찾는 데 3일밖에 남지 않았어요.

P: 흠... 강연을 아예 안 하는 것은 생각해봤니? 그게 가장 쉬운 해결책일 수도 있단다.

S: 음, 저도 그것에 대해 생각해봤는데, 학생들이 실망할까 봐 걱정이에요. 그들은 강연을 듣는 것을 기대하고 있거든요.

P: 알겠다. Daniels 교수님은 어떠니? 가능하실 수도 있어.

S: 교수님께서 3일 안에 강연을 준비하실 수 있을 것 같으신가요?

P: 상황에 따라 다르겠지... 음, 그나저나, 강연이 무엇에 관한 거니?

S: 음, Cooper 박사님께서 선생님으로서의 경험에 대해 말씀하실 예정이었어요.

P: Daniels 교수님은 그걸 하실 수 있을 거야, 그렇게 생각하지 않니? 오랫동안 가르쳐 오셨거든... 내가 대신해서 여쭤봐 줄까?

S: 감사합니다, 교수님. 하지만, 어, 제가 그분께 직접 여쭤봐야 할 것 같아요.

P: 좋아. 지금 사무실에 계실 거야... 사무실은 어디 있는지 아니?

S: 네, 어, 제가 사실 지난 학기에 그분의 수업 중 하나를 들었거든요. 그래서, 그곳이 어디에 있는지 알아요. 다시 한번 감사합니다, 교수님.

department 명 학과, 부서   dinner party 만찬회, 디너파티
talk 명 강연, 연설   attend 동 참석하다   conference 명 학회
solution 명 해결책, 해법   disappointed 형 실망한

---

1 학생의 문제는 무엇인가?
   (A) 그녀는 교수를 만날 수 없다.
   (B) 그녀는 중요한 저녁 식사에 빠져야 한다.
   (C) 그녀는 발표자를 찾아야 한다.
   (D) 그녀는 강연을 준비할 시간이 없다.

2 Daniels 교수에 대한 교수의 의견은 무엇인가?
   (A) 그는 그녀의 강의를 즐겨 듣는다.
   (B) 그는 그녀가 너무 바쁠 것이라고 생각한다.
   (C) 그는 그녀가 경험이 적은 것을 걱정한다.
   (D) 그는 그녀가 일을 잘 할 수 있다고 생각한다.

3 학생은 왜 지난 학기의 수업을 언급하는가?
   (A) 강의가 너무 어려웠다고 불평하기 위해
   (B) 그녀가 사무실을 어떻게 찾는지 안다고 말하기 위해
   (C) 그녀가 주제에 대해 잘 알고 있음을 나타내기 위해
   (D) 강연을 듣는 것에 대한 그녀의 관심을 설명하기 위해

Listening Practice 2   본문 p.99

1 (C)   2 (C)   3 (B)   4 (D)

Note-taking
Earth's Geological Structure
- Crust: Contains rocks and soil
- Mantle: Mostly solid rock, but constantly moving
- Outer core: A liquid-like material
- Inner core: Heavy and solid

Listen to part of a lecture in a geology class.

P: We live on Earth's surface, so we probably do not think about what is underneath very often. But, uh, Earth's structure is important because it makes life on Earth possible. ¹So, let's learn about Earth's geological structure and its three different layers... the crust, the mantle, and the core.

Let's start from the outside. The outer layer of Earth is the crust. The crust is the layer that we can see. It contains rocks and soil, and this is where all of the plants grow. ²But surprisingly, it's actually quite small. Uh, it makes up only around 1.4 percent of Earth.

Next is the mantle. The mantle is mostly solid rock. It is around 2,900 kilometers thick. ³The mantle is heavier than the crust. Thus, the crust floats on the mantle like oil floats on water... uh, because oil is lighter than water. Um, even though the mantle is mostly solid, it is constantly moving. Natural forces, such as gravity, cause the rock to move. Some sections of the rock go over or under the others. When they rub together, this creates heat. So it can be very hot, and the rock can turn to liquid. When this happens, the hot liquid rock can move up to the surface... like in a volcanic eruption.

Lastly, there is the core. The core is in the center of Earth. The pressure in the core is very high. So, this makes the core extremely hot. Some parts of the core are as hot as the Sun! The core can be divided into two parts... the outer core and the inner core. The outer core consists of a liquid-like material. But, the inner core is heavy and solid. The inner core is mostly composed of heavy metals, mainly iron. [4]However, everything we know about the core has been learned indirectly. We cannot examine the core directly because it's too deep to reach. And to tell you the truth, I don't think we ever will...

지질학 강의의 일부를 들으시오.

P: 우리는 지구의 표면에 살고 있기 때문에, 아마도 그 아래에 무엇이 있는지에 대해서는 자주 생각하지 않을 것입니다. 하지만, 어, 지구의 구조는 지구상에 생명체가 있는 것을 가능하게 하기 때문에 중요하죠. 그러면, 지구의 지질 구조와 그것의 세 가지 다른 층에 대해 배워봅시다... 지각, 맨틀, 그리고 핵에 대해서요.

밖에서부터 시작하죠. 지구의 바깥쪽 층은 지각입니다. 지각은 우리가 볼 수 있는 층이에요. 그것에는 바위와 흙이 있는데, 여기가 모든 식물들이 자라는 곳이죠. 하지만 놀랍게도, 그것은 사실 꽤 작답니다. 어, 그것은 지구의 약 1.4%만을 차지해요.

다음은 맨틀입니다. 맨틀은 대부분 단단한 암석이에요. 그것의 두께는 약 2,900킬로미터입니다. 맨틀은 지각보다 무겁죠. 따라서, 어, 기름이 물보다 가벼워서 물 위에 뜨는 것처럼 지각은 맨틀 위에 떠 있습니다... 음, 맨틀이 대부분 고체이기는 하지만, 그것은 끊임없이 움직이고 있습니다. 중력과 같은 자연의 힘이 그 암석을 움직이게 하거든요. 그 암석의 어떤 부분들은 다른 부분들 위에 또는 아래에 있습니다. 그것들이 서로 마찰하면, 이것은 열을 발생시킵니다. 그래서 그것은 매우 뜨겁게 될 수 있고, 바위가 액체로 변할 수도 있죠. 이것이 일어나면, 뜨거운 액체 암석은 표면 쪽으로 위로 이동할 수 있습니다... 화산 폭발과 같은 것으로요.

마지막으로, 핵이 있습니다. 핵은 지구의 중심에 있죠. 핵 내부의 압력은 매우 높습니다. 그래서, 이것은 핵을 극도로 뜨겁게 만들죠. 핵의 어떤 부분들은 태양만큼 뜨겁습니다! 핵은 두 부분으로 나눠질 수 있는데요... 외핵과 내핵이에요. 외핵은 액체 같은 물질로 구성되어 있어요. 하지만, 내핵은 무겁고 단단합니다. 내핵은 대부분 중금속, 주로 철로 이루어져 있어요. 하지만, 우리가 핵에 대해 알고 있는 모든 것은 간접적으로 알게 된 것이에요. 핵에 닿기에는 그것이 너무 깊이 있어서 직접 조사할 수 없거든요. 그리고 사실대로 말하자면, 저는 우리가 결코 할 수 없을 것이라고 생각해요...

underneath 囲 ~의 아래에, 밑에　structure 명 구조
geological 형 지질(학)의　crust 명 지각　mantle 명 맨틀
core 명 핵　mostly 囲 대부분의, 주로　solid 형 단단한; 명 고체
float 동 뜨다, 떠다니다　constantly 囲 끊임없이　gravity 명 중력
rub 동 마찰하다, 문지르다　volcanic eruption 화산 폭발
outer core 외핵　inner core 내핵　heavy metal 중금속
indirectly 囲 간접적으로　examine 동 조사하다

1 강의의 주된 주제는 무엇인가?
　(A) 지구가 다양한 층으로 구성된 이유
　(B) 지구의 표면이 어떻게 생명체가 있는 것을 가능하게 하는지
　(C) 지구의 지질 구조
　(D) 지구 표면의 구성

2 강의에 따르면, 지각에 대한 설명으로 옳은 것은?
　(A) 그것은 사람의 눈에는 보이지 않는다.
　(B) 그것은 단단한 암석으로 이루어져 있다.
　(C) 그것은 지구에서의 비중이 아주 작다.
　(D) 그것은 바다에 있는 것보다 육지에 있는 것의 두께가 더 두껍다.

3 교수는 왜 기름과 물을 언급하는가?
　(A) 두께의 차이에 대한 이유를 제공하기 위해
　(B) 두 층의 관계를 설명하기 위해
　(C) 맨틀이 항상 움직이고 있다는 것을 보여주기 위해
　(D) 층의 높은 온도를 강조하기 위해

4 지구의 핵에 대한 교수의 의견은 무엇인가?
　(A) 두 부분은 규모가 아마 같을 것이다.
　(B) 그것에는 과학자들이 생각하는 것보다 더 많은 성분이 포함되어 있다.
　(C) 그 안에 있는 물질들은 매우 가치가 크다.
　(D) 그것을 직접 연구하는 것은 불가능할 것이다.

Listening Practice 3　　본문 p. 101

1 (A)　　2 (C)　　3 (B)

Note-taking

Student's Problem
University writing is different from high school.

Professor's Suggestion
• Decide on the main topic → Write an outline
• Make a clear plan
• Attend my writing workshop

Listen to a conversation between a student and a professor.

S: Hi, Professor Brown. I have something I need to talk to you about.
P: No problem. My door is always open.
S: Thanks, Professor. [1]Well, the problem is... I don't know how to start writing my paper. University writing is so different from writing in high school.
P: Yes, that's a common problem for first-year students. [2]Um, let me give you some suggestions.
S: I'd really appreciate it, Professor.
P: [2]Yes, so, the first thing is to decide on the main topic of your paper. Then, write an outline. That way, you can always remember what's important.
S: That's interesting... Um, what else should I do?
P: [2]OK, next, make sure that you have a clear plan...

S: What do you mean by a clear plan?

P: ²Well, I'm saying that you should plan your time well. If you don't schedule time to work on your paper, you may not finish in time.

S: I see. OK...

P: ²And lastly, if you ever feel confused again, come see me right away or speak to the other students in class. I also suggest showing your first draft to a couple of other people. You can ask for their opinions. This can help you see things differently.

S: I like that, Professor. Thank you.

P: ³Why don't you attend my writing workshop? I have plenty more advice. So, it could be very helpful.

S: Definitely. Can I sign up right away?

학생과 교수 사이의 대화를 들으시오.

S: 안녕하세요, Brown 교수님. 교수님과 이야기할 것이 있어요.

P: 물론이지. 나는 항상 맞이할 준비가 되어 있단다.

S: 감사합니다, 교수님. 음, 문제는... 보고서 쓰는 것을 어떻게 시작해야 할지 모르겠다는 거예요. 대학 글쓰기는 고등학교에서의 글쓰기와 너무 다르네요.

P: 그래, 그건 1학년 학생들에게 흔한 문제지. 음, 네게 몇 가지 조언을 해주마.

S: 정말 감사합니다, 교수님.

P: 그래, 자, 첫 번째는 보고서의 주된 주제를 결정하는 거야. 그리고 나서, 개요를 쓰렴. 그렇게 하면, 네가 무엇이 중요한지 항상 기억할 수 있을 거란다.

S: 흥미롭군요... 음, 제가 무엇을 더 해야 하나요?

P: 좋아, 다음은, 명확한 계획이 있는지 확실히 해두는 거야...

S: 명확한 계획이라는 게 무슨 뜻인가요?

P: 음, 내 말은 네가 시간을 잘 계획해야 한다는 거야. 만약 네가 네 보고서를 쓸 시간을 정해두지 않는다면, 제시간에 끝내지 못할 수도 있거든.

S: 그렇군요. 알겠습니다...

P: 그리고 마지막으로, 만약 네가 다시 혼란스러워지면, 즉시 나를 보러 오거나 수업의 다른 학생들과 이야기해 보렴. 네가 쓴 첫 초안을 다른 사람들 몇 명에게 보여주는 것도 추천해. 그들의 의견을 물어볼 수 있지. 이건 네가 보는 관점을 달리 하는데 도움이 될 거란다.

S: 좋네요, 교수님. 감사합니다.

P: 내 글쓰기 워크숍에 참석하는 건 어떠니? 조언이 더 많이 있단다. 그래서, 그것은 매우 도움이 될 수도 있어.

S: 물론이죠. 지금 바로 신청할 수 있나요?

---

suggestion 명 조언, 제안   in time 제시간에
confused 형 혼란스러운, 혼란스러워하는   opinion 명 의견
workshop 명 워크숍   plenty 부 많이   sign up 신청하다, 참가하다

---

1 학생의 문제는 무엇인가?
   (A) 그녀는 보고서를 쓰는 데 도움이 필요하다.
   (B) 그녀는 다른 학교로 옮기고 싶어 한다.
   (C) 그녀는 수업 내용을 이해하지 못한다.
   (D) 그녀는 과제에 대한 파일 몇 개를 잃어버렸다.

2 교수는 어떻게 학생을 돕는가?
   (A) 글을 작성할 주제들을 추천함으로써
   (B) 다른 사람들의 작업물을 예시로 보여줌으로써
   (C) 따라 할 세부적인 조언들을 제공함으로써
   (D) 다른 학생의 경험을 이야기함으로써

3 워크숍에 참석하는 것에 대한 학생의 태도는 무엇인가?
   (A) 그녀는 그것이 도움이 될지 확신하지 못한다.
   (B) 그녀는 기꺼이 그것에 참여할 것이다.
   (C) 그녀는 그것이 시간이 너무 많이 걸릴 것이라고 생각한다.
   (D) 그녀는 그것에 대해 다른 사람들에게 말해주고 싶어 한다.

Listening Practice 4   본문 p.103

1 (A)   2 (B)   3 (B)   4 (C)

Note-taking
Different Western Calendars
- Roman calendar: Based on the moon's cycle
- Julian calendar: An extra day added to February every third year
- Gregorian calendar: An extra day once every four years

Listen to part of a lecture in a history class.

P: As you probably know, the Gregorian calendar is the most commonly used calendar today. Um, it was first introduced in 1582. ¹But before this, the Western world used different calendars for more than 1,600 years. I want to take some time this morning to look at how they developed.

The first one was the Roman calendar. It had 355 days in a year. This was because it was based on the moon's cycle, which is how long it takes for the moon to go around Earth. However, the calendar's length was shorter than a solar year... That's, uh, the period of time for Earth to make a complete circle around the Sun. ²This created problems because the calendar did not match the seasons of the year. People got very confused as a result. For instance, farmers sometimes celebrated harvest festivals in the middle of winter instead of in the fall.

So, in 46 BC, the Roman dictator Julius Caesar introduced a new system known as the Julian calendar. ³The purpose of the Julian calendar was to make sure that the calendar year matched the solar year. So, he created a calendar with 365 days, uh, by including an extra day, February 29. This extra day was added to February every third year. Um, this was because the Romans believed that the solar year lasted for 365.25 days. Unfortunately, they made a small mistake... It is actually 365.242 days. As a result, this calendar did not match the seasons, either.

This issue was finally solved by the Gregorian calendar. It includes an extra day once every four years instead of every three years. ⁴This calendar was named for Pope Gregory XIII, who ordered a new calendar system in 1582. And it's a good thing he did... Otherwise, we'd probably still be using a less accurate calendar today.

역사학 강의의 일부를 들으시오.

P: 여러분이 아마 알고 있듯이, 그레고리력은 오늘날 가장 흔하게 사용되는 달력입니다. 음, 그것은 1582년에 처음 도입되었어요. 하지만 이것 이전에, 서구 세계는 1,600년 넘게 다른 달력들을 사용했죠. 저는 그것들이 어떻게 발전했는지에 대해 오늘 아침에 시간을 갖고 살펴보고자 합니다.

첫 번째는 로마력입니다. 그것은 1년에 355일이 있었는데요. 이는 그것이 달이 지구 주위를 도는 데 걸리는 기간인 달의 주기에 기초했기 때문이죠. 하지만, 달력의 길이는 태양년보다 짧았는데요... 그것은, 어, 지구가 태양 주위를 완전히 돌 때까지의 기간이죠. 그 달력은 한 해의 계절들과 일치하지 않았기 때문에 이는 문제를 일으켰어요. 그 결과 사람들은 매우 혼란스러워했죠. 예를 들어, 농부들은 때때로 가을 대신 한겨울에 추수 감사제를 기념하기도 했어요.

그래서, 기원전 46년에는, 로마의 독재자 율리우스 카이사르가 율리우스력으로 알려진 새로운 체계를 도입했어요. 율리우스력의 목적은 달력의 일년이 태양년과 일치하도록 하는 것이었죠. 그래서, 그는 2월 29일이라는 하루를 더 포함시킴으로써, 어, 365일이 있는 달력을 만들었죠. 이 추가적인 하루는 3년마다 2월에 추가되었어요. 음, 이것은 로마인들이 태양년이 365.25일 동안 지속된다고 믿었기 때문이죠. 안타깝게도, 그들은 작은 실수를 했습니다... 그건 실제로는 365.242일이거든요. 결과적으로, 이 달력도 계절들과 일치하지는 않았어요.

이 문제는 그레고리력에 의해 마침내 해결되었어요. 그것은 3년마다가 아닌 4년마다 한 번씩 추가적인 하루를 포함시켰어요. 이 달력은 교황 그레고리오 13세의 이름을 따서 이름 지어졌는데, 그는 1582년에 새로운 달력 체계를 명령했죠. 그리고 그가 그렇게 한 것은 다행스러운 일이에요... 그렇지 않았다면, 우리는 오늘날에도 여전히 덜 정확한 달력을 사용하고 있었을 겁니다.

Gregorian calendar 그레고리력 commonly 「튀」 흔하게, 흔히
introduce 「동」 도입하다; 소개하다 Western 「형」 서구의, 서양의
Roman calendar 로마력 cycle 「명」 주기; 순환
be based on ~에 기초하다 solar year 태양년
period of time 기간 match 「동」 일치하다 celebrate 「동」 기념하다
harvest festival 추수 감사제 dictator 「명」 독재자
Julian calendar 율리우스력 pope 「명」 교황

1 강의의 주된 주제는 무엇인가?

(A) 서양 달력들의 발전
(B) 율리우스력의 장점들
(C) 달력이 오랫동안 사용된 이유들

(D) 태양력과 음력의 차이점

2 교수는 율리우스력을 어떻게 소개하는가?

(A) 계절들 간의 차이점에 대해 말함으로써
(B) 이전 달력에 대한 문제를 이야기함으로써
(C) 일년의 일수를 세는 과정을 설명함으로써
(D) 율리우스 카이사르의 업적들을 묘사함으로써

3 율리우스 카이사르는 왜 새로운 달력을 도입했는가?

(A) 로마인들 사이에서 더 많은 인기를 얻기 위해
(B) 태양년과 달력의 일년을 일치시키기 위해
(C) 로마인들에게 더 긴 휴일을 제공하기 위해
(D) 농부들에게 식량을 재배할 시간을 더 많이 주기 위해

4 교황 그레고리오 13세에 대한 교수의 의견은 무엇인가?

(A) 그는 시스템을 바꾸지 말았어야 했다.
(B) 그는 율리우스력을 이해하지 못했다.
(C) 그는 중요한 개선을 했다.
(D) 그는 더 많은 존경을 받았어야 했다.

---

iBT Listening Test 1

본문 p. 105

1 (A)   2 (C)   3 (B)   4 (C)

Note-taking

Student's Question

Wants to know if I've met all of the graduation requirements

Employee's Answer

You haven't completed a required class for your major.
→ Take the class this semester, and sign up right away

Listen to a conversation between a student and a registrar's office employee.

M: Excuse me, is this the registrar's office? I was hoping you could help me.

W: Yes, of course. What's your question?

M: ¹It's about the graduation requirements. Um, I'm not sure if I've met all of them. I want to be sure because this is supposed to be my last year here.

W: All right. ²If you give me your student ID, I can check on my computer.

M: Oh, I don't have my ID right now. It's back at my dorm room. But, um, I know my student ID number. It's, uh, 1860-4112.

W: ²That's fine. OK, so... I see here that you've paid all your class fees. There's no problem there.

M: Yes, I made all the payments at the beginning of the semester.

W: That's good. Hmm... ⁴However, it seems you haven't completed a required class for your major.

M: Oh, I thought so. I don't remember which class it is, though. Is it a history class?

W: Actually, it's a class on government.

M: Oh, right. ³I think I planned to take it last year, but I was busy. I'm on the university's football team.

W: I understand. You must have been busy with practices and games... Anyway, you can still take the class this semester if you like. I guess it will be your last chance.

M: Right. I hope the class isn't full yet.

W: Let me see... Yes, there are a few spots left, but you should sign up right away. The class could fill up quickly.

M: OK. I'll sign up right now, then.

학생과 학적과 직원 사이의 대화를 들으시오.

M: 실례합니다, 여기가 학적과인가요? 혹시 저를 도와주실 수 있나 해서요.

W: 네, 물론이죠. 무엇이 궁금하신가요?

M: 졸업 요건에 관한 건데요. 음, 제가 그것들을 모두 충족했는지 확실하지 않아서요. 올해가 이곳에서의 마지막 해야야 해서 저는 확실히 알고 싶어요.

W: 알겠습니다. 학생증을 주시면, 제 컴퓨터로 확인할 수 있어요.

M: 아, 제가 지금 학생증이 없어요. 저기 제 기숙사 방에 있거든요. 하지만, 음, 제 학생증 번호는 알아요. 어, 1860-4112예요.

W: 괜찮습니다. 좋아요, 자... 여기 보니까 수업료는 다 내셨네요. 거기에는 문제가 없습니다.

M: 네, 학기 초에 모든 지불금을 냈거든요.

W: 잘하셨네요. 흠... 그런데, 전공의 한 필수 수업을 마치지 못한 것 같네요.

M: 아, 그럴 줄 알았어요. 그런데, 어떤 수업인지 기억이 안 나네요. 역사학 수업인가요?

W: 사실, 그것은 정부에 관한 수업이에요.

M: 오, 맞아요. 제가 작년에 그것을 들으려고 계획했던 것 같은데, 바빴어요. 저는 대학의 축구팀에 있거든요.

W: 이해해요. 연습과 경기들로 바빴겠어요... 어쨌든, 원하신다면 이번 학기에 아직 그 수업을 들을 수 있어요. 이게 학생의 마지막 기회가 될 것 같군요.

M: 맞아요. 아직 강의가 다 차지 않았으면 좋겠네요.

W: 어디 봅시다... 네, 자리가 몇 개 남았는데, 바로 신청하셔야 해요. 그 수업은 금방 찰 수 있거든요.

M: 좋아요. 그럼, 지금 바로 신청할게요.

---

requirement ⓝ 요건, 필요조건   dorm ⓝ 기숙사   class fee 수업료
payment ⓝ 지불(금), 납입   major ⓝ 전공   required ⓐ 필수의
government ⓝ 정부   spot ⓝ 자리; 점

1 학생은 왜 학적과를 찾아가는가?
  (A) 몇 가지 요건에 대해 문의하기 위해
  (B) 새 학생증을 요청하기 위해
  (C) 학부 건물로 가는 길을 알아보기 위해
  (D) 수업에 대한 지불금을 내기 위해

2 직원은 어떻게 학생을 돕는가?
  (A) 그에게 새로운 신분증을 줌으로써
  (B) 몇 가지 지침을 인쇄함으로써
  (C) 정보를 검색함으로써
  (D) 그가 양식을 작성하는 것을 도와줌으로써

3 학생은 왜 대학의 축구팀을 언급하는가?
  (A) 그가 운동을 잘한다는 것을 암시하기 위해
  (B) 그가 왜 수업을 들을 수 없었는지를 설명하기 위해
  (C) 그가 활동에 참여하기를 원한다는 것을 확실히 하기 위해
  (D) 졸업식에 불참한 이유를 대기 위해

대화의 일부를 다시 듣고 질문에 답하시오.

W: However, it seems you haven't completed a required class for your major.

M: Oh, I thought so. I don't remember which class it is, though.

4 학생은 이렇게 말함으로써 무엇을 의미하는가:
  M: Oh, I thought so. I don't remember which class it is, though.
  (A) 그는 수업이 필수적이어야 한다고 생각한다.
  (B) 그는 자신이 수업을 마친 것을 기억해냈다.
  (C) 그는 자신이 수업을 듣지 않았다는 것을 이미 알고 있었다.
  (D) 그는 전에 같은 정보를 들은 적이 있다.

---

iBT Listening Test 2   본문 p. 108

1 (C)   2 (D)   3 (A)   4 (C)   5 (B)

Note-taking

Cause of City Planning in the US

Large increase in the populations of many cities
→ Needed to improve living conditions

What Government Did
- Improved public health and safety
  e.g. Built pipes for clean water, put up lights for safer streets
- Built housing that was not expensive
- Built outdoor areas for leisure and recreation
  e.g. Playgrounds, sports centers, parks

Listen to part of a lecture in a city planning class.

P: OK... In the past, most cities in the United States were created naturally by settlers. This means that people built structures wherever it was convenient for them. As you can imagine, this was very unorganized and random. ¹But in the 19th century, as the Industrial Revolution began, the US government started planning cities. Let's look at how this happened.

²Well, one of the key factors that led to this

was the large increase in the populations of many cities. This happened because millions of immigrants and people from the countryside moved to cities. Uh, they wanted to live close to the factories that were looking for people to work. However, there were not enough houses and facilities for all of the new people. Cities became dirty, crowded, and dangerous.

³So, what did the government do to improve living conditions? Well, it first tried to improve public health and safety. For instance, many people got sick from drinking dirty water, so the government built pipes for clean water. Also, um, streets were unsafe at night because it was dark. So, the government put up lights to make the streets safer... ³What else? Well, many of the people moving to the city were not rich. So the government had to build housing that was not expensive. All of these things required planning. Government officials had to decide where to build everything in an organized way.

³Now, was this all? No, the government also built outdoor areas for leisure and recreation. ⁴People needed somewhere to enjoy breaks from work, to get together, and to exercise. So, the government used public spending not only for necessities but also for leisure and recreation... Therefore, it built playgrounds for children and, uh, sports centers for adults. It also used a lot of land for parks. The most famous example of this is Central Park in New York City, which first opened in 1858. ⁵It cost millions of dollars just to get the land. However, Central Park was hugely successful. It has become a place for people to escape the busy city environment. It's also now a major tourist attraction.

도시 계획학 강의의 일부를 들으시오.

P: 자... 과거에, 미국의 대부분의 도시들은 이주민들에 의해 자연스럽게 만들어졌습니다. 이는 사람들이 그들에게 편리한 곳이면 어디든 건축물들을 지었다는 것을 의미하죠. 여러분이 상상할 수 있듯이, 이것은 매우 체계적이지 않고 마구잡이였습니다. 그러나 19세기에, 산업혁명이 시작되면서, 미국 정부는 도시를 계획하기 시작했어요. 이런 일이 어떻게 일어났는지 살펴봅시다.

음, 이것을 이끈 주요 요인들 중 하나는 많은 도시에서 인구가 크게 증가한 것이었습니다. 이것은 수백만 명의 이민자들과 시골 지역에서 온 사람들이 도시로 이주하면서 발생했어요. 어, 그들은 일할 사람을 찾고 있던 공장들 근처에 살고 싶어 했죠. 하지만, 새로운 사람들 모두를 위한 집과 시설이 충분하지 않았어요. 도시들은 더럽고, 붐비고, 위험해졌죠.

그래서, 정부는 생활 여건을 개선하기 위해 무엇을 했을까요? 음, 그것은 처음에 공중위생과 안전을 개선하려고 노력했습니다. 예를 들어, 많은 사람들이 더러운 물을 마셔서 병에 걸리자, 정부는 깨끗한 물을 위해 배관을 설치했어요. 또한, 음, 거리가 밤에 어두웠기 때문에 위험했는데요. 그래서, 정부는 거리를 더 안전하게 만들기 위해 전등을 설치했어요... 또 뭐가 있을까요? 음, 도시로 이주하는 사람들 중 다수는 부유하지 않았습니다. 그래서 정부는 비싸지 않은 주택을 지어야 했죠. 이 모든 것들은 계획이 필요했습니다. 국가 공무원들은 체계적인 방법으로 모든 것을 어디에 지을지 결정해야 했어요.

자, 이게 다였을까요? 아뇨, 정부는 또한 여가와 오락을 위한 야외 공간들을 만들었어요. 사람들은 일에서 벗어나 휴식을 즐기고, 함께 모이고, 운동을 할 수 있는 장소가 필요했죠. 그래서, 정부는 공공 지출을 필수적인 것뿐만 아니라 여가와 오락에 대해서도 사용했습니다... 따라서, 그들은 아이들을 위한 놀이터와, 어, 어른들을 위한 스포츠 센터를 만들었어요. 그들은 또한 공원을 위해 많은 땅을 사용했죠. 이것의 가장 유명한 예는 1858년에 처음 개장한 뉴욕의 센트럴 파크입니다. 그 땅을 얻는 데에만 수백만 달러가 들었어요. 하지만, 센트럴 파크는 매우 성공적이었어요. 그곳은 사람들이 바쁜 도시 환경에서 벗어날 수 있는 장소가 되었죠. 그곳은 이제 주요 관광 명소이기도 합니다.

settler 명 이주민, 정착민   convenient 형 편리한
random 형 마구잡이의, 무작위의   Industrial Revolution 산업혁명
population 명 인구   immigrant 명 이민자
countryside 명 시골 지역   facility 명 시설
crowded 형 붐비는   living conditions 생활 여건
public health 공중위생   unsafe 형 위험한, 안전하지 못한
housing 명 주택   government official 국가 공무원
leisure 명 여가   recreation 명 오락, 레크리에이션
public spending 공공 지출   necessities 명 필수적인 것, 필수품
successful 형 성공적인, 성공한   attraction 명 명소, 관광지

1 강의는 주로 무엇에 관한 것인가?

(A) 도시에 사는 것의 장점들
(B) 미국 수도의 건설
(C) 미국 도시 계획의 발전
(D) 산업 혁명의 영향

2 교수에 따르면, 미국 도시들의 인구는 왜 증가했는가?

(A) 도시들은 공장을 짓기 위해 이민자들이 필요했다.
(B) 도시 밖의 집들이 너무 비쌌다.
(C) 이민자들이 집을 살 수 있는 돈을 받았다.
(D) 근로자들이 일자리를 찾기 위해 다른 지역에서 왔다.

3 강의는 어떻게 구성되었는가?

(A) 교수가 질문들을 하고 그것들에 답한다.
(B) 교수가 겪은 개인적인 경험에 대해 말한다.
(C) 교수가 이상적인 도시의 특징들을 묘사한다.
(D) 교수가 두 개의 다른 도시들을 비교 및 대조한다.

4 교수는 정부에 관해 무엇을 암시하는가?

(A) 그들은 처음에는 공장을 많이 허용하지 않았다.
(B) 그들은 도시로 이주하는 사람들의 수를 통제했다.
(C) 그들은 기본적으로 필요한 것 이상을 제공하려고 노력했다.
(D) 그들은 더 많은 관광객들을 끌어들이기 위해 공원들을 지었다.

5 센트럴 파크에 대한 교수의 의견은 무엇인가?

(A) 그것은 짓기가 어려웠다.
(B) 그것은 비싼 비용을 들일 가치가 있었다.
(C) 그것은 개선이 조금 필요하다.
(D) 그것은 환경에 좋다.

Vocabulary Review
본문 p. 112

1 status
2 float
3 crowded
4 leisure
5 attraction
6 celebrate
7 successful
8 payment
9 in time
10 (B)
11 (C)
12 (B)
13 (A)
14 (D)

CHAPTER 06
Connecting Contents

Example
본문 p. 115

A. Yes: (A), (C) No: (B), (D)
B. Yes: (B), (D) No: (A), (C)

A.
Note-taking
Student's Question
Finished my summary → What's next?

Things to Discuss in Essay
- What the book can teach us in the historical context
- How the book was written

Listen to a conversation between a student and a professor.

P: Hi, Beth. Did you have a question about writing your essay?
S: Well, Professor Adams, I finished my summary of the book, *The Blind City*. But, I'm not sure what to do next.
P: Yes, well... [A]A summary is necessary, but the essay should also talk about what the book can teach us.
S: Um, like the book's main message?
P: Yes, but also about the historical context. The book was written in 1929. So, what was happening during that time in America's history?
S: OK. [C]I should do more research about that, then.
P: Exactly. Your essay should explain why the book was important for, uh, readers back then...
S: All right... Is there anything else I should include?
P: You should also discuss how the book was written. Um, like what the writer did to make his book effective.

학생과 교수 사이의 대화를 들으시오.

P: 안녕, Beth. 에세이를 쓰는 것에 대해 궁금한 것이 있었니?
S: 음, Adams 교수님, 저는 '블라인드 시티'라는 책의 요약은 끝냈어요. 그런데, 다음에 무엇을 해야 할지 모르겠어요.
P: 그래, 음... 요약도 필요하지만, 에세이는 책이 우리에게 무엇을 가르쳐 줄 수 있는지에 대해서도 이야기해야 한단다.
S: 음, 책의 주된 메시지 같은 것이요?
P: 그래, 하지만 역사적 맥락에 대해서도 말이야. 그 책은 1929년에 쓰였지. 그렇다면, 미국 역사에서 그 기간 동안 무슨 일이 일어나고 있었을까?
S: 네. 그렇다면, 제가 그것에 대해 더 많은 조사를 해야겠군요.
P: 그래. 네 에세이는 그 책이 왜 그 당시 독자들에게, 어, 중요했는지 설명해 줘야 해...
S: 알겠습니다... 제가 포함해야 할 또 다른 것이 있을까요?
P: 그 책이 어떻게 쓰였는지에 대해서도 이야기해야 한단다. 음, 저자가 책이 유용하도록 하기 위해 무엇을 했는지처럼 말이야.

summary 명 요약   context 명 맥락
research 명 조사, 연구   writer 명 저자, 작가

다음의 항목이 학생이 그녀의 에세이를 쓸 때 해야 할 일로 언급된 것인지를 표시하시오. 각 항목에 적절한 칸을 클릭하시오.

	예	아니오
(A) 책의 요약을 포함하기	V	
(B) 책을 다른 책들과 비교하기		V
(C) 미국 역사를 조사하기	V	
(D) 저자의 삶을 서술하기		V

B.
Note-taking
Effects of Globalization
- Positive: Can easily travel anywhere, make products cheaply and deliver them quickly
- Negative: Bad for the environment and helps spread ideas like terrorism

Listen to part of a lecture in a sociology class.

P: Nowadays, people around the world are connected to each other in many ways... This happened because of a process known as globalization.
There are both positive and negative effects of this. For instance, people can easily travel anywhere in the world. [B]Also, companies can make products cheaply and deliver them to customers more quickly than before. And advanced technologies help people communicate and enjoy culture... All of these, um, are positive. But, globalization can have negative effects, too. Um, for example, many people travel on airplanes and companies move products on ships. [C]This is bad for the environment because of pollution. [D]And, um, globalization doesn't just help people spread good ideas. It helps them spread bad ones too, like terrorism.

사회학 강의의 일부를 들으시오.

P: 오늘날, 전 세계 사람들은 많은 방식으로 서로 연결되어 있습니다... 이것은 세계화라고 알려진 과정 때문에 일어났죠.

여기에는 긍정적인 효과와 부정적인 효과가 모두 있습니다. 예를 들어, 사람들은 세계 어디든 쉽게 여행할 수 있어요. 또한, 기업들은 제품을 저렴하게 제작하고 이전보다 더 빠르게 고객에게 전달할 수 있죠. 그리고 첨단 기술은 사람들이 소통하고 문화를 즐길 수 있도록 도와줘요... 이 모든 것들은, 음, 긍정적이에요. 하지만, 세계화에는 부정적인 효과도 있어요. 음, 예를 들어, 많은 사람들이 비행기로 여행을 하고 기업들은 배로 제품을 옮기죠. 이것은 오염으로 인해 환경에 좋지 않습니다. 그리고, 음, 세계화는 사람들이 좋은 사상만 퍼뜨리는 데 도움이 되는 것이 아니에요. 그것은 테러리즘과 같은 나쁜 것들을 퍼뜨리는 데 도움이 되기도 하죠.

globalization 명 세계화   cheaply 부 저렴하게, 싸게
advanced technology 첨단 기술, 선진 기술
pollution 명 오염   spread 동 퍼뜨리다   terrorism 명 테러리즘

강의에서, 교수는 세계화의 몇몇 효과들을 언급한다. 다음의 항목이 효과로 언급된 것인지를 표시하시오. 각 항목에 적절한 칸을 클릭하시오.

	예	아니오
(A) 그것은 국가들 간의 경쟁을 증가시킨다.		V
(B) 그것은 제품을 더 빠르게 배달할 수 있도록 한다.	V	
(C) 그것은 환경에 좋다.		V
(D) 그것은 나쁜 사상이 퍼지게 한다.	V	

Listening Practice 1
본문 p. 117

1 (C)   2 (B)   3 Yes: (A), (C) No: (B), (D)

Note-taking
Student's Problem
Can't find a book for a sociology class

Employee's Answer
Sells books about biology, chemistry, and physics
→ Go to the bookstore in the sociology department building

Listen to a conversation between a student and an employee in the university bookstore.

M: Excuse me. ¹I can't find a book I need for my class.
W: Oh, what's the title of the book? I can look for it on my computer.
M: Um... It's called *Analysis of Structure*.
W: OK... Let me check... Hmm, that's strange. It seems we don't have the book. Um, to make sure, could you give me the author's name?
M: Um, yes... I believe it's, uh, Kay Fielding.
W: ²Are you sure about that name? I'm still not getting any results.
M: That's what it says on this lesson plan I got from class.
W: Oh, could I see that?
M: Of course... I really hope you can find the book. ³ᶜMy class starts on Monday. But, I'm worried I won't be ready.
W: Aha! I see what the problem is. Is this for a sociology class?
M: Yes, that's right. ³ᴬI have to take a class in sociology, so I signed up for Introduction to Sociology this semester.
W: Well, this bookstore only sells books about biology, chemistry, and physics. You need to go to the bookstore in the sociology department building.
M: Oh, I'm sorry. I didn't know that there were different bookstores... I'm new here.
W: It's not a problem. Let me give you directions to the right building.
M: Thanks so much.

대학 서점에서 학생과 직원 사이의 대화를 들으시오.

M: 실례합니다. 제가 수업에 필요한 책을 못 찾겠어요.
W: 아, 그 책의 제목이 무엇이죠? 제 컴퓨터로 찾아볼 수 있어요.
M: 음... 그것은 '구조 분석'이에요.
W: 네... 확인해 볼게요... 흠, 이상하군요. 저희가 그 책을 가지고 있지 않은 것 같은데요. 음, 확실히 하기 위해서, 저자 이름을 알려주시겠어요?
M: 음, 네... 제가 알기로는, 어, 케이 필딩이에요.
W: 그 이름이 확실한가요? 여전히 아무 결과도 나오지 않고 있네요.
M: 제가 수업 시간에 받은 이 수업 계획서에 그렇게 적혀있어요.
W: 오, 그것을 제가 볼 수 있을까요?
M: 물론이죠... 그 책을 꼭 찾아주셨으면 좋겠어요. 제 수업이 월요일부터 시작하거든요. 하지만, 제가 준비가 안 되어 있을까봐 걱정이에요.
W: 아하! 무엇이 문제인지 알겠네요. 이것은 사회학 수업을 위한 건가요?
M: 네, 맞아요. 저는 사회학 수업을 들어야 해서, 이번 학기에 사회학 개론을 신청했거든요.
W: 음, 이 서점은 생물학, 화학, 그리고 물리학에 관한 책만 판매해요. 학생은 사회학과 건물에 있는 서점에 가야 해요.
M: 오, 죄송해요. 다른 서점이 있는 줄은 몰랐네요... 저는 여기 새로 왔거든요.
W: 괜찮아요. 제가 올바른 건물로 가는 길을 알려드릴게요.
M: 정말 감사합니다.

lesson plan 수업 계획서, 학습 계획안   sign up for ~을 신청하다
biology 명 생물학   chemistry 명 화학   physics 명 물리학
direction 명 가는 길, 길 안내, 방향

1 대화는 주로 무엇에 관한 것인가?

(A) 학교 컴퓨터를 사용하는 것
(B) 수업에 등록하는 것
(C) 수업을 위한 물품을 찾는 것
(D) 학교의 요건을 이해하는 것

2 학생은 왜 수업 계획서를 언급하는가?

(A) 학교 활동에 대해 이야기하기 위해
(B) 어떤 정보를 확인하기 위해
(C) 또 다른 요청을 하기 위해
(D) 실수를 설명하기 위해

3 대화에서, 학생은 몇 가지 정보를 제공한다. 다음의 항목이 제공된 것인지를 표시하시오. 각 항목에 적절한 칸을 클릭하시오.

	예	아니오
(A) 수업명	V	
(B) 그의 교수의 이름		V
(C) 수업이 시작하는 날	V	
(D) 그가 공부하고 있는 전공		V

Listening Practice 2   본문 p. 119

1 (A)   2 (C)   3 (B)   4 (C)-(A)-(B)-(D)

Note-taking
Four Stages of Housefly Development
1. A mother fly lays up to 500 eggs.
2. Develops into a maggot, which is like a worm.
3. Grows into a pupa, covered in a hard outer skin.
4. A fly breaks out of its shell.

Listen to part of a lecture in a biology class.

P: I'm guessing many of you have seen houseflies at least once before. About 90 percent of flies that fly around our houses are houseflies. ¹Houseflies go through four different stages of life.

The lifecycle begins with the egg. ⁴ᶜThe mother lays up to 500 eggs, and this process takes three to four days to complete.

These eggs then develop into the next stage... a maggot. ²Um, like a worm, a maggot has no legs. It looks like a grain of rice. ⁴ᴬAt first, the color of the maggots is white, but it changes into, um, a darker color as they grow. Here is a picture that shows this... Can you see the black dots forming on its skin? ³Maggots have a number of tiny holes covering the body. These connect to tubes that lead to the lungs and provide oxygen.

Now, let's move on to the third stage. Each maggot will eventually grow into a pupa. ⁴ᴮA pupa is similar to a maggot, but it is covered in a hard outer skin. The color of the outer skin is slightly yellow at first, but it continues to get darker. And when the pupa is fully grown, it, uh, becomes a black color.

⁴ᴰAfter this, the fly inside the shell will break out using part of its head. This shows that they've reached the last stage and are adults. These flies are the fully grown version that we have all seen. You know, they have black skin and red eyes... And they have six legs and one pair of wings. Their wings make them different from other insects... This is because most insects have two pairs of wings.

Anyway, this whole process takes about seven to ten days... And within 24 hours, adult flies start the cycle again. Female flies will lay eggs after three days.

생물학 강의의 일부를 들으시오.

P: 여러분 중 대다수가 이전에 적어도 한 번은 집파리를 본 적이 있을 거예요. 우리의 집 주위를 날아다니는 파리들의 약 90퍼센트가 집파리거든요. 집파리는 생의 네 가지 다른 단계를 거칩니다.

생의 주기는 알에서 시작합니다. 어미는 알을 500개까지 낳는데, 이 과정은 완료하는 데에 3일에서 4일이 걸려요.

이 알들은 그 후 다음 단계로 성장합니다... 구더기로요. 음, 지렁이처럼, 구더기는 다리가 없어요. 그것은 쌀알처럼 생겼죠. 처음에, 구더기의 색은 흰색이지만, 자라면서 더 어두운색으로, 음, 변합니다. 여기 이것을 보여주는 사진이 있어요... 여러분은 그것의 피부에 형성된 검은 점들이 보이시나요? 구더기는 수많은 작은 구멍들이 몸을 덮고 있어요. 이것들은 폐로 이어져서 산소를 공급하는 관들에 연결됩니다.

이제, 세 번째 단계로 넘어갑시다. 각각의 구더기는 마침내 번데기로 자랄 거예요. 번데기는 구더기와 비슷하지만, 단단한 외피로 덮여 있어요. 외피의 색은 처음에는 약간 노랗지만, 계속해서 어두워집니다. 그리고 번데기가 완전히 자라면, 그것은, 어, 검은색이 되죠.

이후, 껍질 안의 파리는 머리의 일부를 사용해서 빠져 나옵니다. 이는 그것들이 마지막 단계에 도달해서 성체가 되었음을 보여주죠. 이 파리들이 우리 모두가 본 완전히 성장한 형태입니다. 알다시피, 그것들은 검은색 피부와 붉은 눈을 가졌죠... 그리고 그것들은 여섯 개의 다리와 한 쌍의 날개를 가지고 있어요. 날개가 그것들이 다른 곤충들과 다르게 하는 점인데요... 이는 대부분의 곤충이 두 쌍의 날개를 가지고 있기 때문이죠.

어쨌든, 이 모든 과정은 약 7일에서 10일 정도 걸립니다... 그리고 24시간 안에, 성체 파리들은 다시 이 주기를 시작해요. 암컷 파리는 3일 후면 알을 낳을 겁니다.

housefly 명 집파리   lifecycle 명 생의 주기
develop 동 성장하다   maggot 명 구더기
worm 명 지렁이; 벌레   a grain of rice 쌀알   dot 명 점
tube 명 관   lung 명 폐   pupa 명 번데기   slightly 부 약간
shell 명 껍질, 껍데기   break out (of) (~을) 깨뜨리고 빠져나오다

1 강의의 주된 주제는 무엇인가?

   (A) 흔한 곤충의 생의 주기
   (B) 집파리의 식습관
   (C) 집파리의 흔한 서식지
   (D) 곤충이 인간의 삶에 미치는 영향

2 교수는 왜 쌀알을 언급하는가?

   (A) 어린 집파리의 먹이를 밝히기 위해
   (B) 파리를 보기 어려운 이유를 보여주기 위해
   (C) 구더기의 모습을 설명하기 위해
   (D) 파리가 어떻게 농작물에 피해를 줄 수 있는지를 보여주기 위해

3 교수에 따르면, 구더기의 몸에 있는 구멍들은 어떤 역할을 하는가?

   (A) 그것들은 구더기의 색깔을 바꾼다.
   (B) 그것들은 구더기의 폐로 산소를 들여보낸다.
   (C) 그것들은 구더기의 체형을 결정한다.
   (D) 그것들은 구더기가 먹이를 먹는 것을 돕는다.

4 강의에서, 교수는 집파리의 발달 단계들을 설명한다. 아래의 단계들을 올바른 순서대로 나열하시오. 각 답변을 해당하는 곳으로 끌어다 놓으시오.

단계 1	(C) 약 500개의 알을 낳는다.
단계 2	(A) 피부가 어두워진다.
단계 3	(B) 단단한 외피가 발달한다.
단계 4	(D) 머리를 사용하여 껍질을 깬다.

Listening Practice 3   본문 p. 121

1 (D)   2 (A)   3 Yes: (A), (B) No: (C), (D)

Note-taking
Student's Request
Wants to join the international food festival

Instructions
1. Fill out a registration form
2. Prepare samples for the cafeteria staff to try
3. Give a list of the ingredients

Listen to a conversation between a student and a director of the student cafeteria.

M: Excuse me. ¹I heard there will be an international food festival soon. Is that true?

W: Yes. It will happen here in the cafeteria. There will be booths serving traditional food from different countries. However, the event has been moved to next month.

M: Really? I thought the festival was this month!

W: Well, um, the students have asked for more time to prepare. Are you interested in joining?

M: Yes. I want to serve traditional food from Brazil.

W: Wonderful. ³ᴬHere's a registration form that you'll need to fill out... Um, what will you be making?

M: I want to make Brazilian-style cheese bread and chocolate balls.

W: Those sound delicious! ²Will you be making them yourself?

M: Yes. My mother taught me how to make them.

W: That's excellent. ³ᴮUm, you'll also have to prepare samples for the cafeteria staff to try. Can you bring some on Friday?

M: Sure! How much should I make?

W: Um, five small samples of each dish will be fine. Of course, you'll have to make a larger amount for the food festival.

M: I understand.

W: I look forward to trying the samples... Oh, and one more thing. ³ᴰPlease give us a list of the ingredients as well. We're going to order what the participants need before the festival. That way, uh, students have one less thing to prepare.

M: I'll do that! Thanks!

학생과 학생 식당 책임자 사이의 대화를 들으시오.

M: 실례합니다. 곧 국제 음식 축제가 열린다고 들었는데요. 그게 사실인가요?

W: 네. 여기 교내식당에서 열릴 거예요. 다양한 나라의 전통 음식을 제공하는 부스들이 있을 거랍니다. 하지만, 행사가 다음 달로 옮겨졌어요.

M: 정말요? 저는 그 축제가 이번 달인 줄 알았거든요!

W: 그게, 음, 학생들이 준비할 시간을 더 달라고 요청해서요. 참여하는 것에 관심이 있으신가요?

M: 네. 저는 브라질의 전통 음식을 제공하고 싶어요.

W: 멋지네요. 여기 작성하셔야 할 신청서가 있어요... 음, 무엇을 만드실 건가요?

M: 저는 브라질식 치즈 빵과 초콜릿 볼을 만들고 싶어요.

W: 맛있겠네요! 직접 만드실 건가요?

M: 네. 저희 어머니께서 그것들을 만드는 방법을 가르쳐 주셨거든요.

W: 훌륭하군요. 음, 교내식당 직원들이 시식해볼 샘플도 준비하셔야 하는데요. 금요일에 좀 가져오실 수 있나요?

M: 물론이죠! 얼마나 만들어야 할까요?

W: 음, 각 요리마다 소량의 샘플 다섯 개면 됩니다. 물론, 음식 축제를 위해서는 더 많은 양을 만드셔야 하지만요.

M: 알겠습니다.

W: 샘플 시식이 기대되네요... 아, 그리고 한 가지 더요. 저희에게 재료 목록도 주세요. 저희가 축제 전에 참가자들이 필요한 것을 주문할 거예요. 그래야, 어, 학생들이 준비할 것이 하나 줄죠.

M: 그렇게 할게요! 감사합니다!

---

cafeteria 몡 교내식당   booth 몡 부스   serve 동 제공하다
traditional 형 전통의   registration form 신청서

dish 명 요리; 접시   ingredient 명 재료   participant 명 참가자

1 화자들은 주로 무엇을 논의하고 있는가?

(A) 학교 교내식당을 이용하는 방법
(B) 교내식당에서 어떤 음식을 파는지
(C) 유학생을 위한 혜택들
(D) 음식 축제에 참여하는 방법

2 남자는 왜 그의 어머니를 언급하는가?

(A) 그가 어떻게 요리를 만드는 법을 배웠는지 설명하기 위해
(B) 그가 도움이 필요할 것이라는 것을 보여주기 위해
(C) 행사에 누가 참석할 것인지 언급하기 위해
(D) 그가 축제에 참여하고 싶어 하는 이유를 나타내기 위해

3 대화에서, 여자는 남자에게 지시사항을 전달한다. 다음의 항목이 지시사항인지를 표시하시오. 각 항목에 적절한 칸을 클릭하시오.

	예	아니오
(A) 신청서 작성하기	V	
(B) 음식 샘플 준비하기	V	
(C) 부모의 허락 받기		V
(D) 요리 재료를 사기		V

Listening Practice 4   본문 p. 123

1 (C)   2 (B)   3 (B)
4 Logging: (B), (D) Mining: (A) Introducing animals: (C)

Note-taking
European Settlers' Activities and Effects in Australia
- Logging → Habitat loss, soil loss, and dry weather
- Mining → Pollution of streams and rivers, and toxic chemicals
- Animals from overseas → Lowered biodiversity

Listen to part of a lecture in an ecology class.

P: ¹Europeans began to settle in Australia in 1788. And, um, since that time, they have changed the environment in various ways. Uh, now let's talk about how their activities affected it.

Well... first, European settlers did a lot of logging, uh, which means that they cut down large sections of forest. They did this for wood to build houses and towns. ²But they mainly did it to remove trees for agriculture. It was usually done in areas near the coast because the soil there was good for farming. ⁴ᴮCutting down forests, however, caused habitat loss, and forest animals had to move to new areas. Trees also protect soil. ⁴ᴰSo, uh, removing the trees caused the soil to disappear. Removing trees also caused long periods of dry weather, and the deserts in Australia got larger and larger...

Another major activity of the settlers was mining. Many miners moved to Australia to search for gold because they believed they would become rich. ⁴ᴬBut mining caused the pollution of streams and rivers. This killed many fish. It also released toxic chemicals into the soil, so plants could no longer grow.

Now, the outcome of this next part will surprise you. ³Settlers introduced animals, such as rabbits and dogs, from overseas. You might think that increasing the number of new species living in Australia would be good, right? For instance, um, if there are lots of different animals and plants, you have high biodiversity. ³/⁴ᶜBut, actually, by introducing foreign animals, settlers lowered biodiversity. Rabbits ate native plants and seeds, and dogs killed birds and destroyed their eggs. In the end, these animals led to the extinction of more than 100 native Australian species.

생태학 강의의 일부를 들으시오.

P: 유럽인들은 1788년에 호주에 정착하기 시작했습니다. 그리고, 음, 그때 이후로, 그들은 다양한 방식으로 환경을 변화시켰죠. 어, 이제 그들의 활동이 그것에 어떻게 영향을 미쳤는지 얘기해 봅시다.

음... 먼저, 유럽 정착민들은 많은 벌목을 했는데, 어, 이는 그들이 숲의 많은 부분의 나무를 잘라냈다는 것을 의미해요. 그들은 집과 마을을 짓기 위한 목재를 위해 이것을 했죠. 그러나 그들은 주로 농사를 짓기 위해 나무를 제거했습니다. 그것은 주로 해안 근처의 지역에서 행해졌는데 그곳의 토양이 농사를 짓기에 좋았기 때문이에요. 하지만, 숲을 벌목하는 것은 서식지 감소를 야기했고, 숲의 동물들은 새로운 지역으로 이동해야 했습니다. 나무는 토양도 보호하는데요. 그래서, 어, 나무를 제거하는 것은 토양이 사라지도록 만들었죠. 나무를 제거하는 것은 또한 오랜 기간의 건조한 날씨를 야기했고, 호주의 사막은 점점 더 커졌어요...

정착민들의 또 다른 주요 활동은 광산업이었어요. 많은 광부들이 금을 찾기 위해 호주로 이주했는데, 그들이 부자가 될 것이라고 믿었기 때문이었죠. 그러나 광산업은 하천과 강의 오염을 야기했습니다. 이것은 많은 물고기들이 죽게 했죠. 그것은 또한 독성 화학물질을 토양으로 방출해서, 식물들이 더 이상 자라날 수 없었습니다.

자, 이 다음 부분의 결과는 여러분을 놀라게 할 겁니다. 정착민들은 해외로부터 토끼와 개와 같은 동물들을 들여왔어요. 여러분은 호주에 사는 새로운 생물 종의 수를 늘리는 것이 좋을 거라고 생각할 수도 있겠어요, 그렇죠? 예를 들어, 음, 만약 많은 다양한 동물들과 식물들이 있다면, 높은 생물 다양성이 있는 것이니까요. 하지만, 사실, 외래 동물을 들여옴으로써, 정착민들은 생물 다양성을 감소시켰습니다. 토끼는 토종 식물과 씨앗을 먹었고, 개는 새를 죽이고 그것들의 알을 부쉈죠. 결국, 이 동물들은 100종 이상의 호주 토착종들을 멸종으로 이끌었습니다.

settle 동 정착하다; 해결하다   logging 명 벌목
cut down 자르다, 벌목하다   agriculture 명 농사, 농업
habitat 명 서식지   loss 명 감소, 상실
mining 명 광산업   toxic 형 독성의, 유독성의
biodiversity 명 생물 다양성   foreign 형 외래의, 외국의
lead to ~로 이끌다, 이어지다   extinction 명 멸종
native species 토착종

1 강의의 주된 주제는 무엇인가?
  (A) 호주의 식물과 동물의 다양성
  (B) 호주의 다양한 종류의 생태계
  (C) 유럽인들이 호주의 환경에 미친 영향
  (D) 호주에서의 유럽인 정착의 역사

2 교수는 대부분의 농업 지역에 관해 무엇이라고 말하는가?
  (A) 그곳들에는 원래 토양이 거의 없었다.
  (B) 그곳들은 바다와 가까웠다.
  (C) 그곳들은 마을에서 멀리 떨어져 있었다.
  (D) 그곳들은 결국 사막이 되었다.

3 교수는 왜 토끼와 개를 언급하는가?
  (A) 이 동물들이 어떻게 유럽인들로부터 피해를 입었는지를 설명하기 위해
  (B) 외래 동물들과 그것들의 영향에 대한 예를 들기 위해
  (C) 유럽인 정착 이후 생물 다양성이 증가했음을 보여주기 위해
  (D) 유럽 정착민들이 종종 반려동물들을 키웠다는 것을 강조하기 위해

4 교수는 몇 가지 인간의 활동과 각각의 결과에 대해 언급한다. 각 활동의 결과를 표시하시오. 각 항목에 적절한 칸을 클릭하시오.

	벌목	광산업	동물 도입
(A) 하천과 강의 오염		V	
(B) 동물 서식지의 감소	V		
(C) 토착종의 멸종			V
(D) 토양의 감소	V		

iBT Listening Test 1
본문 p. 125

1 (B) **2** (C) **3** (C)
4 Yes: (B), (D) No: (A), (C)

Note-taking
Student's Question
Wants to know about the role of election volunteers

What Volunteers Do
- Help with preparations like setting up tables
- Check student IDs
- Help students use voting machines

Listen to a conversation between a student and a professor.

S: Hi, Professor Melrose! Could I talk to you about the student election?
P: Sure, Olivia. What would you like to know?
S: Um, so, I know it's happening soon, but, uh, I'm interested in becoming a volunteer. ¹Could you tell me about the role of election volunteers?
P: All right. I can explain it to you. It's really quite simple.
S: Do we have to help with preparations like, uh, setting up tables?
P: That's a part of it, yes. ⁴ᴮBut, um, more importantly, you'll be checking student IDs. We have to be sure that everyone who participates is a student at this school.
S: That's because only students are allowed to vote, right?
P: Yes, exactly. Um, and next, well, have you ever used a voting machine before?
S: No, I haven't, but I think I can learn.
P: That's fine. ²The school is going to have an orientation for all the volunteers. ⁴ᴰUm, someone will teach you everything about the voting machines. That way, you can help students use them on election day.
S: Great! I think I can do all of that... Um, so how do I sign up?
P: I have a form right here. You can complete it whenever you like. Just return it to me before the end of the week.
S: Thanks, Professor! ³Oh, could I get a second form? My friend would also like to volunteer.
P: Certainly. We're still looking for six to eight more volunteers.
S: Understood, Professor Melrose. I know some other students who might be interested. I'll tell them to sign up as well.

학생과 교수 사이의 대화를 들으시오.

S: 안녕하세요, Melrose 교수님! 학생 선거에 대해 이야기 좀 할 수 있을까요?
P: 물론이지, Olivia. 무엇이 알고 싶니?
S: 음, 그러니까, 그것이 곧 있을 거라는 건 알지만, 어, 저는 자원 봉사자가 되는 것에 관심이 있어요. 선거 자원 봉사자들의 역할에 대해 말씀해 주실 수 있나요?
P: 알겠단다. 설명해 줄 수 있지. 그건 사실 꽤 간단해.
S: 저희가 테이블을 세우는 것처럼, 어, 준비를 도와야 하나요?
P: 그것도 한 부분이지, 맞아. 하지만, 음, 더 중요한 건, 학생증을 확인하는 거야. 우리는 참여하는 모든 사람이 이 학교의 학생이라는 것을 확실히 해야 하거든.
S: 그건 학생들만 투표할 수 있기 때문이죠, 그렇죠?
P: 맞아, 정확해. 음, 그리고 다음으로, 자, 전에 투표 집계기를 사용해 본 적이 있니?
S: 아니요, 안 써봤지만, 배울 수 있을 것 같은데요.
P: 괜찮아. 학교에서 모든 자원 봉사자들을 위한 예비 교육이 있을 거야. 음, 누군가가 투표 집계기에 대한 모든 것을 가르쳐 줄 거란다. 그렇게 해서, 네가 선거일에 학생들이 그것들을 사용하는 것을 도울 수 있겠지.
S: 좋아요! 그걸 다 할 수 있을 것 같아요.. 음, 그럼 제가 어떻게 신청하

나요?
P: 바로 여기 서류가 있어. 네가 원할 때 언제든지 그것을 작성하면 돼. 이번 주가 끝나기 전에만 나한테 돌려주렴.
S: 감사합니다, 교수님! 아, 서류를 하나 더 받을 수 있을까요? 제 친구도 자원 봉사를 하고 싶어 해서요.
P: 물론이지. 우리는 여전히 6명에서 8명의 자원 봉사자들을 더 찾고 있단다.
S: 알겠습니다, Melrose 교수님. 제가 관심 있어 할 만한 다른 학생들을 알고 있어요. 제가 그들에게도 신청하라고 말할게요.

election 몡 선거   volunteer 몡 자원 봉사자; 동 자원 봉사를 하다
role 몡 역할   preparation 몡 준비   set up ~을 세우다, 건설하다
voting machine 투표 집계기   orientation 몡 예비 교육, 오리엔테이션
election day 선거일

1 화자들은 주로 무엇을 논의하고 있는가?
 (A) 등록 과정에 대한 문제점들
 (B) 학생 자원 봉사자들이 무엇을 할 것인지
 (C) 학교 선거의 결과
 (D) 학교 단체에 가입하는 방법

2 교수에 따르면, 학교는 무엇을 할 계획인가?
 (A) 더 많은 투표 집계기를 설치하기
 (B) 학교 밖에 넓은 공간을 빌리기
 (C) 몇몇 학생들에게 예비 교육을 제공하기
 (D) 행사 마감일을 변경하기

3 학생은 왜 또 다른 신청서를 언급하는가?
 (A) 그녀는 첫 번째 것에 실수를 했다.
 (B) 그녀는 몇몇 정보를 확인해야 한다.
 (C) 그녀는 도움을 주고 싶어 하는 친구가 있다.
 (D) 그녀는 두 가지 활동에 참여하기를 원한다.

4 다음의 항목이 선거 자원 봉사자들의 역할로 언급된 것인지를 표시하시오.
각 항목에 적절한 칸을 클릭하시오.

	예	아니오
(A) 학생들에게 서류 제공하기		V
(B) 학생증 확인하기	V	
(C) 득표 수 세기		V
(D) 학생들이 기계를 사용하는 것을 돕기	V	

iBT Listening Test 2
본문 p. 128

1 (C)   2 (C)   3 (B)
4 Realism: (B), (D) Impressionism: (A), (C)   5 (C)

Note-taking
Realism
• Represented the real world

• Focused on ordinary subjects in the present time
e.g. Jean-Francois Millet

Impressionism
• Created a general impression of what an artist saw
• Happy and pleasant scenes
e.g. Claude Monet

Listen to part of a lecture in an art class.

P: ¹Today, we're going to talk about a couple of major movements in art history. ¹/²These are Realism and Impressionism. And my examples will be from French art in particular.

As the name suggests, Realists tried to create art that represented the real world. What I mean is, um, how most people saw the world. Before, art focused only on the wealthy class or great events of the past. ⁴ᴮBut, um, Realists focused on ordinary subjects in the present time. These included common people, like workers in a factory... ⁴ᴰThe focus was on ordinary life, which the Realists tried to present in accurate detail. They were almost like photographers because of how they represented life...

In contrast, Impressionists created art based on, well, their impressions. ⁴ᴬImpressionists did not try to capture every detail. Instead, the artists would create a general impression of what they saw. ⁴ᶜUsually, the subjects were shown in happy and pleasant scenes like a picnic or a party... Either way, Impressionists wanted to give an impression of a brief moment, like, um, the way sunlight looks in a field of flowers at sunset...

²So, now for an example of each... ³Jean-Francois Millet was a Realist painter. His works mostly showed the life of farmers. He had a clear intention to represent farmers at work realistically. The clothes, the fields, and even the sky looked real. It was as if you were inside the painting with the subjects when you looked at it... uh, like you were a part of the painting...

Now, I'm sure you are all familiar with the next one... Claude Monet. Monet is famous for his paintings of the countryside of France. In fact, the Impressionist movement was named after one of his early paintings, uh, called *Impression, Sunrise*. This work shows a red sun far away and, uh, its reflection in the water. There are some boats in the picture, but there is almost no detail. ⁵The lines are quickly drawn and the colors are not carefully mixed together... The scene is mostly a gray fog. Overall, it seems as if the painting was done in a hurry.

미술학 강의의 일부를 들으시오.

P: 오늘, 우리는 미술 역사에 있어 두 가지 주요한 운동에 대해 이야기할 것입니다. 이것들은 사실주의와 인상주의에요. 그리고 특히 프랑스 미술에서 예시들을 가져올 겁니다.

이름에서 알 수 있듯이, 사실주의자들은 현실 세계를 나타내는 예

술을 창조하고자 했습니다. 제 말은, 음, 대부분의 사람들이 세상을 보는대로요. 이전에, 예술은 부유한 계층이나 과거의 위대한 사건들에만 초점을 맞췄죠. 하지만, 음, 사실주의자들은 현재의 평범한 대상에 초점을 맞췄어요. 이것은 공장의 노동자들과 같은 평범한 사람들을 포함했죠. 초점이 평범한 삶에 있었는데, 사실주의자들은 이를 정확히 세부적으로 나타내려고 노력했습니다. 그들이 삶을 표현했던 방식으로 인해 그들은 마치 사진작가와도 같았죠...

그에 반해서, 인상주의자들은, 음, 그들의 인상을 바탕으로 예술을 창조했습니다. 인상주의자들은 모든 세부 묘사를 정확히 담아내려고 노력하지 않았어요. 대신, 그 예술가들은 그들이 본 것에 대한 대략적인 인상을 창조하곤 했어요. 보통, 대상들은 소풍 또는 파티와 같은 행복하고 즐거운 장면 안에 있는 것을 보여주었습니다... 어떤 경우든, 인상주의자들은 짧은 순간에 대한 인상을 주고 싶어했는데요, 음, 해질녘 꽃밭에 햇빛이 비치는 모습처럼요...

자, 이제 각각의 예시로... 장 프랑수아 밀레는 사실주의 화가였어요. 그의 작품들은 대부분 농부들의 삶을 보여주었습니다. 그는 분명한 의도를 가지고 일터의 농부들을 현실적으로 나타내려고 했습니다. 옷, 들판, 그리고 심지어 하늘도 진짜처럼 보였죠. 그것을 보면 마치 그림 안에 그 대상들과 함께 있는 것 같았어요... 어, 마치 그 그림의 일부인 것처럼...

자, 여러분 모두 다음 건 익숙할 것입니다... 클로드 모네인데요. 모네는 프랑스의 시골 지역을 그린 그림으로 유명하죠. 실제로, 인상주의 운동은 '인상, 해돋이'라고 불리는, 어, 그의 초기 그림들 중 하나에서 이름을 땄어요. 이 작품은 멀리 있는 붉은 태양과, 어, 물에 비친 그것의 모습을 보여줍니다. 그림에 몇 개의 배가 있기는 하지만, 세부 묘사가 거의 없죠. 선들은 빠르게 그리고 색깔들은 세심하게 섞지 않습니다... 풍경 대부분은 회색 안개예요. 전체적으로, 그 그림은 급히 그린 것처럼 보이죠.

Realism 명 사실주의   Impressionism 명 인상주의
in particular 특히   represent 동 나타내다, 표현하다; 대표하다
wealthy 형 부유한   subject 명 대상, 주제
capture 동 정확히 담아내다; 포획하다   general 형 대략적인, 일반적인
pleasant 형 즐거운, 쾌적한   scene 명 장면, 풍경; 현장
intention 명 의도, 의사   fog 명 안개   in a hurry 급히, 서둘러

1 강의의 주된 주제는 무엇인가?
  (A) 인상주의의 창시자
  (B) 프랑스 미술의 인기
  (C) 두 가지 중요한 예술 운동
  (D) 가장 유명한 프랑스 예술가들

2 강의는 어떻게 구성되어 있는가?
  (A) 각기 다른 예술가들의 다양한 목표들을 강조함으로써
  (B) 한 예술가가 다른 예술가의 작품에 어떻게 영향을 미쳤는지 이야기함으로써
  (C) 두 가지 예술 양식을 설명하고 예시들을 제공함으로써
  (D) 다른 두 나라의 예술 양식을 비교함으로써

3 장 프랑수아 밀레의 예술작품의 대상에 대한 예시는 무엇인가?
  (A) 사교행사에 있는 사람들
  (B) 밭에 있는 농부들
  (C) 알록달록한 풍경들
  (D) 꽃밭들

4 다음의 항목이 사실주의 혹은 인상주의 중 어떤 것에 대한 설명인지를 표시하시오.
각 항목에 적절한 칸을 클릭하시오.

	사실주의	인상주의
(A) 모든 세부 묘사를 담아내지 않았다		V
(B) 평범한 사람들과 같은 대상에 초점을 맞췄다	V	
(C) 즐겁고 행복한 장면을 보여줬다		V
(D) 삶을 진실되게 나타내려고 했다	V	

5 모네의 '인상, 해돋이'에 대한 교수의 의견은 무엇인가?
  (A) 그것은 시간이 지나면서 더 중요해졌다.
  (B) 그것은 모네의 성격을 보여준다.
  (C) 그것은 완성하는 데 많은 시간이 걸리지 않았다.
  (D) 그것은 모네의 일생 동안 유명해지지 않았다.

Vocabulary Review
본문 p. 132

1 extinction   2 toxic   3 summary
4 settle   5 participant   6 spread
7 lead to   8 preparation   9 cheaply
10 (A)   11 (C)   12 (D)
13 (B)   14 (C)

CHAPTER 07
Inference

Example
본문 p. 135

A. (C)   B. (D)

A.

Note-taking
Student's Situation
Applied for the student exchange program

Missing Requirements
• Letter of recommendation from a professor
• One-page essay

Listen to a conversation between a student and a university employee at the registrar's office.

W: Hi, my name is Elizabeth Moore. I'm here about the student exchange program in Germany. I applied last week.

M: Ah, yes, Ms. Moore. We received your application form and your school transcript. However, you're missing some other requirements.

W: Oh, really? Could you tell me what they are?

M: Well, we need a letter of recommendation from a professor. It should include something about your German language skills.

W: OK. I thought Professor Muller was going to submit that for me. I'll ask him about that right after I leave here.

M: And another thing is the one-page essay. Um, it should be about why you want to join the student exchange program.

W: All right. I'll work on that later tonight.

학적과에서 학생과 교직원 사이의 대화를 들으시오.

W: 안녕하세요, 제 이름은 Elizabeth Moore입니다. 독일 교환학생 프로그램 때문에 왔어요. 지난주에 지원했거든요.

M: 아, 네, Moore씨. 학생의 지원서와 성적증명서는 받았어요. 하지만, 몇 가지 다른 요건들이 누락되었네요.

W: 아, 정말요? 그것들이 무엇인지 말씀해 주시겠어요?

M: 음, 교수님의 추천서가 필요합니다. 그건 학생의 독일어 실력에 대한 내용을 포함해야 해요.

W: 알겠습니다. 저는 Muller 교수님이 저를 위해 그걸 제출해 주실 줄 알았어요. 제가 여기를 나간 후에 바로 교수님께 그것에 대해 여쭤볼게요.

M: 그리고 또 다른 것은 한 페이지짜리 에세이예요. 음, 그건 교환학생 프로그램에 참여하고 싶은 이유에 대한 것이어야 해요.

W: 알겠습니다. 이따가 밤에 그걸 쓸게요.

---

student exchange program 교환학생 프로그램
apply (동) 지원하다, 신청하다 application form 지원서, 신청서
school transcript 성적증명서
letter of recommendation 추천서, 추천장

학생은 다음에 무엇을 할 것인가?

(A) 에세이 수정하기
(B) 지원서 복사하기
(C) 교수와 대화하기
(D) 언어 시험 보기

B.

Note-taking

Functions of Longhouses
- For sleeping and storing food
- Held large community gatherings
  e.g. Political meetings, traditional ceremonies

Listen to part of a lecture in an anthropology class.

P: The longhouse was a long, narrow house built by the Iroquois people. The Iroquois people were a group of Native Americans. They became known as the People of the Longhouse because, well, they built many longhouses and lived in them.

Longhouses were very large structures. Some were even longer than a football field! Many families lived together in one longhouse. Sometimes, there were 20 or more families in a single house. Longhouses were also used to store food, like dried meat and corn. But, uh, they weren't just for sleeping and storing food. They had another important function... Large community gatherings like political meetings and traditional ceremonies were held in longhouses. Today, some Iroquois people still use longhouses for those reasons.

인류학 강의의 일부를 들으시오.

P: 롱하우스는 이로쿼이족 사람들이 지은 길고 좁은 집이었습니다. 이로쿼이족 사람들은 아메리카 원주민 집단이었는데요. 그들은 롱하우스를 많이 짓고 거기서 살았기 때문에, 음, 롱하우스의 사람들로 알려지게 되었습니다.

롱하우스는 매우 큰 건물이었어요. 몇몇은 심지어 축구장보다 더 길었답니다! 많은 가족들이 한 채의 롱하우스에서 함께 살았습니다. 때때로, 한 집에 20가구 혹은 그 이상의 가족들이 있었어요. 롱하우스는 말린 고기와 옥수수 같은 식량을 저장하는 데에도 사용되었어요. 하지만, 어, 그것들은 단지 잠을 자고 식량을 저장하기 위한 것만은 아니었죠. 그것들은 또 다른 중요한 기능이 있었어요... 정치적 모임과 전통 의식과 같은 큰 공동체 모임들이 롱하우스에서 열렸죠. 오늘날, 몇몇 이로쿼이족 사람들은 이러한 이유들로 여전히 롱하우스를 사용합니다.

Iroquois (형) 이로쿼이족의; (명) 이로쿼이족
Native American 아메리카 원주민   structure (명) 건물, 구조물
football field 축구장   store (동) 저장하다   function (명) 기능
community (명) 공동체; 주민   political (형) 정치적인, 정치의
ceremony (명) 의식

교수는 롱하우스에 관해 무엇을 암시하는가?

(A) 그것들은 오늘날 더 이상 사용되지 않는다.
(B) 그것들은 돌과 점토로도 만들어진다.
(C) 그것들은 농장 가축들을 기르는 데 사용되었다.
(D) 그것들은 이로쿼이족 생활의 중심지였다.

Listening Practice 1   본문 p. 137

1 (C)   2 Suggested: (C), (D) Not Suggested: (A), (B)
3 (C)

Note-taking

Professor's Suggestion

Submit your essay for the history department's monthly publication
→ Remove the section on Turkey's modern history
→ Discuss Turkey's ancient history some more

Listen to a conversation between a student and a professor.

P: Thank you for coming, Allan. I want to talk to you about your history essay on Turkey.
S: Sure, Professor Perlman. Uh, is there something wrong with it?
P: Actually, it's excellent. [1]I think you should submit it for the history department's monthly publication.
S: Oh? Is it really that good?
P: Absolutely. It has some great points that were well supported by your research.
S: Thank you, Professor. Is there anything I should do before submitting the essay?
P: [2A]Well, the length is fine, but there is a part that needs to be changed.
S: OK. Which part?
P: Well, I'd like you to remove the section on its modern history... Another student will write an article about that.
S: All right. But I'm worried that my essay might not have enough content then.
P: [2C]Yes, so you will need to discuss Turkey's ancient history some more.
S: Hmm... OK. What exactly should I write about?
P: [2C]I think you should focus on, uh, how Turkey's location affected its history. As you know, it's located between Asia and Europe.
S: Thanks, Professor. I'll start as soon as possible. [3]I just need to return some books to the library first.
P: Good. [2D]While you're there, maybe you can find some books on Turkey's ancient history.

S: 흠... 알겠습니다. 제가 정확히 무엇에 대해 써야 하나요?
P: 나는 네가 터키의 위치가 그것의 역사에 어떤 영향을 미쳤는지에 대해, 어, 초점을 맞춰야 한다고 생각한단다. 알다시피, 그곳은 아시아와 유럽 사이에 위치해 있잖니.
S: 감사해요, 교수님. 최대한 빨리 시작하겠습니다. 제가 일단 도서관에 책을 반납하기만 하면 돼서요.
P: 좋아. 네가 거기 있는 동안, 터키의 고대 역사에 관한 책들을 몇 권 찾아볼 수도 있겠구나.

Turkey 명 터키 submit 동 제출하다
history department 역사학과 publication 명 간행물, 출판물
support 동 입증하다, 지지하다 article 명 글, 기사
ancient 형 고대의

1 화자들은 주로 무엇을 논의하고 있는가?
  (A) 교수가 글을 쓰는 것을 돕는 것
  (B) 수업을 위한 조사를 하는 것
  (C) 간행물을 위한 에세이를 준비하는 것
  (D) 발표 주제를 변경하는 것

2 대화에서, 교수는 학생이 반영해야 할 몇 가지 변경사항을 제안한다. 다음의 항목이 제안사항인지를 표시하시오. 각 항목에 적절한 칸을 클릭하시오.

	제안됨	제안 안 됨
(A) 에세이의 길이를 늘리기		V
(B) 다른 학생을 인터뷰하기		V
(C) 특정 주제에 초점을 맞추기	V	
(D) 책을 몇 권 찾기	V	

3 학생은 다음에 무엇을 할 것인가?
  (A) 전문가에게 연락하기
  (B) 시험공부 하기
  (C) 도서관 방문하기
  (D) 웹사이트 확인하기

학생과 교수 사이의 대화를 들으시오.

P: 와줘서 고맙구나, Allan. 터키에 대한 네 역사 에세이에 대해 이야기하고 싶단다.
S: 물론이죠, Perlman 교수님. 어, 그것에 무슨 문제라도 있나요?
P: 사실, 훌륭해. 난 네가 그걸 역사학과의 월간 간행물에 제출해야 한다고 생각한단다.
S: 오? 그게 정말 그렇게 괜찮은가요?
P: 그렇고말고. 그것은 네 조사로 잘 입증된 몇 가지 훌륭한 요점들이 있어.
S: 감사합니다, 교수님. 에세이를 제출하기 전에 제가 해야 할 일이 있을까요?
P: 음, 길이는 괜찮은데, 바꿔야 할 부분이 있단다.
S: 좋아요. 어떤 부분인가요?
P: 음, 그것의 현대사에 관한 부분을 삭제했으면 한다... 다른 학생이 그것에 대한 글을 쓸 거거든.
S: 알겠습니다. 하지만 그럼 제 에세이의 내용이 충분하지 않을까 걱정되네요.
P: 그래, 그래서 네가 터키의 고대 역사에 대해 좀 더 얘기해야 할 거야.

Listening Practice 2
본문 p.139

1 (C) **2** (B), (C) **3** (A) **4** (C)

Note-taking
How Social Spiders Hunt
Hunt as a group and build two kinds of webs
• Main web: Spread out like a net
• Another web: Acts as a trap
→ Can quickly find the trapped prey
→ Can kill larger prey

Listen to part of a lecture in a biology class.

P: [1]Next, I'm going to introduce you to some very interesting spiders. They are called *Anelosimus eximius*, a type of social spider. Most spiders

CHAPTER 07 | Inference

like to stay alone, but these spiders live in large groups in some rainforests of South America. ¹Let's focus on some features of their social behavior.

These spiders build huge webs in the rainforest. Thousands of spiders live together in these webs. ²They do various tasks, like, uh, make webs and repair damaged parts of the web. They also take care of baby spiders...

But the most interesting task that they do is hunt as a group. These spiders build two kinds of webs. Their main web is spread out like a net. Below that there is another web, but this one is shaped like a bowl and acts as a trap. This is brilliant because, uh, after insects get caught in the main web, they fall into the trap. Once the prey is trapped, the spiders then do something amazing. ³They all move toward the prey together. First, they move a short distance, and then they stop... They do this repeatedly. The spiders look like dancers giving an organized performance on a stage...

With every motion, the spiders can feel the movements of the trapped prey. In this way, every spider knows where to find the trapped prey quickly. Working as a group also helps them kill larger prey... Um, you see, social spiders are very small. That's why they usually attack their prey in large numbers. ⁴In some cases, they can catch prey that is over 700 times their own weight! So, there is usually more than enough food for all of them...

생물학 강의의 일부를 들으시오.

P: 다음으로, 여러분에게 아주 흥미로운 거미들을 소개할 거예요. 그것들은 사회적 거미의 일종으로, 'Anelosimus eximius'라고 불립니다. 대부분의 거미들은 홀로 있는 것을 좋아하지만, 이 거미들은 남아메리카의 일부 열대 우림에서 큰 무리를 지어 살아요. 그것들의 사회적 습성의 몇 가지 특징에 집중해 봅시다.

이 거미들은 열대 우림에 거대한 거미줄을 만듭니다. 수천 마리의 거미들이 이 거미줄에서 함께 살죠. 그것들은 거미줄을 만들고 거미줄의 손상된 부분을 고치는 등, 어, 다양한 일을 합니다. 그것들은 새끼 거미도 돌보죠...

하지만 그것들이 하는 가장 흥미로운 일은 집단으로 사냥하는 것입니다. 이 거미들은 두 종류의 거미줄을 만들어요. 그것들의 주 거미줄은 그물처럼 펼쳐져 있죠. 그 아래에는 또 다른 거미줄이 있는데, 이것은 그릇처럼 생겨서 덫의 역할을 합니다. 이것은 기발한데요, 왜냐하면, 어, 곤충들이 주 거미줄에 걸린 후에, 덫 안으로 떨어지기 때문이죠. 먹이가 덫에 걸리면, 거미들은 놀라운 일을 해요. 그것들은 다 같이 먹이쪽으로 움직이는데요. 먼저, 그것들은 짧은 거리를 갔다가, 그리고 나서 멈춥니다... 그것들은 이것을 반복적으로 해요. 그 거미들은 마치 무대 위에서 조직적인 공연을 하는 무용수들처럼 보이죠...

매 동작마다, 거미들은 덫에 걸린 먹이의 움직임을 느낄 수 있어요. 이런 식으로, 모든 거미는 덫에 걸린 먹이를 어디에서 빠르게 찾을 수 있는지 알 수 있죠... 집단으로 움직이는 것은 그것들이 더 큰 먹이를 사냥하는 데에도 도움이 됩니다... 음, 그러니까, 사회적 거미는 매우 작아요. 이것이 그것들이 보통 많은 수로 먹이를 공격하는 이유죠. 어떤 경우에는, 그것들은 자신의 몸무게의 700배가 넘는 먹이를 잡을 수 있어요! 그래서, 보통은 그것들 전부에게 충분하고도 남을 양의 식량이 생기죠...

---

social 혱 사회적인, 사회의   rainforest 몡 열대 우림
South America 남아메리카   behavior 몡 습성, 행동
web 몡 거미줄   damaged 혱 손상된, 손해를 입은
net 몡 그물; 망사   bowl 몡 그릇   trap 몡 덫
brilliant 혱 기발한, 훌륭한   organized 혱 조직적인, 정리된
motion 몡 동작, 움직임   movement 몡 움직임

1 강의의 주된 주제는 무엇인가?
    (A) 사회적 거미가 어떻게 거미줄을 만드는지
    (B) 남아메리카의 다양한 종류의 거미
    (C) 사회적 거미의 특별한 습성
    (D) 두 거미 종들의 유사성

2 교수에 따르면, 거미들이 하는 두 가지 일은 무엇인가? 2개의 답을 고르시오.
    (A) 다른 동물들로부터 거미줄을 보호하기
    (B) 거미줄을 만들고 고치기
    (C) 새끼 거미를 돌보기
    (D) 새 집 찾기

3 교수는 왜 무대 위의 공연을 이야기하는가?
    (A) 사회적 거미가 어떻게 먹이를 잡는지 설명하기 위해
    (B) 거미줄이 어떻게 만들어지는지 보여주기 위해
    (C) 거미가 얼마나 빨리 움직이는지 묘사하기 위해
    (D) 사회적 거미가 집단으로 사는 이유를 설명하기 위해

4 교수는 거미들의 먹이에 관해 무엇을 암시하는가?
    (A) 거미들은 보통 그것을 먹기 전에 저장한다.
    (B) 거미들은 때때로 그것을 위해 서로 싸운다.
    (C) 그것은 종종 거미들이 필요로 하는 것보다 더 많은 식량을 제공한다.
    (D) 그것은 때때로 거미들의 덫에서 탈출한다.

Listening Practice 3   본문 p. 141

1 (A)   2 (C)   3 (D)

Note-taking
Student's Problem
Couldn't find a poetry collection for an English literature class

Librarian's Response
• Lost our only copy of the book
• Try our interlibrary loan system

Listen to a conversation between a student and a librarian.

M: Excuse me. I'm writing an essay for my English literature class. ¹So, I need a poetry collection called *The Tennis Court Oath*. It's by John Ashbury. Could you help me find it?

W: Umm... Did you check the library's website? You can search by the book's title or author.

M: Actually, I already did. There is supposed to be one copy here. But I couldn't find it on the shelves.

W: Just a moment... Ah, I see. It's marked as missing.

M: What do you mean?

W: Uh, it means we've lost our only copy of the book. But the library has ordered a new one.

M: OK. When do you think it will arrive? My paper is due next Friday, so I really need the book.

W: Uh, I'm sorry, but it will take at least two weeks to get here.

M: Oh, no. Is there nothing I can do? It's too late to change the topic of my essay.

W: ²Why don't you try our interlibrary loan system? Our library is part of an interlibrary program. ²/³If you submit a request for a book, a partner library will send it to us. Uh, if it's not checked out. I'm sure one of the other libraries will have it.

M: Thank you so much for your help! ³I'll do that now.

학생과 사서 사이의 대화를 들으시오.

M: 실례합니다. 저는 제 영문학 수업을 위해 에세이를 쓰고 있는데요. 그래서, '테니스 코트의 서약'이라는 시집이 필요합니다. 존 애쉬베리의 작품이에요. 찾는 것을 도와주시겠어요?

W: 음... 도서관 웹사이트는 확인해 보셨나요? 책의 제목이나 저자로 검색하실 수 있어요.

M: 사실, 이미 해봤어요. 여기에 한 권이 있어야 되는데요. 그런데 그걸 책꽂이에서 찾을 수 없었어요.

W: 잠시만요... 아, 그렇군요. 그것이 분실된 것으로 표시되어 있네요.

M: 무슨 말씀이신가요?

W: 어, 저희가 유일한 그 책 한 권을 잃어버렸다는 뜻이에요. 하지만 도서관에서 새 책을 주문했어요.

M: 알겠습니다. 언제쯤 도착할 것 같으세요? 제 보고서가 다음 주 금요일까지라서, 그 책이 꼭 필요해요.

W: 어, 죄송하지만, 여기 오는데 적어도 2주는 걸릴 거예요.

M: 오, 어떡하죠. 제가 할 수 있는 일은 없나요? 제 에세이의 주제를 바꾸기에는 너무 늦었어요.

W: 저희의 도서관 상호대차 제도를 이용해 보시는 건 어떨까요? 저희 도서관이 도서관 상호 프로그램의 일원이거든요. 학생이 책에 대한 요청서를 제출하면, 협력 도서관에서 그것을 저희에게 보내줄 거예요. 어, 그것이 대출되지 않았다면요. 분명 다른 도서관 중 한 곳은 그것을 가지고 있을 거예요.

M: 도와주셔서 정말 감사합니다! 지금 바로 할게요.

English literature 영문학　poetry collection 시집
search 동 검색하다, 찾아보다　copy 명 권, 복사본
missing 형 분실된, 없어진
interlibrary loan system 도서관 상호대차 제도　request 명 요청(서)

1 학생은 왜 사서와 이야기하는가?
　(A) 책을 찾는 데 도움을 요청하기 위해
　(B) 도서관 웹사이트의 이용 방법을 알아보기 위해
　(C) 도서관에서 분실물을 찾기 위해
　(D) 그가 빌린 책을 반납하기 위해

2 사서는 왜 도서관 상호대차 제도를 언급하는가?
　(A) 프로그램에 대해 불평하기 위해
　(B) 최근의 실수를 설명하기 위해
　(C) 학생에게 선택지를 제공하기 위해
　(D) 도서관이 개선되고 있음을 보여주기 위해

3 학생은 다음에 무엇을 할 것인가?
　(A) 인터넷에서 시를 찾아보기
　(B) 대학 서점 방문하기
　(C) 그의 교수님과 이야기하러 가기
　(D) 책에 대해 요청하기

Listening Practice 4　본문 p.143

1 (C)　**2** (B)　**3** (D)　**4** (B)

Note-taking

Innovations by Jacques Cousteau
- Aqua-Lung: A breathing device that allowed divers to move freely and take better pictures
- A new underwater camera: Light, easy to hold, with a waterproof case

Listen to part of a lecture in a photography class.

P: Since the 19th century, underwater photography has been an important art form and a scientific tool. At first, it had many problems. The equipment was limited and color was difficult to capture underwater. ¹/³Then, a French photographer named Jacques Cousteau introduced innovations that influenced and improved underwater photography. Let's discuss those today.

³The first innovation was the Aqua-Lung. It was a breathing device that Cousteau developed in 1946 with Emile Gagnan, a French engineer. The Aqua-Lung allowed divers to move more freely because they did not have to use difficult and heavy equipment. ²It also helped them take better pictures. When they breathed out air, the, uh, air bubbles went behind their head. The bubbles didn't block their view, which allowed them to take clearer pictures.

³Another innovation was in cameras. Before, most cameras didn't work very well underwater.

They were, uh, slow and easily damaged by water. ⁴They also produced low-quality images. Well, in 1957, Cousteau and a Belgian inventor named Jean de Wouters developed a new kind of underwater camera. It was better in every way. It was light and easy to hold... But what made this camera so special was its waterproof case. This made the camera completely waterproof, which helped underwater photography significantly!

³With these innovations, Cousteau explored the deep oceans and shared what he saw with viewers. This helped people have a better understanding of the underwater world.

사진학 강의의 일부를 들으시오.

P: 19세기부터, 수중 사진은 중요한 예술 형태이자 과학적인 도구가 되어왔습니다. 처음에, 그것은 많은 문제점이 있었어요. 장비는 제한되어 있었고 물속에서 색을 정확히 담아내기가 어려웠죠. 그러다, 자크 쿠스토라는 한 프랑스 사진작가가 수중 사진에 영향을 주고 발전시킨 발명품들을 선보였는데요. 오늘은 그것들에 대해 논의합시다.

첫 번째 발명품은 아쿠아렁이었어요. 그것은 쿠스토가 1946년에 프랑스 기술자인 에밀 가냥과 함께 개발한 호흡 장치였죠. 아쿠아렁은 잠수부들이 어렵고 무거운 장비를 사용하지 않아도 돼서 더 자유롭게 움직일 수 있게 해주었습니다. 그것은 또한 더 좋은 사진을 찍을 수 있도록 해주었죠. 그들이 숨을 내쉬면, 그, 어, 기포가 머리 뒤로 갔어요. 기포들이 그들의 시야를 막지 않았는데, 이것이 더 선명한 사진을 찍을 수 있게 해주었죠.

또 다른 혁신은 카메라에 있었어요. 이전에는, 대부분의 카메라가 물속에서 잘 작동하지 않았어요. 그것들은, 어, 속도가 느리고 물에 의해 쉽게 손상되기도 했죠. 그것들은 또한 저품질의 이미지를 만들어냈어요. 음, 1957년에, 쿠스토와 장 드 바우터스라는 벨기에 발명가는 새로운 종류의 수중 카메라를 개발했는데요. 그것은 모든 면에서 더 좋았습니다. 그것은 가볍고 잡기가 쉬웠죠... 하지만 이 카메라를 정말 특별하게 만든 것은 방수 케이스였습니다. 이것은 카메라가 완전히 방수가 되도록 했는데, 이는 수중 사진에 큰 도움을 주었어요!

이러한 발명품들로, 쿠스토는 깊은 바다를 탐험했고 그가 본 것을 관객들과 공유했어요. 이것은 사람들이 수중 세계를 더 잘 이해하는 데 도움이 되었습니다.

underwater photography 수중 사진(술)
capture (동) 정확히 담아내다; 포획하다
photographer (명) 사진작가   innovation (명) 발명품, 혁신
breathing (명) 호흡   engineer (명) 기술자; 기사   diver (명) 잠수부
air bubble 기포   view (명) 시야; 견해   Belgian (형) 벨기에의
waterproof (형) 방수의   viewer (명) 관객, 시청자

1 강의는 주로 무엇에 관한 것인가?
  (A) 세상을 바꾼 과학적인 발견들
  (B) 물속에서 사진을 찍기 위해 사용되는 방법들
  (C) 한 사람이 수중 사진술에 미친 영향
  (D) 자연 다큐멘터리에서 사진의 역할

2 교수에 따르면, 아쿠아렁의 한 가지 장점은 무엇이었는가?

  (A) 그것은 누구나 쉽게 고칠 수 있었다.
  (B) 그것은 사진작가들에게 더 선명한 시야를 주었다.
  (C) 그것은 몇몇 새로운 발명품에 영감을 주었다.
  (D) 그것은 물 밖에서도 유용했다.

3 교수는 강의를 어떻게 구성하는가?
  (A) 서로 다른 두 탐사를 비교함으로써
  (B) 사진술의 발전을 보여줌으로써
  (C) 유명한 사진작가들의 이름을 언급함으로써
  (D) 몇몇 발명품들의 영향에 대해 이야기함으로써

4 교수는 쿠스토의 카메라에 관해 무엇을 암시하는가?
  (A) 그것은 이전 카메라들보다 크기가 더 컸다.
  (B) 그것은 고품질의 이미지를 만들어냈다.
  (C) 그것은 전부 금속으로 만들어졌다.
  (D) 그것은 아쿠아렁에 부착할 수도 있었다.

iBT Listening Test 1   본문 p. 145

1 (D)   2 (C)   3 Yes: (A), (D) No: (B), (C)   4 (A)

Note-taking
Student's Problem
Missed the midterm exam because of an accident
→ Wants to take a makeup test

Professor's Answer
Tests can be missed for students' own medical reasons.
→ Will review your academic scores

Listen to a conversation between a student and a professor.

S: Hi, Professor Brown. ¹I'm sorry about missing yesterday's midterm exam. Um, do you think I could take a makeup test?

P: Hello, Carol. We can talk about that. But why couldn't you take it yesterday?

S: There was an accident. My grandmother fell down the stairs, and, uh, I had to take her to the hospital.

P: Oh, I'm sorry to hear that. I hope it's nothing serious.

S: Well, she broke her wrist, but she's doing fine. The doctors fixed her up, and she returned home today.

P: OK, good... Now, about the test...

S: Yes, I was wondering if you would let me take a makeup test. I'm prepared to take it at any time.

P: ²Well, students can usually only miss tests for their own medical reasons. That's the university's policy. Um, makeup tests for other reasons are sometimes allowed, but only in special cases.

S: I understand, Professor. ³A/⁴Um, what if I called my grandmother's doctor and asked for a doctor's note? It will show that I was at the hospital yesterday.

P: ³ᴬThat could help, but I don't think it will be enough.

S: ³ᴰBut if you check my overall score, it's quite good... And I've never missed a test or assignment before.

P: ³ᴰYes, that might help. I'll have to review your academic scores again, though. Um, if your scores are good and you've worked hard in class, I may allow you to take a makeup test.

S: Thank you, Professor. ⁴I'll let you know about the doctor's note in a few minutes.

학생과 교수 사이의 대화를 들으시오.

S: 안녕하세요, Brown 교수님. 어제 중간고사를 못 보아서 죄송합니다. 음, 제가 추가 시험을 볼 수 있을까요?

P: 안녕, Carol. 그것에 대해 이야기해 볼 수 있단다. 그런데 어제 왜 그것을 볼 수 없었니?

S: 사고가 있었어요. 저희 할머니께서 계단에서 굴러 떨어지셔서, 어, 제가 병원에 데려다 드려야 했거든요.

P: 오, 그것 참 유감이구나. 심각한 일이 아니어야 할 텐데.

S: 음, 할머니께서 손목이 부러지셨지만, 괜찮으세요. 의사들이 할머니를 치료해서, 오늘 집에 돌아오셨어요.

P: 그래, 잘됐구나... 이제, 시험에 대해서...

S: 네, 교수님께서 제가 추가 시험을 볼 수 있게 해주실 수 있는지 궁금해요. 전 언제든지 볼 준비가 되어 있어요.

P: 음, 학생들은 보통 본인의 건강상의 이유로만 시험을 못 보는 게 가능해. 그게 대학의 방침이야. 음, 다른 이유로 인한 추가 시험이 가끔 허용되지만, 특별한 경우에만 그렇단다.

S: 알겠습니다, 교수님. 음, 제가 할머니의 의사에게 전화해서 의사 진단서를 달라고 하면 어떨까요? 제가 어제 병원에 있었다는 것을 보여줄 거예요.

P: 그게 도움이 될 수도 있겠지만, 충분하지 않을 것 같구나.

S: 하지만 제 전체적인 점수를 보시면, 꽤 괜찮은 편이에요. 그리고 저는 시험이나 과제를 한 번도 놓친 적이 없고요.

P: 그래, 그것도 도움이 될 것 같네. 그래도, 네 학업 성적을 다시 한 번 검토해 봐야겠어. 음, 네 성적이 좋고 수업 시간에 열심히 했다면, 추가 시험을 보도록 허락해 줄 수도 있겠구나.

S: 감사합니다, 교수님. 잠시 후에 의사 진단서에 대해 알려드릴게요.

makeup test 추가 시험   fall down the stairs 계단에서 굴러 떨어지다
wrist 몡 손목   prepared 혱 준비가 된
medical 혱 건강상의, 의학의   policy 몡 방침, 정책
doctor's note 의사 진단서   overall 혱 전체적인, 종합적인
academic 혱 학업의

1 학생의 문제는 무엇인가?
   (A) 그녀는 병원에 가야 한다.
   (B) 그녀는 과제에 대해 기록한 것을 잃어버렸다.
   (C) 그녀는 수업에서 낮은 점수를 받았다.
   (D) 그녀는 중요한 시험을 치지 않았다.

2 교수는 대학 방침에 관해 무엇이라고 말하는가?
   (A) 그것은 최근에 변경되었다.
   (B) 일부 학생들이 그것에 대해 불평했다.
   (C) 그것은 일부 상황에서는 예외가 허용된다.
   (D) 일부 교수들은 그것에 동의하지 않는다.

3 학생의 사례에 도움이 될 수 있는 방안들은 무엇인가? 다음의 항목이 방안인지를 표시하시오.
   각 항목에 적절한 칸을 클릭하시오.

	예	아니오
(A) 의사 진단서 보여주기	V	
(B) 추가 과제 제출하기		V
(C) 더 많은 수업 토론에 참여하기		V
(D) 좋은 전체적인 점수 갖기	V	

4 학생은 다음에 무엇을 할 것인가?
   (A) 의사에게 전화하기
   (B) 몇 가지 서류 작성하기
   (C) 그녀의 할머니를 방문하기
   (D) 시험 준비하기

iBT Listening Test 2   본문 p. 148

1 (D)   2 (B)   3 (C)   4 (D)   5 (C)

Note-taking
1939 ~ 1940
Nazi-Soviet Pact: A secret agreement for control of Eastern Europe countries
→ Soviet Union took control of the Baltic countries.

1986
People escaped from the Baltic countries to the West.
→ Held protests every year on August 23

1989
Baltic Chain: The Baltic people formed a human chain.
→ The Baltic countries declared independence.

Listen to part of a lecture in a history class.

P: What happened in Eastern Europe during the Cold War? Um, in 1989, two years before the Cold War ended, three countries wanted independence from the Soviet Union. These were Estonia, Latvia, and Lithuania. Now, these countries are called the Baltic countries because they are near the coast of the Baltic Sea. ¹The Baltic countries organized a protest that became known as the Baltic Chain.

¹ᐟ²Before we talk about this in detail, let's review some key events that led to this protest... The first one happened on August 23, 1939. This was when Nazi Germany and the Soviet Union made

an agreement called the Nazi-Soviet Pact. This agreement promised that they would not attack one another. ³It also included a secret agreement for control of countries in Eastern Europe. So, in 1940, the Soviet Union took control of the Baltic countries.

²By 1986, many people who were unhappy with the situation escaped from the Baltic countries to the West. There, they held protests every year on August 23, which was the same day that the Nazi-Soviet Pact was signed. They wanted to tell the world about the harm caused by the Soviet Union... Meanwhile, people who remained in the Baltic countries learned about these protests in the West and decided to hold their own. They planned their protest for August 23, 1989. This was the 50th anniversary of the Nazi-Soviet Pact. This protest became the Baltic Chain.

⁴The Baltic Chain was actually a human chain. Many people formed a long line while holding each other's hands... And there was a reason why the protest was done in this way. The Baltic people believed that a violent protest would cause more violence from the Soviet Union. ⁵So, instead of choosing violence, two million people held hands in a long line. This line went across all three Baltic countries and was over 675 kilometers long. Now, imagine a human chain that long... It must have been quite a sight! Well, various news media reported on the event and helped spread its message. This message was that the people of the Baltic countries wanted independence... Only seven months after the Baltic Chain, Lithuania became the first of these countries to declare independence. It was followed by Estonia and Latvia.

역사학 강의의 일부를 들으시오.

P: 냉전 동안 동유럽에서는 무슨 일이 일어났을까요? 음, 냉전이 끝나기 2년 전인 1989년에, 세 나라가 소련으로부터 독립을 원했습니다. 이 나라들은 에스토니아, 라트비아, 그리고 리투아니아였죠. 자, 이 나라들은 발트해의 해안 근처에 있기 때문에 발트 국가라고 불립니다. 발트 국가들은 발트의 사슬이라고 알려진 시위를 조직했어요.

이것에 대해 자세히 이야기하기 전에, 이 시위를 야기한 몇 가지 주요 사건들을 살펴봅시다... 첫 번째는 1939년 8월 23일에 일어났습니다. 이것은 나치 독일과 소련이 독소불가침조약이라고 불리는 협정을 맺었을 때였어요. 이 협정에서 그들은 서로를 공격하지 않겠다고 약속했어요. 그것은 또한 동유럽 국가들을 통제하는 것에 대한 비밀 협정을 포함했죠. 그래서, 1940년에, 소련은 발트 국가들을 장악했습니다.

1986년까지, 그 상황에 불만이 있던 많은 사람들이 발트 국가들에서 서부 지역으로 탈출했어요. 그곳에서, 그들은 매년 8월 23일에 시위를 열었는데, 이는 독소불가침조약이 서명된 날과 같은 날이었죠. 그들은 소련이 초래한 피해에 대해 세상에 알리고 싶었던 거예요... 한편, 발트 국가들에 남아있던 사람들은 서부 지역에서 일어난 이 시위들에 대해 알게 되었고 그들 자신의 시위를 열기로 결심했어요. 그들은 1989년 8월 23일에 그들의 시위를 계획했습니다. 이 날은 독소불가침조약을 맺은지가 50년이 된 날이었어요. 이 시위가 발트의 사슬이 되었습니다.

발트의 사슬은 사실 인간 사슬이었습니다. 많은 사람들이 서로의 손을 잡은 채 긴 줄을 섰어요... 그리고 시위가 이런 식으로 진행된 데는 이유가 있었죠. 발트 사람들은 폭력적인 시위가 소련의 폭력을 더 유발할 것이라고 믿었어요. 그래서, 폭력을 선택하는 대신, 2백만 명의 사람들이 긴 줄을 서서 손을 잡았습니다. 이 줄은 세 발트 국가를 모두 가로질렀고 길이가 675킬로미터가 넘었어요. 자, 이렇게 긴 인간 사슬을 상상해 보세요... 그것은 정말 놀라운 광경이었겠죠! 음, 다양한 뉴스 매체들이 그 사건에 대해 보도했고 그것의 메시지를 퍼뜨리는 것을 도왔어요. 이 메시지는 발트 국가의 사람들이 독립을 원한다는 것이었죠... 발트의 사슬 이후 겨우 7개월 후에, 리투아니아는 이 국가들 중 독립을 선언한 첫 번째 국가가 되었습니다. 에스토니아와 라트비아가 그 뒤를 이었죠.

---

independence 똉 독립   Soviet Union 소련
Estonia 똉 에스토니아   Latvia 똉 라트비아
Lithuania 똉 리투아니아   Baltic Sea 발트해
protest 똉 시위, 항의   Baltic Chain 발트의 사슬
agreement 똉 협정   Nazi-Soviet Pact 독소불가침조약
take control of ~을 장악하다   violent 휑 폭력적인
media 똉 매체   report 통 보도하다, 알리다
declare 통 선언하다

1 강의는 주로 무엇에 관한 것인가?

   (A) 냉전의 이유들
   (B) 발트 국가의 정치인들
   (C) 냉전 동안의 유럽의 역할
   (D) 대규모 시위의 뒷이야기

2 교수는 발트의 사슬을 어떻게 소개하는가?

   (A) 정치인들에게 있어서 그것의 중요성을 설명함으로써
   (B) 그것을 초래한 사건들을 설명함으로써
   (C) 다른 나라들의 사건과 비교함으로써
   (D) 그것을 시작한 지도자들에 대해 이야기함으로써

3 독소불가침조약의 중요성은 무엇이었는가?

   (A) 그것은 나치로부터 발트 국가들을 보호하는 데 도움을 주었다.
   (B) 그것은 소련에 일부 독일 영토를 주었다.
   (C) 그것은 소련이 발트 국가들을 장악하도록 했다.
   (D) 그것은 결국 2차 세계 대전의 종결로 이어졌다.

4 교수는 발트의 사슬에 관해 무엇을 암시하는가?

   (A) 그것은 서부 지역에 있는 사람들에 의해 조직되었다.
   (B) 그것은 소련을 폭력적으로 만들었다.
   (C) 그것은 많은 사람들이 발트 국가들을 떠나도록 만들었다.
   (D) 그것은 평화로운 형태의 시위였다.

강의의 일부를 다시 듣고 질문에 답하시오.

P: So, instead of choosing violence, two million people held hands in a long line. This line went across all three Baltic countries and was over 675 kilometers long. Now, imagine a human chain that long... It must have been quite a sight!

5 교수는 왜 이렇게 말하는가:
P: It must have been quite a sight!

(A) 그가 시위를 직접 봤다는 것을 암시하기 위해
(B) 시위가 텔레비전에 방영되지 않았다고 말하기 위해
(C) 시위의 규모를 강조하기 위해
(D) 시위에 대한 보도들이 틀렸다는 것을 설명하기 위해

Vocabulary Review 본문 p. 152

1 ceremony	2 ancient	3 innovation
4 waterproof	5 publication	6 store
7 medical	8 Violent	9 protest
10 (C)	11 (A)	12 (B)
13 (A)	14 (D)	

Actual Test 1

PART 1. Passage 1 본문 p. 154

1 (C)   2 (C)   3 (A)
4 Yes: (A), (D)   No: (B), (C)   5 (C)

Note-taking

Student's Problem
Wants to find a part-time job related to journalism major
→ Will help future career

Professor's Suggestion
• Apply for an internship
• Get a job with *Reflections* magazine
  → Looking for a student assistant

Listen to a conversation between a student and a professor.

S: Hi, Professor Neville. Could I ask you something? ¹Um, I need to find a part-time job that's related to my journalism major. Do you know of any jobs like that?

P: Hi, Carla. Well, I know it's too late to work as a campus reporter. Those jobs are usually taken in the first semester... Um, what are you doing now?

S: I'm working in the campus café... The job is OK, but I want to find something that will help my future career.

P: I understand. ⁴ᴬHave you considered applying for an internship?

S: I have, but I'm too busy. ²/⁴ᴮI'd have to work full-time as an intern, but I need to take some courses this summer break to graduate. That's why I only want a part-time job... ⁴ᶜUm, are you looking for a research assistant for a project?

P: I'm sorry, Carla, but there aren't any new projects right now. Hmm... ⁴ᴰHowever, you might be able to get a job with *Reflections* magazine. That's the magazine for students who have graduated from our university.

S: Yes! I've seen copies of the magazine on campus. That would be great!

P: Um, yes, but before you get too excited, I should warn you. They're looking for a student assistant. So, you will probably do small tasks like make phone calls and copy documents.

S: Oh, right... Well, that's better than nothing.

P: ³Yes, it's still a good job to consider. You'll be able to see what professional reporters do. And if you work hard, you may get a chance to write your own articles eventually. That would help your future career.

S: That's right! ⁵Um, can I go to their office now and ask them about the position?

P: Actually, let me call first. The magazine usually hires more experienced students. I'll talk to the editor and tell her that you did good work in class.

S: I really appreciate that, Professor. I'll wait to hear from you then.

학생과 교수 사이의 대화를 들으시오.

S: 안녕하세요, Neville 교수님. 뭐 좀 여쭤봐도 될까요? 음, 저는 제 신문방송학 전공과 관련된 아르바이트직을 찾아야 하는데요. 그런 일자리를 알고 계시나요?

P: 안녕, Carla. 음, 캠퍼스 기자로 일하기에 너무 늦었다는 건 안단다. 그 일자리들은 보통 1학기 중에 자리가 다 차서 말이야... 음, 지금은 무엇을 하고 있니?

S: 캠퍼스 카페에서 일하고 있어요... 일은 괜찮지만, 저는 제 미래 진로에 도움이 될 만한 것을 찾고 싶어서요.

P: 이해한단다. 인턴직에 지원하는 것은 고려해 봤니?

S: 해봤는데, 제가 너무 바빠서요. 인턴으로는 전시간 일을 해야 할 텐데, 졸업하기 위해서는 이번 여름 방학에 몇몇 강의들을 들어야 하거든요. 그게 제가 아르바이트직만 원하는 이유예요... 음, 프로젝트 연구 조교를 찾고 계신 중인가요?

P: 미안하지만, Carla, 지금은 새로운 프로젝트가 없단다. 흠... 하지만 '리플렉션스' 잡지사에서 일자리를 구할 수 있을지도 모르겠구나. 그것은 우리 대학을 졸업한 학생들을 위한 잡지란다.

S: 네! 캠퍼스에서 그 잡지를 몇 부 본 적 있어요. 좋을 것 같아요!

P: 음, 그래, 하지만 너무 들뜨기 전에, 미리 알려줘야겠구나. 그들은 학생 조교를 찾고 있단다. 그래서, 아마 전화를 하거나 문서를 복사하는 것과 같은 작은 일들을 하게 될 거야.

S: 오, 그렇군요... 음, 그래도 안 하는 것보다는 낫겠죠.

P: 맞아, 그래도 고려해 볼 만한 괜찮은 일자리야. 전문 기자들이 하는 일을 볼 수 있을 거고. 그리고 만약 열심히 한다면, 언젠가 네

기사를 쓸 수 있는 기회를 얻을지도 몰라. 그건 네 미래 진로에 도움이 되겠지.

S: 맞아요! 음, 제가 지금 그들의 사무실에 가서 그 일자리에 대해 물어봐도 될까요?

P: 아니, 내가 먼저 전화해보마. 그 잡지사는 보통 경험이 더 많은 학생들을 고용하거든. 내가 편집장과 이야기해서 네가 수업 시간에 잘했다고 전할게.

S: 정말 감사합니다, 교수님. 그럼 연락 기다리겠습니다.

part-time job 아르바이트직 journalism 명 신문방송학, 저널리즘
major 명 전공   reporter 명 기자
internship 명 인턴직, 인턴사원 근무 (기간)
research assistant 연구 조교   warn 동 미리 알려주다, 주의하다
student assistant 학생 조교   eventually 부 언젠가, 결국
hire 동 고용하다; 빌리다   editor 명 편집장

1 학생은 왜 교수를 찾아가는가?
(A) 그녀는 진로를 결정하는 데 더 많은 시간이 필요하다.
(B) 그녀는 캠퍼스에서 일하는 것에 대해 생각하고 있다.
(C) 그녀는 자신의 전공과 관련된 일자리를 원한다.
(D) 그녀는 졸업 후에 무엇을 해야 할지 모른다.

2 학생은 왜 여름 동안 인턴직을 할 수 없는가?
(A) 그녀는 가족과 함께 여행을 간다.
(B) 그녀는 프로젝트를 진행할 것이다.
(C) 그녀는 몇몇 수업들을 들어야 한다.
(D) 그녀는 몇 가지 요건을 충족하지 못한다.

3 교수는 학생 조교 일자리에 대한 그의 생각을 어떻게 밝히는가?
(A) 그것이 어떻게 이후의 진로에 영향을 미칠 수 있는지 설명함으로써
(B) 다른 학생의 경험을 설명함으로써
(C) 그것이 어떻게 학생의 성적을 향상시킬 수 있는지 보여줌으로써
(D) 그것이 많은 힘든 일을 수반한다고 주의를 줌으로써

4 교수는 학생을 돕기 위해 몇 가지 제안을 한다. 다음의 항목이 교수가 언급한 제안인지를 표시하시오.
각 항목에 적절한 칸을 클릭하시오.

	예	아니오
(A) 인턴 기자로 지원하기	V	
(B) 방학 동안 전시간 근무직을 찾기		V
(C) 연구 프로젝트와 관련해서 교수를 돕기		V
(D) 학교 관련 잡지사에서 일하기	V	

대화의 일부를 다시 듣고 질문에 답하시오.

S: Um, can I go to their office now and ask them about the position?

P: Actually, let me call first. The magazine usually hires more experienced students. I'll talk to the editor and tell her that you did good work in class.

5 교수는 왜 이렇게 말하는가:
P: Actually, let me call first.
(A) 그는 일자리에 대해 다른 교수들의 의견을 묻고 싶다.
(B) 그는 편집장이 경험이 충분하지 않다고 생각한다.
(C) 그는 학생이 일자리를 갖게 될 가능성을 높이고 싶다.
(D) 그는 편집장이 사무실에 없을 수도 있다고 생각한다.

PART 1. Passage 2 본문 p. 156

6 (B)   7 (C)   8 (B)   9 (C)
10 (D)-(B)-(A)-(C)   11 (B)

Note-taking

Photosynthesis
: A process that plants make their own energy
→ Needs four things: Chlorophyll, sunlight, water and carbon dioxide

How Plants Do Photosynthesis
1. Plants consume water from the soil.
2. Leaves absorb carbon dioxide from the air.
3. Chlorophyll uses sunlight to produce sugars.
4. Plants release oxygen from their leaves.

Listen to part of a lecture in a biology class.

P: Animals, including humans, produce energy by eating food. Then, how about plants? [6]Actually, plants make their own energy. In this lecture, we're going to focus on how plants do this. [8]They use a process called photosynthesis...

Plants need four things to do this. The first is chlorophyll. [7]Chlorophyll is the chemical that causes plants to be green in color. It exists in the plants' cells. Uh, the other three things are sunlight, water, and carbon dioxide. The process of photosynthesis goes like this... [10D]First, plants consume water from the soil through their roots. [10B]Next, the leaves absorb carbon dioxide from the air. Uh, there are tiny holes on the surface of the leaves, and the carbon dioxide enters these... Once the plants absorb the carbon dioxide, they then use energy from sunlight. This is when the chlorophyll becomes important. [10A]Chlorophyll uses sunlight to produce sugars, which are the plants' food. These sugars provide the energy for plants to grow and heal themselves. Some of the sugars are used immediately, and some are stored for later... [10C]And, uh, the final step is... uh, plants release oxygen from their leaves. It goes out through little holes, just like the carbon dioxide comes in...

S: [9]So, uh, the carbon dioxide and oxygen parts... I guess that's how plants breathe...

P: Well, yes and no... We don't call it breathing in plants. We call it respiration. But, actually, this is a helpful way to understand it. Unlike people, plants need to "breathe in" carbon dioxide, and they need to "breathe out" oxygen. So, plant respiration is exactly the opposite of how you and I breathe...

Anyway, photosynthesis is influenced by several factors. I've already mentioned two of these, sunlight and carbon dioxide. If there is not enough sunlight, photosynthesis occurs very slowly. Similarly, there has to be enough carbon dioxide. [11]Now, the other factor is temperature. Plants cannot easily perform photosynthesis in extreme temperatures. So, it depends on the weather, climate, and seasons...

[8]Now, photosynthesis is important for all life. Why is this? Well, this is because plants store carbon dioxide. As you might know, too much carbon dioxide in the air can cause global warming. So, by removing carbon dioxide from the air, plants can help prevent climate change. And, uh, by releasing oxygen, they also improve the air quality for all of us.

생물학 강의의 일부를 들으시오.

P: 인간을 포함해서, 동물은 음식을 섭취함으로써 에너지를 생산하죠. 그렇다면, 식물은 어떨까요? 사실, 식물은 스스로 에너지를 만들어요. 이번 강의에서는, 식물이 어떻게 이것을 하는지에 집중할 거예요. 그것들은 광합성이라고 불리는 과정을 이용합니다...

식물이 이것을 하기 위해서는 네 가지가 필요해요. 첫 번째는 엽록소입니다. 엽록소는 식물이 녹색을 띠도록 하는 화학물질인데요. 그것은 식물의 세포 안에 존재해요. 어, 다른 세 가지는 햇빛, 물, 그리고 이산화탄소입니다. 광합성의 과정은 이렇게 진행돼요... 먼저, 식물이 그것들의 뿌리를 통해 흙으로부터 물을 섭취합니다. 다음으로, 잎들이 공기 중의 이산화탄소를 흡수해요. 어, 잎의 표면에는 작은 구멍들이 있는데, 이산화탄소가 이것들 안으로 들어가죠... 식물이 이산화탄소를 흡수하고 나면, 그것들은 그 후 햇빛에서 나온 에너지를 사용해요. 이때 엽록소가 중요해집니다. 엽록소는 햇빛을 이용해 당을 생산하는데, 이것이 식물의 먹이입니다. 이 당은 식물이 자라고 스스로 치유할 수 있는 에너지를 제공하죠. 당의 일부는 바로 쓰이고, 일부는 나중을 위해 저장됩니다... 그리고, 어, 마지막 단계는... 어, 식물이 잎에서 산소를 방출해요. 이것은 작은 구멍들을 통해 나가요, 꼭 이산화탄소가 들어오는 것 같이요...

S: 그러면, 어, 이산화탄소와 산소 부분이... 그게 식물이 숨 쉬는 방법이겠네요...

P: 음, 그렇기도 하고 아니기도 해요... 식물의 경우 우리는 그걸 숨쉬기라고 부르지 않거든요. 우리는 그것을 호흡이라고 불러요. 하지만, 사실, 이게 그것을 이해하는 데 도움이 되는 방법이기는 해요. 사람과 달리, 식물은 이산화탄소를 "들이마셔야" 하고, 산소를 "내쉬어야" 하니까요. 그래서, 식물의 호흡은 여러분과 제가 숨 쉬는 방법과는 정확히 반대인 거죠...

어쨌든, 광합성은 몇 가지 요인에 의해 영향을 받죠. 제가 이미 이 중 두 가지를 언급했죠, 햇빛과 이산화탄소에요. 만약 햇빛이 충분하지 않으면, 광합성은 매우 천천히 일어나요. 마찬가지로, 이산화탄소가 충분히 있어야 합니다. 자, 다른 요인은 온도예요. 식물은 극단적인 온도에서는 광합성을 쉽게 할 수 없거든요. 그래서, 그것은 날씨, 기후, 계절에 달려 있어요...

자, 광합성은 모든 생명체에게 중요하죠. 왜 그럴까요? 음, 이것은 식물이 이산화탄소를 저장하기 때문이에요. 여러분도 알겠지만, 공기 중의 과도한 이산화탄소는 지구 온난화를 일으킬 수 있어요. 그래서, 공기 중의 이산화탄소를 제거함으로써, 식물은 기후 변화를 막는 데 도움을 줄 수 있죠. 그리고, 어, 산소를 방출함으로써, 그것들은 우리 모두를 위해 공기의 질을 향상시키기도 합니다.

---

photosynthesis 명 광합성   chlorophyll 명 엽록소
chemical 명 화학물질   cell 명 세포; 작은 방
carbon dioxide 이산화탄소   consume 동 섭취하다, 먹다
root 명 뿌리   absorb 동 흡수하다   surface 명 표면
immediately 부 바로, 즉시   release 동 방출하다; 풀어 주다
breathing 명 숨쉬기   respiration 명 호흡   climate 명 기후
global warming 지구 온난화

6 강의의 주된 주제는 무엇인가?

(A) 식물이 스스로 먹이를 만들어내는 이유
(B) 식물이 에너지를 만들어내는 방법
(C) 식물이 어떻게 환경에 도움이 되는지
(D) 인간에게 있어 식물의 중요성

7 교수는 엽록소에 관해 무엇이라고 말하는가?

(A) 그것은 식물의 주요 영양소다.
(B) 그것은 일부 식물에는 없다.
(C) 그것은 식물을 녹색으로 만든다.
(D) 그것은 식물의 뿌리에서 생산된다.

8 교수는 강의를 어떻게 구성하는가?

(A) 식물의 성장 단계를 강조함으로써
(B) 과정 하나를 설명하고 그것의 중요성을 설명함으로써
(C) 문제 하나를 언급하고 가능한 해결책들을 제시함으로써
(D) 생태계에서의 식물의 두 가지 역할을 비교함으로써

강의의 일부를 다시 듣고 질문에 답하시오.
S: So, uh, the carbon dioxide and oxygen parts... I guess that's how plants breathe...
P: Well, yes and no... We don't call it breathing in plants. We call it respiration. But, actually, this is a helpful way to understand it.

9 교수는 이렇게 말함으로써 무엇을 의미하는가:
P: Well, yes and no...

(A) 그녀는 학생의 대답이 창의적이라고 생각한다.
(B) 그녀는 학생들이 다른 예시들을 생각해내기를 바란다.
(C) 그녀는 학생의 의견이 완전히 옳다고 생각하지 않는다.
(D) 그녀는 질문이 주제와 직접적으로 관련이 있는지 확신하지 못한다.

10 강의에서, 교수는 광합성의 단계들을 설명한다. 아래의 단계들을 올바른 순서대로 나열하시오.
각 답변을 해당하는 곳으로 끌어다 놓으시오.

단계 1	(D) 물이 뿌리를 통해 섭취된다.
단계 2	(B) 공기에서 이산화탄소가 흡수된다.
단계 3	(A) 햇빛을 이용해 당이 생산된다.
단계 4	(C) 산소가 잎에서 방출된다.

11 교수는 광합성을 하는 식물의 능력에 관해 무엇을 암시하는가?

(A) 그것은 이산화탄소가 너무 많으면 제한된다.
(B) 그것은 매우 덥고 추운 환경에서 감소한다.
(C) 그것은 보통 모든 계절에서 거의 동일하다.
(D) 그것은 흐리거나 비가 오는 날 향상된다.

PART 2. Passage 1
본문 p. 158

1 (C)   2 (D)   3 (B)   4 (D)   5 (C)

Note-taking

Student's Request
Wants to change his major; economics
→ Has to be something related to business

Advisor's Suggestion
Consider choosing marketing as a major
- Fill out some forms
- Read a brochure to learn more about the classes

Listen to a conversation between a student and an academic advisor.

M: Excuse me. Could you help me out? ¹I'm interested in changing my major, but I'm not sure what to do. I'm currently majoring in economics.

W: Yes, I can help you change your major. But, uh, why do you want to change it now?

M: Oh, well, I took some economics classes in the first semester and, uh, realized that I'm not really interested in the subject.

W: I see... Why did you choose it in the first place?

M: ²My goal is to start a small business after college. Um, and one of my friends told me that learning economics would help.

W: Yes, it can be useful. But many people who have that as a major become researchers after college. Clearly, that is not what you want to do.

M: Um, yeah, it's really not for me. Besides, I found the economics lectures too boring and difficult.

W: OK, so that's decided... ³But what do you want to study instead?

M: Honestly, I'm still not sure. But, uh, it definitely has to be something related to business.

W: Let's try this... Among all your past classes, which one interested you the most?

M: Oh, that's easy! The answer has to be marketing. I have a lot of ideas about how to promote companies and products.

W: ⁴Great! Then you should consider choosing marketing as a major. It sounds more suitable for you.

M: Can I select that as my major right now?

W: It's not that simple. You'll need to fill out some forms first... Here, why don't you take these with you and bring them back when you're done?

M: OK, I can do that. Is there anything else I should know about?

W: ⁵Um, take this brochure about the marketing program, too. You can read it to learn more about the classes you're going to take.

M: All right, thanks. I'll do that now.

학생과 지도 교수 사이의 대화를 들으시오.

M: 실례합니다. 저를 좀 도와주실 수 있나요? 제가 전공을 바꾸는 것에 관심 있는데, 어떻게 해야 할지 모르겠어요. 저는 현재 경제학을 전공하고 있어요.

W: 네, 제가 전공을 바꾸는 것을 도와드릴 수 있어요. 그런데, 어, 왜 지금 바꾸려는 거죠?

M: 아, 음, 제가 첫 학기에 경제학 수업을 몇 개 들었는데, 어, 그 학과에 별로 흥미가 없다는 것을 깨달았거든요.

W: 그렇군요... 처음에 왜 그걸 선택하셨나요?

M: 제 목표는 대학 이후에 작은 사업을 시작하는 거예요. 음, 그리고 제 친구들 중 한 명이 경제학을 배우면 도움이 될 거라고 했거든요.

W: 네, 유용할 수 있죠. 하지만 그걸 전공으로 하는 많은 사람들이 대학 이후에 연구원이 돼요. 확실히, 그것은 학생이 하고 싶은 것이 아니죠.

M: 음, 네, 저한테는 정말 맞지 않아요. 게다가, 경제학 강의는 너무 지루하고 어렵다고 느꼈어요.

W: 좋아요, 그럼 그것은 결정됐군요... 그런데 대신 무엇을 공부하고 싶나요?

M: 솔직히, 아직 잘 모르겠어요. 하지만, 어, 그것은 확실히 비즈니스와 관련된 것이어야 해요.

W: 이렇게 한번 해보죠... 이전의 모든 수업들 중에서, 어떤 것이 가장 흥미로웠나요?

M: 오, 그건 쉬워요! 정답은 마케팅일 수 밖에 없어요. 저는 회사와 제품을 홍보하는 방법에 대한 많은 아이디어를 가지고 있거든요.

W: 좋네요! 그렇다면 학생은 마케팅을 전공으로 선택하는 것을 고려해보는 게 좋겠어요. 그게 학생에게 더 적합할 것 같네요.

M: 지금 바로 그것을 제 전공으로 선택할 수 있나요?

W: 그렇게 간단하지는 않아요. 먼저 몇 가지 서류를 작성해야 해요... 여기, 이것들을 가져가서 다 하면 다시 가져오시는 게 어때요?

M: 네, 그렇게 할 수 있어요. 제가 알아야 할 또 다른 것이 있을까요?

W: 음, 마케팅 강의 계획에 관한 이 책도 가져가세요. 수강할 수업에 대해 더 자세히 알아보려면 그걸 읽으시면 됩니다.

M: 네, 감사합니다. 지금 할게요.

economics 명 경제학   subject 명 학과; 주제
business 명 사업, 비즈니스   researcher 명 연구원
honestly 부 솔직히   marketing 명 마케팅   promote 동 홍보하다
suitable 형 적합한   brochure 명 책자
program 명 강의 계획, 프로그램

1. 남자는 왜 여자와 이야기하는가?
   (A) 학교를 그만두는 것에 대한 조언을 얻기 위해
   (B) 복수전공을 하는 것에 대해 알아보기 위해
   (C) 전공을 변경하는 것에 대해 문의하기 위해
   (D) 그가 수강했던 몇몇 강의들에 대해 불평하기 위해

2. 남자는 대학 이후 무엇을 할 계획인가?
   (A) 비즈니스 수업 가르치기
   (B) 대학원에 가기
   (C) 대기업에서 일하기
   (D) 사업을 시작하기

3. 여자는 왜 남자에게 그의 이전 수업들에 대해 물어보는가?
   (A) 그의 성과를 평가하기 위해
   (B) 그의 관심사를 확인하기 위해
   (C) 그에게 몇몇 요건들을 상기시키기 위해
   (D) 그가 프로그램에 참여할 자격이 있는지 보기 위해

4. 남자의 결정에 대한 여자의 태도는 무엇인가?
   (A) 그녀는 그가 경제학 수업을 더 들어야 한다고 생각한다.
   (B) 그녀는 그가 변화에 대한 준비가 되어 있지 않다고 걱정한다.
   (C) 그녀는 그의 친구가 좋은 조언을 했다는 것에 동의한다.
   (D) 그녀는 그가 그의 선택에 만족할 것이라고 생각한다.

5. 남자는 다음에 무엇을 할 것인가?
   (A) 몇 가지 아이디어들을 제안하기
   (B) 교수의 사무실에 방문하기
   (C) 서류를 읽기
   (D) 그의 친구들과 이야기하기

PART 2. Passage 2   본문 p. 160

6 (C)   7 (B)   8 (C)
9 Supply: (B), (C) Demand: (A), (D)   10 (D)   11 (D)

Note-taking
The Law of Supply and Demand
- Price goes up.
  → Demand: Consumers buy a product <u>less</u>.
  → Supply: Sellers make <u>more</u> products to sell.
- Factors that affect supply and demand
  → Demand: <u>Preferences</u> of consumers and how much <u>money</u> they have
  → Supply: Cost of <u>materials</u> and paying <u>workers</u>

Listen to part of a lecture in an economics class.

P: When we go shopping, we want the best price, right? Well... what determines prices? ⁶According to one economic theory, it is supply and demand. The law of supply and demand is a way to describe the relationship between buyers and sellers... Let's explore this law in detail...

First, according to the law of demand, buyers want a product less if the price is high. ⁷So, if the prices of goods go up, people buy them less. But what about the law of supply? What happens to supply if prices are high?

S: Um, I think supply should go up... uh, because sellers can make more money if prices are high.

P: Exactly. ⁸If sellers can make higher profits, then they will make more products to sell. So according to the law of supply, if prices are high, sellers make more products. But, let's say that prices are low. What happens then? Well, buyers will usually want more products, so demand will be high. At the same time, sellers make less money, so supply will be low... As you can see, prices influence both supply and demand in opposite ways. If the price of a product is too high, demand will be low, but supply will be high. And if the price of a product is too low, then supply will be low, but demand will be high.

There are other factors that affect supply and demand as well. ⁹ᴮ/⁹ᶜFirst of all, supply is affected by production costs. These include the cost of materials and the cost of paying workers. If the materials you need to make a product are expensive and your workers' salaries are high, then it will cost more to make a product. ⁹ᴬOn the other hand, demand is mainly influenced by consumers. For instance, the preferences of consumers play a big role since what they want often changes. ⁹ᴰAlso, how much money they have affects demand. Naturally, people will buy more if they have more money to spend...

Because of these factors, supply and demand are usually different. ¹⁰However, imagine that supply and demand are equal. For instance, sellers want to sell 100 products, and consumers want to buy 100 products, too. When this occurs, we say that the price is ideal. This price is called the equilibrium price. ¹¹We can find this ideal price easily with a graph. For example, let's take a look at this graph...

경제학 강의의 일부를 들으시오.

P: 우리가 쇼핑할 때, 우리는 가장 좋은 가격을 원해요, 그렇죠? 음... 무엇이 가격을 결정할까요? 한 경제 이론에 따르면, 그것은 공급과 수요입니다. 공급과 수요의 법칙은 구매자와 판매자 간의 관계를 설명하는 하나의 방법이죠... 이 법칙에 대해 자세히 살펴봅시다...

먼저, 수요의 법칙에 따르면, 구매자들은 가격이 높으면 제품을 덜 원합니다. 그래서, 물건들의 가격이 오르면, 사람들은 그것들을 덜 사죠. 하지만 공급의 법칙은 어떨까요? 가격이 높으면 공급은 어떻게 될까요?

S: 음, 저는 공급이 증가할 거라고 생각해요... 어, 왜냐하면 판매자들은 가격이 높으면 더 많은 돈을 벌 수 있으니까요.

P: 정확해요. 판매자들은 더 높은 수익을 낼 수 있다면, 판매할 제품들을 더 많이 만들 거예요. 그래서 공급의 법칙에 따르면, 가격이 높으면, 판매자들은 더 많은 제품을 만듭니다. 하지만 가격이 낮다고 해봅시다. 그러면 어떻게 될까요? 음, 구매자들은 보통 더 많

은 제품을 원할테니, 수요가 많을 거예요. 동시에, 판매자들은 더 적은 돈을 벌기 때문에, 공급은 낮을 것입니다... 보다시피, 가격은 공급과 수요 모두에 서로 반대되는 방식으로 영향을 미칩니다. 제품의 가격이 너무 높으면, 수요는 낮지만, 공급은 높을 것입니다. 그리고 제품의 가격이 너무 낮으면, 공급은 낮겠지만, 수요는 높을 거예요.

공급과 수요에 영향을 미치는 다른 요인들도 있습니다. 우선, 공급은 생산 비용의 영향을 받아요. 여기에는 자재 비용과 근로자 급여 비용이 포함되죠. 제품을 만드는 데 필요한 자재가 비싸고 근로자들의 급여가 높으면, 제품을 만드는 데 비용이 더 많이 듭니다. 반면에, 수요는 주로 소비자의 영향을 받아요. 예를 들어, 소비자들이 원하는 것은 종종 바뀌기 때문에 그들의 취향은 큰 역할을 하죠. 또한, 그들에게 돈이 얼마나 많이 있는지도 수요에 영향을 줍니다. 당연히, 사람들은 쓸 수 있는 돈이 더 많으면 더 많이 살 테니까요...

이러한 요인들 때문에, 공급과 수요는 보통 다릅니다. 하지만, 공급과 수요가 동일하다고 상상해 보세요. 예를 들어, 판매자들이 100개의 제품을 팔고 싶어 하고, 소비자들도 100개의 제품을 사고 싶어 하는 거죠. 이럴 때, 우리는 가격이 이상적이라고 말합니다. 이 가격은 균형가격이라고 불려요. 우리는 그래프를 통해 이 이상적인 가격을 쉽게 찾을 수 있는데요. 예를 들어, 이 그래프를 살펴봅시다...

economic 형 경제의 theory 명 이론 supply 명 공급
demand 명 수요; 요구 buyer 명 구매자 seller 명 판매자
profit 명 수익, 이익 at the same time 동시에
influence 통 영향을 미치다; 명 영향 production 명 생산
cost 명 비용, 값 materials 명 자재 salary 명 급여
play a role 역할을 하다, 역할을 맡다 naturally 부 당연히, 물론
ideal 형 이상적인 equilibrium price 균형가격

6 강의의 주된 주제는 무엇인가?

(A) 기업과 소비자 모두에게 이상적인 가격
(B) 고객이 특정 제품을 선호하는 이유
(C) 구매자와 판매자에 대한 경제 이론
(D) 생산자가 가격을 결정하는 방법

7 교수에 따르면, 제품들의 가격이 오르면 어떤 일이 일어나는가?

(A) 수요가 증가한다.
(B) 사람들이 그것들을 덜 산다.
(C) 판매자들이 그것들을 덜 공급한다.
(D) 그것들의 품질이 향상된다.

강의의 일부를 다시 듣고 질문에 답하시오.
P: If sellers can make higher profits, then they will make more products to sell. So according to the law of supply, if prices are high, sellers make more products. But let's say that prices are low.

8 교수는 왜 이렇게 말하는가?

P: But let's say that prices are low.

(A) 이론의 약점을 비판하기 위해
(B) 일반적인 문제를 지적하기 위해
(C) 반대되는 개념을 소개하기 위해
(D) 더 명확한 예시를 제시하기 위해

9 교수는 공급과 수요에 영향을 미치는 요인들을 설명한다. 다음의 항목이 공급 또는 수요 중 어떤 것과 관련이 있는지를 표시하시오. 각 항목에 적절한 칸을 클릭하시오.

	공급	수요
(A) 소비자의 취향		V
(B) 자재 비용	V	
(C) 근로자 급여 비용	V	
(D) 사람들이 보유한 돈의 양		V

10 교수에 따르면, 균형가격은 무엇인가?

(A) 그것은 대부분의 소비자가 선호하는 가격이다.
(B) 그것은 판매자들이 수익을 덜 낼 때의 가격을 말한다.
(C) 그것은 최저의 가격이다.
(D) 그것은 공급과 수요가 같을 때의 가격을 말한다.

11 교수는 다음에 무엇을 할 것인가?

(A) 또 다른 경제 이론 소개하기
(B) 학생들에게 몇 가지 질문을 하기
(C) 경제 문제를 설명하기
(D) 학생들에게 그래프를 보여주기

PART 2. Passage 3   본문 p. 162

12 (C)   13 (B)   14 (B)   15 (B)   16 (B)
17 (C)

Note-taking
1667

The Paris Salon
• Open to the certain people from the upper class.
• Showed only artwork of graduates from the Royal Academy

19th Century

Private galleries and salons
• Creative and experimental artists e.g. Monet, Van Gogh
• Development of new art movements like Impressionism

Listen to part of a lecture in an art history class.

P: So... let's continue our discussion of French art... As we learned last time, art became very popular during the Renaissance. This was because wealthy people began helping artists. At first, individuals would personally give money to support the French arts and culture. ¹²However, by the 17th century, the royal family also started to support the arts. This led to an art exhibition called the Paris Salon. Let's talk about its history...

¹³In French, the word *salon* originally referred to a reception room in a large house. In other words, it was a place to receive guests. But over time, its meaning changed. A salon became a space to view and appreciate beauty. And this is what the

Paris Salon was. Now, the Paris Salon opened in 1667. But, uh, it wasn't open to the general public. Only certain people from the upper class could attend. Um, think of it as a private art gallery... [14]The Paris Salon took place in a room called the *Salon Carré* in the Louvre Palace. It displayed the artwork of young talented artists. And in the beginning, these artists had to be someone who graduated from the Royal Academy of Painting and Sculpture, which was the best art school at the time. Other artists were not allowed to submit their work...

By the late 1700s, this attitude slightly changed. The Paris Salon was open to the broader public. Also, artists who were not from the Royal Academy could participate. But the art style was still limited. [15]The judges selected the artwork for display, and they usually preferred artwork in a traditional style. So, all the works in the salon looked very similar. They were always about historical subjects in a realistic style. Therefore, more creative artists were usually rejected, which is a shame.

Then, in the 19th century, private galleries and salons began to appear, and their number increased. And, uh, artists became more creative and experimental. [16]In fact, many of them strongly opposed the traditional art style of the Paris Salon. They thought it did not allow them to freely express themselves. So, many popular artists like Monet and Van Gogh created private exhibitions that were different from the Paris Salon. [17]They eventually led to the development of new movements like Impressionism. And because of the popularity of new art movements, the Paris Salon began to decline by the 1880s. We'll talk more about some of these new art forms in the next class...

미술사학 강의의 일부를 들으시오.

P: 자... 프랑스 미술에 대한 논의를 계속해 봅시다... 지난 시간에도 배웠듯이, 미술은 르네상스 시대에 아주 인기를 끌었죠. 이것은 부유한 사람들이 화가들을 돕기 시작했기 때문이었는데요. 처음에는, 개개인이 사적으로 프랑스의 예술과 문화를 지원하기 위해 돈을 기부했습니다. 하지만, 17세기에 이르러서는, 왕실에서도 예술을 지원하기 시작했어요. 이것은 파리 살롱이라고 불리는 미술 전시회로 이어지게 됐고요. 그 역사에 대해 이야기해 봅시다...

프랑스어로, '살롱'이라는 단어는 원래 큰 집에 있는 응접실을 의미했습니다. 다시 말해, 손님을 맞이하는 장소였죠. 하지만 시간이 지나면서, 이것의 의미는 바뀌었습니다. 살롱은 아름다움을 보고 감상할 수 있는 공간이 되었어요. 그리고 파리 살롱이 바로 이런 곳이었죠. 자, 파리 살롱은 1667년에 문을 열었습니다. 하지만, 어, 그것은 일반 대중에게 공개되지는 않았죠. 오직 상류층의 특정 사람들만 참석할 수 있었거든요. 음, 개인 미술관이라고 생각하면 돼요... 파리 살롱은 루브르 궁전에 있는 '살롱 카레'라는 방에서 열렸습니다. 그곳은 젊은 재능 있는 화가들의 작품을 전시했어요. 그리고 초기에는, 이 화가들은 왕립 회화 조각원을 졸업한 사람이어야 했는데, 이곳은 당시 최고의 예술 학교였어요. 다른 화가들은 작품을 제출하는 것이 허락되지 않았죠...

1700년대 후반에 이르러서는, 이러한 태도가 약간 바뀌게 됐는데요. 파리 살롱은 더 많은 대중들에게 개방됐어요. 또한, 왕립원 출신이 아닌 화가들도 참여할 수 있었죠. 하지만 미술 양식은 여전히 한정되어 있었어요. 심사위원들이 전시될 작품을 선정했는데, 그들은 보통 전통적인 양식의 작품을 선호했어요. 그래서, 살롱에 있는 모든 작품들은 매우 비슷해 보였죠. 그것들은 항상 역사적인 소재를 사실주의 양식으로 그려낸 것이었어요. 그러므로, 더 창의적인 화가들은 보통 거절당했는데, 이는 아쉬운 일이죠.

그 후, 19세기에, 개인 미술관들과 살롱이 등장하기 시작했고, 그것들의 수가 늘어났어요. 그리고, 어, 화가들은 더 창의적이고 실험적이게 되었죠. 사실, 그들 중 많은 사람들이 파리 살롱의 전통적인 미술 양식에 강하게 반대했어요. 그들은 그것이 그들이 자유롭게 표현하는 것을 못하게 한다고 생각했거든요. 그래서, 모네와 반 고흐 같은 많은 유명한 화가들이 파리 살롱과는 다른 개인 전시회를 열었어요. 그들은 머지않아 인상주의와 같은 새로운 운동의 발전을 이끌었죠. 그리고 새로운 예술 운동의 인기로 인해, 파리 살롱은 1880년대가 되자 쇠퇴하기 시작했습니다. 다음 수업에서는 이러한 새로운 예술 형태들에 대해 더 이야기할 거예요...

Renaissance 명 르네상스　personally 부 사적으로, 개별적으로
exhibition 명 전시(회)　refer to ~을 의미하다, 말하다
reception room 응접실, 거실
appreciate 동 감상하다; 진가를 알아보다
public 명 대중, 일반 사람들　art gallery 미술관
Louvre Palace 루브르 궁전　talented 형 재능 있는
judge 명 심사위원, 심판　realistic 형 사실주의의, 사실적인
experimental 형 실험적인　eventually 부 머지않아; 결국
decline 동 쇠퇴하다, 줄어들다

12 강의의 주된 목적은 무엇인가?

(A) 프랑스에서 미술의 중요성을 보여주기 위해
(B) 특정 프랑스 미술 양식을 묘사하기 위해
(C) 한 미술 전시회의 역사를 설명하기 위해
(D) 독립 화가들의 시초를 설명하기 위해

13 교수는 프랑스 단어 '살롱'에 관해 무엇이라고 말하는가?

(A) 그것은 1600년대에 발명되었다.
(B) 그것의 의미는 시간이 지나면서 변했다.
(C) 그것의 기원은 '공간'을 뜻하는 프랑스어 단어이다.
(D) 그것은 집에서 가장 작은 방을 가리킨다.

14 교수는 초기의 파리 살롱에 관해 무엇이라고 말하는가?

(A) 그것은 미술계의 모든 일원들에게 개방되었다.
(B) 그것은 왕립원 졸업생들의 예술작품에 주력했다.
(C) 그것은 왕실의 일원들을 위한 미술 학교였다.
(D) 그것은 1600년대에 모든 미술 전시회를 닫았다.

15 파리 살롱의 심사위원들에 대한 교수의 태도는 무엇인가?

(A) 그들은 왕실로부터 지원을 받았어야 했다.
(B) 그들은 더 많은 창의적인 화가들을 받아들였어야 했다.
(C) 그들은 예술적 취향이 너무 현대적이었다.
(D) 그들은 전통적인 화가들의 진가를 충분히 알아봐 주지 않았다.

16 교수는 모네와 반 고흐에 관해 무엇을 암시하는가?

(A) 그들의 작품은 파리 살롱에 전시되었다.
(B) 그들은 전통적인 미술에 반대했다.
(C) 그들의 미술은 그들의 일생 동안 인기가 없었다.
(D) 그들은 같은 미술 학교를 졸업했다.

17 교수는 왜 강의에서 인상주의를 언급하는가?

(A) 파리 살롱이 새로운 미술에 관심이 있었음을 보여주기 위해
(B) 왕립원의 중요성을 강조하기 위해
(C) 새로운 미술 운동의 예시를 제공하기 위해
(D) 초기 미술 양식이 인기가 없었다는 것을 강조하기 위해

Actual Test 2

PART 1. Passage 1

본문 p. 164

1 (B)　2 (C)　3 (D)　4 (A)　5 (C)

Note-taking

Student's Problem
Here to pick up a letter of recommendation
→ Can't submit my **application** without the letter

Assistant's Suggestion
Visit the **scholarship** office and explain your **situation**
→ Might be able to **extend** the date of the **deadline**

Listen to a conversation between a student and an assistant.

M: Excuse me. My name is Shawn Kramer and, uh, I'm here to see Professor Miller... Is he in his office?

W: I'm sorry, Mr. Kramer. Professor Miller is currently in South Africa on a work trip. Is there anything you need?

M: I see. [1]Um, I'm here to pick up a letter of recommendation. I need it for my scholarship application. Professor Miller told me to come by today to pick it up.

W: Hold on. [2]The professor gave me some documents before his trip. Let me check... Hmm... I apologize, Mr. Kramer, but there is nothing for you here.

M: Oh, no. Do you think he forgot? [1]I can't submit my application without the letter.

W: When is the deadline for the application?

M: Um, actually, it's this Friday. [3]Do you think you can send the professor an e-mail now? Maybe he can, uh, write the letter while he's in South Africa. He can send it back to me through e-mail.

W: I don't know if that will help. Um, the professor is doing research in a location in the countryside. So, he might not have internet access... And also, he might be too busy to check his e-mails.

M: I understand... But, what else can I do?

W: [4]I would suggest visiting the scholarship office. Someone there might be able to help you if you explain your situation.

M: I don't know about that. Do you think that will help?

W: They might be able to extend the date of the deadline for you.

M: Hmm... I guess I can try.

W: It's only for a few days. The professor will be back on Tuesday next week. And, um, I'll remind him about your request right away.

M: OK, I'll do that later. But, uh, just in case, do you think you could still send him an e-mail?

W: Well, all right. [5]Um, could you give me your e-mail address and phone number?

M: Thanks! I'll write them down for you on this piece of paper.

학생과 조교 사이의 대화를 들으시오.

M: 실례합니다. 제 이름은 Shawn Kramer인데요, 어, 저는 Miller 교수님을 뵈러 왔습니다. 교수님께서 사무실에 계시나요?

W: 죄송합니다, Kramer씨. Miller 교수님은 현재 남아프리카 공화국에 출장 중이세요. 필요한 것이 있으신가요?

M: 그렇군요. 음, 저는 추천서를 가지러 왔어요. 제 장학금 신청에 그게 필요하거든요. Miller 교수님께서 오늘 그것을 가지러 잠깐 들르라고 하셨는데요.

W: 잠시만요. 교수님께서 여행 전에 저에게 몇 가지 서류를 주셨거든요. 확인해 볼게요... 흠... 죄송합니다만, Kramer씨, 여기에는 학생을 위한 게 없네요.

M: 오, 어떡하죠. 교수님께서 잊어버리신 걸까요? 추천서 없이는 신청서를 제출할 수 없는걸요.

W: 신청 마감 기한이 언제인가요?

M: 음, 사실, 이번 주 금요일이에요. 지금 교수님께 이메일을 보내주실 수 있을까요? 교수님께서, 어, 남아프리카 공화국에 계시는 동안 추천서를 써주실 수도 있으니까요. 그걸 제게 이메일로 다시 보내 주시면 되고요.

W: 그게 도움이 될지 모르겠네요. 음, 교수님께서 지방에 있는 곳에서 연구하고 계시거든요. 그래서, 인터넷 접속이 안 될 수도 있어요... 그리고 또, 교수님께서 너무 바쁘셔서 이메일을 확인하실 수 없을지도 모르고요.

M: 알겠습니다... 하지만, 제가 무엇을 더 할 수 있죠?

W: 장학금 담당실을 방문하는 것을 제안할게요. 학생이 상황을 설명하면 그곳에 있는 누군가가 학생을 도울 수 있을지도 몰라요.

M: 그건 잘 모르겠네요. 그게 도움이 될 것 같으신가요?

W: 학생을 위해 마감 기한을 연장해 줄 수도 있을지도 모르죠.

M: 흠... 해 볼 수는 있을 것 같네요.

W: 며칠만 있으면 돼요. 교수님께서 다음 주 화요일에는 돌아오실 거예요. 그리고, 음, 학생의 요청을 제가 곧바로 교수님께 상기시켜 드릴게요.

M: 네, 나중에 그렇게 할게요. 하지만, 어, 혹시 모르니, 그래도 교수님께 이메일을 보내주실 수 있나요?

W: 음, 알겠어요. 음, 이메일 주소와 전화번호를 알려주시겠어요?

M: 감사해요! 제가 이 종이에 그것들을 적어 드릴게요.

South Africa 남아프리카 공화국 scholarship 명 장학금
application 명 신청(서) come by 잠깐 들르다
document 명 서류 extend 동 연장하다, 더 길게 만들다
deadline 명 마감 기한 remind 동 상기시키다

1 남자의 문제는 무엇인가?
  (A) 그는 출장에 함께할 수 없다.
  (B) 그는 서류를 받지 못했다.
  (C) 그는 앞선 약속에 가지 않았다.
  (D) 그는 마감 기한을 잊어버렸다.

2 여자에 따르면, Miller 교수는 출장 전에 무엇을 했는가?
  (A) 몇 가지 요청 수락하기
  (B) 발표 준비하기
  (C) 몇 가지 서류 남겨두기
  (D) 몇몇 약속 취소하기

3 여자는 왜 교수의 연구 장소를 언급하는가?
  (A) 지연의 이유를 밝히기 위해
  (B) 그가 어떤 종류의 일을 하는지 보여주기 위해
  (C) 출장이 오랫동안 이어질 것임을 나타내기 위해
  (D) 일이 어려울 수 있는 이유를 설명하기 위해

4 여자의 제안에 대한 남자의 태도는 무엇인가?
  (A) 그는 그것이 될지 확신하지 못한다.
  (B) 그는 그것이 그의 생각과 비슷하다고 생각한다.
  (C) 그는 그것이 유일한 해결책이라는 것에 동의한다.
  (D) 그는 그것이 너무 많은 시간이 걸릴 것이라고 생각한다.

5 남자는 다음에 무엇을 할 것인가?
  (A) 그의 이메일 확인하기
  (B) 추천서에 서명하기
  (C) 그의 연락처 제공하기
  (D) 캠퍼스에 있는 다른 교수에게 전화하기

PART 1. Passage 2
본문 p. 166

6 (B)   7 (C)   8 (B)   9 (C)
10 Fahrenheit: (D) Celsius: (B) Kelvin: (A), (C)   11 (B)

Note-taking

Fahrenheit
- The oldest system developed in 1724
- Used a mercury thermometer

Celsius
- Based on the melting and boiling points of water
- Almost all countries in the world use this.

Kelvin
- The standard scale in science
- Most detailed and accurate
- Based on the concept of absolute zero

Listen to part of a lecture in a physics class.

P: You may all be familiar with temperature. Simply said, temperature is a measure of how hot or cold something is. [6]Three common scales used to measure temperature are Fahrenheit, Celsius, and Kelvin, and this is the topic of today's lecture.

So, let's start with the first one... the Fahrenheit scale. [10D]It is actually the oldest system. Daniel Gabriel Fahrenheit, a Dutch physicist, developed this scale in 1724. He used a mercury thermometer that he invented to measure changes in temperature. [7]Mercury is a chemical that quickly reacts to small changes in temperature, so it is useful for measuring temperature accurately. On the Fahrenheit scale, water freezes at 32 degrees and boils at 212 degrees. [8]Today, only a few countries still use this system. These include the United States and Liberia...

The next one is Celsius. The Celsius scale was named after a Swedish scientist, Anders Celsius. He developed his scale in 1742. It was based on the melting and boiling points of water in normal conditions of air pressure. Celsius used these specific conditions because he noticed that air pressure affects the boiling point of water. You see, water boils faster when air pressure is low. [9]Anyway, based on Celsius, water freezes at 0 degrees Celsius, and it boils at 100 degrees Celsius. I think this was a major advancement... Uh, zero and 100 are easier to remember than 32 and 212, right? [10B]And I think most of the world agrees with me. In fact, almost all countries in the world use this scale every day...

Finally, there is the Kelvin scale... It was invented by Lord Kelvin, a British philosopher. He started developing it in the late 1840s. Now, the Kelvin scale is the standard scale in science. Scientists prefer it because it is the most detailed and accurate. It is based on the concept of absolute zero. [11]In physics, absolute zero is the coldest possible temperature. Um, actually, it's not quite that simple... but we'll cover this in a later class... For today, just know that absolute zero is 0 degrees Kelvin. Uh, this is why Kelvin is considered the most convenient scale to use by scientists. [10A]There cannot be any negative numbers, or numbers lower than zero. So, this makes it easier to calculate. In, uh, the Kelvin system, water freezes at 273 degrees and boils at 373 degrees... The scale is used in digital photography to measure the temperature of colors. ¹⁰ᶜSimilarly, it is used in astronomy to measure the temperature of stars… It is even used in electronics to measure the temperature of noise… Pretty interesting, huh?

물리학 강의의 일부를 들으시오.

P: 여러분은 아마 모두 온도에 대해 잘 알 것입니다. 간단히 말하면, 온도는 어떤 것이 얼마나 뜨겁거나 차가운지에 대한 척도이죠. 온도를 측정하는 데 사용되는 세 가지 일반적인 단위는 화씨, 섭씨, 켈빈인데, 이것이 오늘 강의의 주제입니다.

자, 첫 번째 것부터 시작해봅시다… 화씨 단위인데요. 이것은 사실 가장 오래된 시스템이에요. 네덜란드의 물리학자인 다니엘 가브리엘 파렌하이트는 1724년에 이 단위를 개발했어요. 그는 그가 발명한 수은 온도계를 사용해서 온도의 변화를 측정했어요. 수은은 온도의 작은 변화에도 빠르게 반응하는 화학물질이라서, 온도를 정확하게 측정하는 데 유용하죠. 화씨 단위에서, 물은 32도에서 얼고 212도에서 끓습니다. 오늘날, 몇몇 나라들만이 여전히 이 시스템을 사용하고 있어요. 여기에는 미국과 라이베리아가 포함되죠…

다음은 섭씨입니다. 섭씨 단위는 스웨덴의 과학자인 안데르스 셀시우스의 이름을 따서 이름 지어졌어요. 그는 1742년에 그의 단위를 개발했습니다. 그것은 기압이 표준인 상태에서 물이 녹고 끓는점을 기준으로 했어요. 셀시우스는 기압이 물의 끓는점에 영향을 미친다는 것을 알았기 때문에 이러한 특정한 조건들을 이용했죠. 그러니까, 기압이 낮으면 물이 더 빨리 끓거든요. 어쨌든, 섭씨를 기준으로, 물은 섭씨 0도에서 얼고, 섭씨 100도에서 끓어요. 저는 이것이 큰 발전이었다고 생각하는데요… 어, 0과 100이 32와 212보다 기억하기 쉽잖아요, 그렇죠? 그리고 전 세계 대부분이 제 의견에 동의할 것 같아요. 사실, 세계의 거의 모든 나라들이 매일 이 단위를 사용하거든요…

마지막으로, 켈빈 단위가 있습니다… 그것은 영국의 철학자인 켈빈 경이 발명했어요. 그는 1840년대 후반에 그것을 개발하기 시작했죠. 자, 켈빈 단위는 과학에서 표준 단위입니다. 과학자들은 그것이 가장 상세하고 정확하기 때문에 선호해요. 그것은 절대 영도의 개념에 기초하고 있어요. 물리학에서, 절대 영도란 최저 온도입니다. 음, 사실, 그렇게 간단하지는 않지만… 이것은 이후의 수업 시간에서 다루도록 하죠. 오늘은, 그냥 절대 영도가 켈빈 0도라는 것만 알아두세요. 어, 켈빈이 과학자들에게 가장 사용하기 편리한 단위로 여겨지는 이유가 바로 이거예요. 음수, 즉 0보다 낮은 숫자가 있을 수 없어요. 그래서, 이것은 계산하기 더 쉽게 만들죠. 어, 켈빈 시스템에서, 물은 273도에서 얼고 373도에서 끓습니다… 이 단위는 디지털 사진술에서 색온도를 측정하는 데 사용돼요. 마찬가지로, 그것은 천문학에서 별의 온도를 측정하는데 사용되죠… 그것은 전자 공학에서 잡음온도를 측정하기 위해 사용되기도 합니다… 꽤 흥미로워요, 그렇죠?

measure 명 척도, 측정; 통 측정하다   scale 명 단위, 규모
Fahrenheit 명 화씨; 형 화씨의   Celsius 명 섭씨; 형 섭씨의
Kelvin 명 켈빈; 형 켈빈의   Dutch 형 네덜란드의
physicist 명 물리학자   mercury 명 수은   thermometer 명 온도계
freeze 통 얼다   boil 통 끓다   Liberia 명 라이베리아
Swedish 형 스웨덴의   be based on ~에 기준을 두다, ~에 기초하다
air pressure 기압   advancement 명 발전   Lord 명 경; 귀족

British 형 영국의   philosopher 명 철학자
absolute zero 절대 영도
temperature of colors (= color temperature) 색온도(광원(빛)의 색을 온도 수치로 나타낸 것)
astronomy 명 천문학   electronics 명 전자 공학
temperature of noise (=noise temperature) 잡음온도(장치/회로/소자의 잡음 성능을 온도 수치로 나타낸 것)

6 강의의 주된 주제는 무엇인가?

  (A) 첫 온도계의 발명
  (B) 온도를 측정하는 다양한 방법들
  (C) 온도에 영향을 미치는 환경적 요인들
  (D) 온도의 역사적인 변화

7 교수에 따르면, 수은이 왜 온도계에 사용되었는가?

  (A) 그것은 절대 얼지 않는다.
  (B) 그것은 찾기가 쉽다.
  (C) 그것은 변화에 민감하다.
  (D) 그것은 천천히 끓는다.

8 교수는 왜 미국과 라이베리아를 언급하는가?

  (A) 온도 측정의 시초를 강조하기 위해
  (B) 몇몇 나라에서 특정 시스템을 사용한다는 것을 나타내기 위해
  (C) 섭씨를 개발한 나라들을 밝히기 위해
  (D) 여러 단위의 정확도를 비교하기 위해

9 섭씨 시스템에 대한 교수의 의견은 무엇인가?

  (A) 그는 그것이 너무 혼란스럽다고 생각한다.
  (B) 그는 더 많은 나라들이 그것을 사용하기를 바란다.
  (C) 그는 그것이 큰 발전이었다고 느낀다.
  (D) 그는 그것이 다른 시스템들보다 덜 정확하다고 생각한다.

10 교수는 각기 다른 측정 단위들에 대해 이야기한다. 다음의 항목이 어떤 유형의 단위를 설명하는지를 표시하시오.
각 항목에 적절한 칸을 클릭하시오.

	화씨	섭씨	켈빈
(A) 음수가 없다			V
(B) 전 세계에서 가장 많이 사용되고 있다		V	
(C) 별의 온도를 측정한다			V
(D) 가장 오래된 시스템이다	V		

강의의 일부를 다시 듣고 질문에 답하시오.

P: In physics, absolute zero is the coldest possible temperature. Um, actually, it's not quite that simple… but we'll cover this in a later class… For today, just know that absolute zero is 0 degrees Kelvin.

11 교수는 이렇게 말함으로써 무엇을 의미하는가:

  P: Um, actually, it's not quite that simple… but we'll cover this in a later class…

  (A) 절대 영도는 최저의 온도가 아니다.
  (B) 학생들은 아직 모든 세부 사항을 알 필요가 없다.
  (C) 교수는 복잡한 개념을 설명할 수 없다.
  (D) 과학자들은 여전히 절대 영도를 연구하고 있다.

PART 2. Passage 1

본문 p.168

1 (D) 2 (B) 3 Suggested: (A), (D) Not Suggested: (B), (C)
4 (A) 5 (C)

Note-taking

Student's Question

Can't find a copy of the book
→ Is it possible to change the date of the quiz?

Professor's Suggestion

- Try searching on the Internet
- Check the campus bookstore
- Try a different university library
- Borrow my personal copy

Listen to a conversation between a student and a professor.

S: Hi, Professor Stewart. Are you busy right now? I have a question about Friday's quiz.

P: Oh, hello, Anita. Not at all... What's your question?

S: ¹Well, um, we're supposed to prepare for the quiz by reading a book about medieval poetry, right? But, um, I can't find a copy of the book. ²Is it possible to change the date of the quiz?

P: Oh, I'm sorry, Anita, but I can't do that. I gave everyone enough time to prepare for the quiz. It would be unfair to the other students if I changed the date now.

S: I understand. Actually, I thought you might say that, but I wanted to ask, anyway. Um, but what should I do about the book?

P: You've probably already checked the school library, right?

S: Yes. That's the first place I went, but all of their copies are out. Um, I guess the other students in class borrowed them.

P: Yes, I see. Hmm... Did you try searching on the Internet?

S: I tried that too, Professor. ⁴I found a copy on one website, but you need to pay for a membership to read it. Those are the website's rules.

P: That's a shame. I think websites should make it easier to get information. ³ᴬHave you checked the campus bookstore as well?

S: Yes. All of their copies are sold out. I really don't know what else to do.

P: ³ᶜMaybe you could try a different library outside the campus.

S: Do you mean a public library?

P: No. I mean a different university library. ⁵Our school librarian can tell you how to do that.

S: Oh! I didn't know that was an option... I guess I could go to the library right now and ask.

P: Yes, but let me know what happens. ³ᴰUh, I don't normally do this, but I do have a personal copy at home that you can borrow. I can bring it for you on Wednesday if you can't find a copy anywhere.

S: OK, Professor. I appreciate it. ⁵I'll be back in around 20 minutes.

학생과 교수 사이의 대화를 들으시오.

S: 안녕하세요, Stewart 교수님. 지금 바쁘신가요? 금요일 퀴즈에 대한 질문이 있어서요.

P: 오, 안녕, Anita. 전혀 아니란다... 질문이 뭐니?

S: 그게, 음, 저희가 중세의 시에 관한 책을 읽어서 퀴즈를 준비해 오기로 되어 있었죠, 그렇죠? 하지만, 음, 그 책을 찾을 수가 없어서요. 퀴즈 날짜를 변경하는 게 가능할까요?

P: 오, 미안하지만, Anita, 그렇게 할 수는 없단다. 모두에게 퀴즈를 준비할 시간을 충분히 주었어. 만약 내가 지금 날짜를 바꾼다면 다른 학생들에게 불공평할 거란다.

S: 알겠습니다. 사실, 교수님께서 그렇게 말씀하실 거라고 생각했는데, 어쨌든, 여쭤보고 싶었어요. 음, 하지만 제가 그 책에 대해서는 어떻게 해야 할까요?

P: 학교 도서관은 이미 확인해 봤을 거야, 그렇지?

S: 네. 거기가 제가 처음 갔던 곳인데, 모든 책들이 대출되었어요. 음, 수업의 다른 학생들이 빌린 것 같아요.

P: 그래, 그렇구나. 흠... 인터넷에 검색은 해봤니?

S: 그것도 해봤어요, 교수님. 한 웹사이트에서 한 권을 찾았는데, 그걸 읽으려면 회원비를 내야 해요. 그게 그 웹사이트의 규정이에요.

P: 그것 참 아쉽구나. 웹사이트들이 정보를 쉽게 얻을 수 있도록 해야 할 텐데. 교내 서점도 확인해 봤니?

S: 네. 그곳의 책들도 품절되었어요. 달리 어떻게 해야 할지 정말 모르겠네요.

P: 캠퍼스 밖의 다른 도서관을 이용해 볼 수도 있겠구나.

S: 공립 도서관을 말씀하시는 건가요?

P: 아니. 내 말은 다른 대학 도서관을 말하는 거란다. 우리 학교 도서관 사서가 어떻게 해야 하는지 알려줄 수 있을 거야.

S: 아! 저는 그게 선택지가 될 줄 몰랐네요... 지금 바로 도서관에 가서 물어보면 되겠어요.

P: 그래, 그런데 어떻게 되는지 알려주렴. 어, 보통 이렇게 하지는 않지만, 집에 네가 빌릴 수 있는 개인용 책이 있단다. 네가 어디에서도 책을 찾을 수 없다면 내가 수요일에 가져다줄 수 있어.

S: 네, 교수님. 감사합니다. 한 20분 후에 다시 올게요.

medieval 형 중세의   poetry 명 시   unfair 형 불공평한; 부당한
membership 명 회원   rule 명 규정, 규칙   sold out 품절의, 매진된
public library 공립 도서관

1 학생은 왜 교수를 찾아가는가?

(A) 퀴즈 결과를 논의하기 위해
(B) 프로젝트에 대한 조언을 구하기 위해
(C) 수업을 위한 책을 추천하기 위해
(D) 시험 준비에 대한 도움을 얻기 위해

2 교수는 왜 퀴즈 날짜를 바꿀 수 없는가?

(A) 그는 학교 규정을 따라야 한다.
(B) 그는 다른 학생들에게도 공평하고자 한다.
(C) 그는 강의를 준비할 시간이 없다.
(D) 그는 그것이 수업 일정에 영향을 줄 것이라고 생각한다.

3 교수는 학생을 돕기 위해 몇 가지 제안을 한다. 다음의 항목이 제안인지를 표시하시오.

각 항목에 적절한 칸을 클릭하시오.

	제안됨	제안 안 됨
(A) 근처 서점에 가기	V	
(B) 웹사이트에 가입하기		V
(C) 공립 도서관을 방문하기		V
(D) 교수님의 책을 빌리기	V	

4 웹사이트에 대한 교수의 의견은 무엇인가?

(A) 그는 그것의 규정에 동의하지 않는다.
(B) 그는 전에 그것을 사용한 적이 있다.
(C) 그는 그것의 인기에 놀랐다.
(D) 그는 그것이 수집한 것에 깊은 인상을 받았다.

5 학생은 다음에 무엇을 할 것인가?

(A) 캠퍼스 서점 방문하기
(B) 도서관 카드 신청하기
(C) 학교 사서와 대화하기
(D) 다른 교수 만나보기

PART 2. Passage 2

본문 p. 170

6 (A) 7 (C) 8 (A) 9 (B) 10 (C) 11 (D)

Note-taking

The Milky Way Galaxy

: A collection of stars, dust, gas, and other objects held together by gravity
- Name: From an ancient myth
- Shape: A spiral
- Size: Only an average size, compared to other galaxies

Listen to part of a lecture in an astronomy class.

P: Did you know that the Sun is a star? In fact, it is just one of many stars. [6]And along with other stars, it is part of the Milky Way Galaxy. Today, I'm going to discuss some features of this galaxy.

So, like other galaxies, the Milky Way Galaxy is a collection of stars, dust, gas, and other objects. Um, these objects are held together by gravity. [7]Think of our solar system... The planets and everything in it stay together as a group. This is due to the Sun's gravity. And galaxies work the same way. At the center of every galaxy is a large black hole with strong gravity.

[8]Now, you may be wondering why our galaxy is called the Milky Way... Well, this comes from an ancient myth. Um, in this myth, a Greek goddess throws milk across the sky. That's what the Milky Way looked like to the ancient Greeks. For the Chinese, it looked like a river made of silver because the white colored stars looked like a curved river. And for some Africans, it looked like a human backbone. So, they called it the backbone of night. However, its actual shape is a spiral. [9]From the side, the Milky Way is shaped like a flat, thin disk with a bump at its center. Imagine a pancake with a fried egg on top. It's thick in the center and gets thinner towards the edge. It looks like this because gravity is strongest near the middle of the galaxy and becomes weaker as you move away. There are also many other different shapes and sizes of galaxies.

[10]Anyway, our solar system is found on one tiny part of the Milky Way. You can hardly see it. It's somewhere between the middle of the galaxy and the edge. In fact, our solar system is over 160 million times smaller than the Milky Way Galaxy. Um, let's say you can travel at the speed of light, which is 300,000 kilometers per second. It will take you 25,000 years to go from our solar system to the middle of the galaxy... And, uh, it would take 100,000 years for you to go from one side of the galaxy to the other. [11]Because of the Milky Way's size, it's impossible to count all of the stars in it. Astronomers say there are hundreds of billions of stars. That is impressive, for sure. But, um, compared to other galaxies, this is only an average size!

천문학 강의의 일부를 들으시오.

P: 여러분은 태양이 별이라는 것을 알고 있었나요? 사실, 그것은 많은 별들 중 단지 하나일 뿐입니다. 그리고 다른 별들과 함께, 그것은 은하수의 일부이죠. 오늘, 저는 이 은하계의 몇 가지 특징에 대해 이야기하려고 합니다.

자, 다른 은하계들처럼, 은하수는 별, 먼지, 가스, 그리고 다른 물체들의 집합체인데요. 음, 이 물체들은 중력에 의해 결합되어 있어요. 우리의 태양계를 생각해보세요... 행성들과 그 안에 있는 모든 것들이 한 무리로 함께 있죠. 이것은 태양의 중력 때문입니다. 그리고 은하계들도 같은 방식으로 작용해요. 모든 은하계의 중심에는 강한 중력을 지닌 큰 블랙홀이 있거든요.

이제, 여러분은 아마도 우리 은하계가 왜 은하라고 불리는지 궁금할 텐데요... 음, 이것은 고대 신화에서 나온 거예요. 음, 이 신화에서, 그리스 여신이 하늘에 우유를 뿌리는데요. 은하는 고대 그리스인들에게 그렇게 보였어요. 중국인들에게는, 하얀색 별들이 굽은 강처럼 보였기 때문에 그것은 은으로 된 강처럼 보였고요. 그리고 어떤 아프리카인들에게는, 그것이 사람의 등뼈처럼 보였죠. 그래서, 그들은 그것을 밤의 등뼈라고 불렀습니다. 하지만, 그것의 실제 모양은 나선형이에요. 측면에서 보면, 은하는 납작하고 얇은 원반 모양에, 중심에 튀어나온 부분이 있죠. 계란 프라이가 위에 얹어진 팬케이크를 상상해보세요. 중앙이 두껍고 가장자리로 갈수록 얇아지죠. 중력이 은하계 중심 부근에서 가장 강하고 멀어질수록 약해지기 때문에 이렇게 보이는 것입니다. 더 다양한 다른 모양과 크기의 은하계들도 있어요.

어쨌든, 우리의 태양계는 은하의 아주 작은 부분에서 발견되는데요. 그것은 거의 보이지 않습니다. 은하계의 중앙과 가장자리 사이 어딘가에 있어요. 실제로, 우리의 태양계는 은하수보다 1억 6천만 배 이상 더 작습니다. 음, 초당 30만 킬로미터인 빛의 속도로 이동할 수 있다고 해봅시다. 우리의 태양계에서 은하계의 한가운데에까지 가는 데 2만 5천 년이 걸릴 겁니다... 그리고, 어, 은하계의 한쪽에서 반대 쪽으로 가는 데에는 10만 년이 걸릴 거예요. 은하의 규모 때문에, 그 안에 있는 모든 별들을 세는 것도 불가능해요. 천문학자들은 수천억 개의 별이 있다고 말하는데요. 그것은 인상적이죠, 확실히요. 하지만, 음, 다른 은하계들과 비교하면, 이것은 겨우 평균 크기랍니다!

Milky Way Galaxy 은하수 feature 명 특징, 특색
galaxy 명 은하계 solar system 태양계 gravity 명 중력
black hole 블랙홀 myth 명 신화 curved 형 굽은, 곡선 모양의
spiral 명 나선형, 나선 disk 명 원반
bump 명 튀어나온 부분; 동 부딪치다 astronomer 명 천문학자

6 강의는 주로 무엇에 관한 것인가?
(A) 은하계의 특징
(B) 태양이 어떻게 형성되었는지
(C) 우주의 크기
(D) 별은 무엇으로 만들어졌는지

7 교수에 따르면, 은하는 우리의 태양계와 어떻게 비슷한가?
(A) 그것들은 독특한 모양을 가지고 있다.
(B) 그것들 모두 행성과 별을 가지고 있다.
(C) 그것들은 중력으로 인해 함께 있다.
(D) 그것들은 밤에 조사하기가 더 쉽다.

8 은하수는 어디에서 이름을 얻었는가?
(A) 옛날이야기로부터
(B) 그리스어 단어로부터
(C) 유명한 천문학자로부터
(D) 중국 설화로부터

9 교수는 은하의 모양을 어떻게 설명하는가?
(A) 사진 하나를 보여줌으로써
(B) 익숙한 물체들을 묘사함으로써
(C) 실험 하나를 소개함으로써
(D) 다른 모양들을 비교함으로써

10 태양계에 대한 교수의 의견은 무엇인가?
(A) 그것은 은하계의 중요한 부분이다.
(B) 그것은 독특한 성질이 있다.
(C) 그것은 알아차리기가 어렵다.
(D) 그것은 특이한 모양과 규모를 가지고 있다.

11 교수는 은하에 관해 무엇을 암시하는가?
(A) 그것의 중력은 고르게 퍼져있다.
(B) 그것은 시간이 지남에 따라 작아질 것이다.
(C) 그것의 별들은 다른 것들보다 더 밝다.
(D) 그것은 가장 큰 은하계 중 하나가 아니다.

PART 2. Passage 3

본문 p. 172

12 (B)   13 (C)   14 (A), (B)   15 (C)   16 (B)   17 (D)

Note-taking

Speed Limit Laws
- 1910: Connecticut, the first state to set a limit for <u>driving speeds</u>
- 1974: A <u>national</u> <u>speed</u> limit law for all states

Alcohol Laws
Made and <u>carried out</u> by states

Traffic Light Laws
Helped drivers avoid accidents in intersections

Seatbelt and Airbag Laws
<u>Combined</u> use of seatbelts and airbags reduced accident <u>deaths</u>.

Listen to part of a lecture in a history class.

P: Before 1900, there were very few automobiles in America. Then, in the early 1900s, more and more cars were produced and sold. However, one outcome of more cars was an increase in accidents. [12]This caused leaders to consider safety laws for the first time. Now, let's look at the evolution of automobile safety laws in America...

Uh, the most common traffic laws to be made were speed limits. Leaders in some states realized that fast driving could cause accidents. [13/14A]So, in 1910, Connecticut became the first state to set a limit for driving speeds. Then, in 1974, a national speed limit law was created for all states. This happened during the middle of an oil crisis, and it was hoped that people would use less gas. [14B]However, it also reduced the number of deaths from traffic accidents. Even though safety was not the original reason for the law, it made driving safer.

Laws for driving after drinking alcohol have a similar history. Laws were first introduced in states like New Jersey, New York, and California in the early 1900s. Drivers who got caught usually paid a fine and spent some time in jail. Though national laws exist, most alcohol-related driving laws are still made and carried out by states. And, uh, the laws in each state are different. [15]In most cases, the alcohol laws for professional drivers like truck drivers are more strict than laws for other drivers.

OK... What else. Oh, the traffic light... Traffic light laws helped drivers avoid accidents in intersections. [16]Without traffic lights, it was extremely hard for drivers to know when to go and when to stop. Colored traffic lights make this simple. Green means go, yellow means slow down, and red means stop... Quite easy, isn't it?

Even with all of these improvements, many people still were badly injured or killed when accidents occurred. Then seatbelt requirements came in the 1960s, and airbag requirements came in the 1990s. Seatbelt and airbag laws could not prevent accidents. But, they became the most effective laws for the safety of people in accidents. [17]In fact, the combined use of seatbelts and airbags reduced automobile accident deaths by 80 percent. So even though your car has an airbag, don't ever forget to wear your seatbelt! They might save your life one day...

역사학 강의의 일부를 들으시오.

P: 1900년 이전에는, 미국에 자동차가 거의 없었습니다. 그 후, 1900년대 초에, 점점 더 많은 자동차가 생산되고 판매되었죠. 그러나, 더 많은 자동차가 생긴 것의 결과 중 하나로 사고의 증가가 있었습니다. 이것은 지도자들이 처음으로 안전법을 고려하게 했어요. 이제, 미국의 자동차 안전법의 발전을 살펴봅시다...

어, 가장 흔하게 제정된 교통 법규는 속도 제한이었는데요. 몇몇 주의 지도자들은 과속 운전이 사고를 일으킬 수 있다는 것을 깨달았죠. 그래서, 1910년에, 코네티컷주는 운전 속도에 제한을 둔 최초의 주가 되었어요. 그러고 나서, 1974년에, 모든 주에 대한 국가 속도 제한법이 만들어졌습니다. 이것은 석유 파동 도중에 일어났는데, 사람들이 휘발유를 덜 쓰도록 하기 위한 것이었어요. 하지만, 그것은 교통사고로 인한 사망자의 수도 줄이게 됐죠. 비록 안전이 그 법이 생긴 원래 이유는 아니었지만, 운전이 더 안전해지도록 했습니다.

음주 운전에 대한 법들도 비슷한 역사를 가지고 있습니다. 1900년대 초에 뉴저지, 뉴욕, 캘리포니아와 같은 주에서 처음 법이 도입되었어요. 적발된 운전자들은 보통 벌금을 내고 감옥에서 시간을 보냈죠. 비록 국법이 존재하지만, 음주와 관련된 대부분의 운전법은 여전히 주에서 만들어지고 시행되고 있어요. 그리고, 어, 각 주마다 법이 다릅니다. 대부분의 경우, 트럭 운전사와 같은 직업 운전자들에 대한 음주법은 다른 운전자에 대한 법보다 더 엄격해요.

네... 또 무엇이 있죠. 아, 신호등... 신호등 법은 운전자들이 교차로에서 사고를 피하는 데 도움이 됐습니다. 신호등 없이는, 운전자들이 언제 가야 하고 언제 멈춰야 하는지 아는 것이 매우 어려웠거든요. 색이 있는 신호등은 이것을 쉽게 해주죠. 녹색은 가라는 의미고, 노란색은 속도를 늦추라는 의미고, 빨간색은 멈추라는 의미죠. 꽤 쉬워요, 그렇죠?

이러한 모든 개선에도 불구하고, 사고가 일어나면 많은 사람들이 여전히 심하게 다치거나 사망했습니다. 그 후 안전벨트에 대한 요구조건이 1960년대에 생기게 됐고, 에어백 요구조건은 1990년대에 생겼습니다. 안전벨트와 에어백 법은 사고를 예방할 수는 없죠. 하지만, 그것들은 사고를 당한 사람들의 안전을 위한 가장 효과적인 법이 되었어요. 실제로, 안전벨트와 에어백을 겸용한 것이 자동차 사고 사망을 80퍼센트 줄여줬습니다. 그러므로 여러분의 자동차에 에어백이 있다고 해도, 안전벨트를 매는 것을 잊지 마세요! 그것들은 언젠가 여러분의 생명을 구할지도 몰라요...

---

automobile 몡 자동차　safety law 안전법　evolution 몡 발전, 진화
traffic 몡 교통　speed limit 속도 제한　national 헝 국가의
oil crisis 석유 파동(1973년, 1978년 두 차례에 걸친 석유 공급 부족 및 가격 상승으로 인해 세계적으로 큰 혼란과 어려움을 겪은 사건)
gas 몡 휘발유; 기체　get caught 적발되다, 잡히다
fine 몡 벌금; 헝 질 높은　carry out ~을 시행하다, ~을 수행하다
strict 헝 엄격한　traffic light 신호등　intersection 몡 교차로
improvement 몡 개선, 향상　seatbelt 몡 안전벨트

12 강의의 주된 주제는 무엇인가?
(A) 미국 자동차 생산의 역사
(B) 미국 자동차 안전 규정의 발전
(C) 자동차 충돌 감소의 중요성
(D) 자동차 사고를 일으키는 요인들

13 교수는 코네티컷주에 관해 무엇이라고 말하는가?
(A) 그곳은 미국에서 최초의 자동차를 생산했다.
(B) 그곳은 1910년에 가장 많은 자동차 사고가 있었다.
(C) 그곳은 속도 제한이 생긴 첫 번째 주였다.
(D) 그곳은 국가 운전법을 만드는 데 도움을 주었다.

14 국가 속도 제한법의 두 가지 특징은 무엇인가?
2개의 답을 고르시오.
(A) 그것은 주에서 자체적인 속도 제한을 도입한 후에 만들어졌다.
(B) 그것은 사고로 인한 사망률을 감소시켰다.
(C) 그것의 속도 제한은 대부분의 주 제한보다 낮았다.
(D) 그것은 석유 파동을 해결하는 데 도움이 되지 않았다.

15 교수는 왜 트럭 운전사 같은 직업 운전자들을 언급하는가?
(A) 일부 운전자가 다른 운전자보다 안전하다는 것을 보여주기 위해
(B) 최악의 자동차 사고의 원인을 강조하기 위해
(C) 법이 어떻게 다르게 적용되었는지 설명하기 위해
(D) 법이 어떻게 더 많은 일자리를 창출했는지 예시를 제공하기 위해

16 신호등에 대한 교수의 태도는 무엇인가?
(A) 그는 그것들의 색이 바뀌어야 한다고 생각한다.
(B) 그는 그것들이 따르기 쉬운 시스템이라고 생각한다.
(C) 그는 그것들이 발전하는 데 오랜 시간이 걸렸다고 느낀다.
(D) 그는 모든 교차로에서 그것들을 사용하길 원한다.

17 교수는 안전벨트와 에어백에 관해 무엇을 암시하는가?
(A) 그것들은 몇몇 주에서는 요구조건이 아니다.
(B) 그것들은 사고를 예방하는 데 유용하다.
(C) 그것들은 동시에 발명되었다.
(D) 그것들은 함께 사용될 때 가장 효과적이다.

HACKERS
APEX
LISTENING
for the
TOEFL iBT Intermediate

Answer Book